MICROSOFT®

EXCEL® 2021 PROGRAMMING

Pocket Primer

Microsoft®
Excel® 2021
Programming
Pocket Primer

Julitta Korol

Mercury Learning and Information
Dulles, Virginia
Boston, Massachusetts
New Delhi

Publisher: David Pallai
MERCURY LEARNING AND INFORMATION
22841 Quicksilver Drive
Dulles, VA 20166
info@merclearning.com
www.merclearning.com
800-232-0223

J. Korol. *Microsoft* Excel 2021 Programming Pocket Primer.
ISBN: 978-1-68392-892-8

The publisher recognizes and respects all marks used by companies, manufacturers, and developers as a means to distinguish their products. All brand names and product names mentioned in this book are trademarks or service marks of their respective companies. Any omission or misuse (of any kind) of service marks or trademarks, etc. is not an attempt to infringe on the property of others.

Library of Congress Control Number: 2022941631

222324321   This book is printed on acid-free paper in the United States of America.

Our titles are available for adoption, license, or bulk purchase by institutions, corporations, etc. For additional information, please contact the Customer Service Dept. at 800-232-0223(toll free).

CONTENTS

Chapter 8 Keeping Track of Multiple Values in Excel VBA Programs: *A Quick Introduction to Creating and Using Collections* 199

Chapter 9 Excel Tools for Testing and Debugging: *A Quick Introduction to Testing VBA Programs*.................... 221

ACKNOWLEDGMENTS

As years pass and we gain more and more knowledge on a particular subject there is a tendency to publish books for people who want to know it all. But the truth is that we really don't have time to read all the printed pages when we are just getting started in a new subject. I thank my publisher, David Pallai, for continuing to publish this smaller book that serves as a starting point for anyone attempting to get into VBA programming in Excel. I hope that you as a reader of this primer book will appreciate this short book and find that the knowledge gained from its pages will not only allow you to continue your programming journey, but also take you places you never thought possible.

I'm also thankful to Jennifer Blaney for her expert management of this book project. I am grateful to the compositor, Swaradha Typesetting, for all of the composition efforts that gave this book the easy-to-follow look and feel.

Julitta Korol
Long Island, New York
August 2022

INTRODUCTION

I've been working with Excel since the very beginning. Database and application concepts were completely new to me, but the Excel interface made it a pleasure to work with almost daily. Step by step I acquired the skills of database management and then programming. I learned the latter by trial and error. When the first consulting opportunity came up to use my Excel skills, I found that I barely knew enough to get started. But challenges do not scare me. I was eager to learn on the job. My first Excel programming project was designing a custom quotation system for an automotive manufacturer. Despite my limited prior exposure to the programming concepts, I was able to deliver a system that automated a big chunk of work for that company. Another project automated several dozens of budget worksheets for a school district. How was I able to do this? I find reading and doing is the first step towards mastering a skill like programming. This book presents enough programming concepts to get you started tackling your own Excel challenges. This is not a book about using Excel. I assume you are already familiar with most tasks that you can achieve using Excel built-in commands. But if you are ready to look beyond the standard user interface, you have come to the right place and have made a decision that will bring a whole set of new possibilities to your Excel experience. So, let's forget the menus for now. Do your own thing. Automating Excel is something everyone can do. With the right training, that is. This book's purpose is to introduce you to the Excel built-in language, known as Visual Basic for Applications (VBA). With VBA you can begin delegating repetitive tasks to Excel while freeing your time for projects that are more fun to do. Besides, knowing how to program these days is a sought-after and lucrative skill.

This book was designed for someone like you who needs to master Excel programming fundamentals without spending too much time. Most of the time all you need is a short book to get you started. It's less overwhelming to deal with a new subject in smaller chunks. The *Programming Pocket Primer* series will show you only the things you need to know to feel at home with VBA. What you learn in this book on Excel programming will apply to, say, Access programming. Just take a quick look my other book, the *Microsoft Access 2021 Programming Pocket Primer*, to see what I mean. How's that for knowledge transfer? Learn in Excel and use it in Excel or other Microsoft 365 applications. I call this sweet learning.

If you are looking for in-depth knowledge of Excel programming (and have time to work through a 1,000-page book), then go ahead and try some of my more complete, programming titles available from MERCURY LEARNING AND INFORMATION.

Excel is about doing and so is this book. So do not try to read it while not at the computer. You can sit, stand, or lie down; it does not matter. But you do need to work with this book. Do the examples, read the explanations. Do this until it becomes easy to do without the step-by-step instructions. Do not skip anything as the concepts in later chapters build on material introduced earlier.

CHAPTER OVERVIEW

Before you get started, allow me to give you a short overview of the things you'll be learning as you progress through this primer book. *Microsoft Excel 2021 Programming Pocket Primer* is divided into nine chapters that progressively introduce you to programming Microsoft Excel.

Chapter 1: Getting Started with Excel VBA–A Quick Start in Excel VBA Programming
In this chapter you learn how you can introduce automation into your Excel worksheets by simply using the built-in macro recorder. You learn about different phases of macro design and execution. You also learn about macro security.

Chapter 2: Excel Programming Environment–A Quick Overview of its Tools and Features
In this chapter you learn almost everything you need to know about working with the Visual Basic Editor window, commonly referred to as VBE. Some of the programming tools that are not covered here are discussed and used in Chapter 9.

Chapter 3: Excel VBA Fundamentals–A Quick Reference to Writing VBA Code
In this chapter you are introduced to the basic VBA concepts such as Microsoft Excel object model and its objects, properties, and methods. You also learn concepts that allow you to store various pieces of information for later use.

Chapter 4: Excel VBA Procedures–A Quick Guide to Writing Function Procedures
In this chapter you learn how to write and execute function procedures. You also learn how to provide additional information to your procedures before they are run. You are introduced to working with some useful built-in functions and methods that allow you to interact with you VBA procedure users.

Chapter 5: Adding Decisions to Excel VBA Programs–A Quick Introduction to Conditional Statements
In this chapter you learn how to control your program flow with several different decision-making statements.

Chapter 6: Adding Repeating Actions to Excel VBA Programs–A Quick Introduction to Looping Statements
In this chapter you learn how you can repeat certain groups of statements using procedure loops.

Chapter 7: Storing Multiple Values in Excel VBA Programs–A Quick Introduction to Working with Arrays
In this chapter you learn the concept of static and dynamic arrays, which you can use for holding various values. You also learn about built-in array functions.

Chapter 8: Keeping Track of Multiple Values in Excel VBA Programs–A Quick Introduction to Creating and Using Collections
In this chapter you learn the basic skills of using collections for tracking and maintaining data in your VBA procedures.

Chapter 9: Excel Tools for Testing and Debugging–A Quick Introduction to Testing VBA Programs
In this chapter you begin using built-in debugging tools to test your programming code and trap errors.

The above nine chapters will give you the fundamental techniques and concepts you will need in order to continue your Excel VBA learning path. The skills obtained in this primer are very portable. They can be utilized in programming other Microsoft 365 applications that also use VBA as their native programming language such as Access, Word, PowerPoint, Outlook, and so on. And when you are ready to get more Excel VBA skills under your belt, you can jump right into Chapter 10 in my more complete book - *Excel 2021 / Microsoft 365 Programming by Example* also available from MERCURY LEARNING AND INFORMATION. (ISBN: 978-1-68392-886-7).

THE COMPANION FILES

The example files for all the hands-on activities in this book are available in the companion files. Replacement files may be downloaded by contacting the publisher at info@merclearning.com. Digital versions of this title are available at *academiccourseware.com* and other digital vendors.

Chapter 1

EXCEL MACROS

A QUICK START IN EXCEL VBA PROGRAMMING

Visual Basic for Applications (VBA) is the programming language built into Microsoft Excel® and other Microsoft® 365® applications. By learning some basic VBA commands, you can start automating many of the mundane routine tasks that you perform in Excel. In this chapter, you acquire the fundamentals of VBA by recording macros and using the Visual Basic Editor to examine and edit the VBA code behind the recorded macro.

MACROS AND VBA

Macros are programs that store a series of commands. When you create a macro, you simply combine a sequence of keystrokes into a single command that you can later "play back." Because macros can reduce the number of steps required to complete tasks, using macros can significantly decrease the time you spend creating, formatting, modifying, and printing your Excel worksheets. You can create macros by using Microsoft Excel's built-in recording tool (Macro Recorder), or you can write them from scratch using Visual Basic Editor, a special development environment built into Excel. You can combine recorded macros with your own programming code to create unique VBA applications that meet your everyday needs. Whether you write or record your programming code in Excel, you'll be utilizing the powerful programming language—Visual Basic for Applications—commonly known as VBA.

Microsoft Excel comes with dozens of built-in, time-saving features that allow you to work faster and smarter. Before you decide to automate a worksheet task with a recorded macro or programming code written from scratch, make sure there is not already a built-in feature that you can use to perform that task. Consider writing your own VBA code or recording a macro when you find yourself performing the same series of actions multiple times or when Excel does not provide a built-in tool to do the job.

Just by learning how to handle Excel's macro recorder and use basic VBA statements and constructs to enhance your macros, you'll be able to automate any part of your worksheet. For example, you can automate data entry by recording a macro that enters headings in a worksheet or replaces column titles with new labels. Adding a little bit of conditional logic to your VBA code will allow you to automatically check for duplicate entries in a specified range of your worksheet. With a macro, you can quickly apply formatting to several worksheets, as well as combine different formats, such as fonts, colors, borders, and shading. Macros will save you keystrokes when it comes to setting print areas, margins, headers, and footers, and selecting special options for printouts.

Excel Macro-Enabled File Formats

When a workbook contains programming code, it should be saved in one of the following macro-enabled file formats:

- Excel Macro-Enabled Workbook (.xlsm)
- Excel Binary Workbook (.xlsb)
- Excel Macro-Enabled Template (.xltm)

If you attempt to save the workbook in a file format that is incompatible with the type of content it includes, Excel will warn you with a message as shown in Figure 1.1.

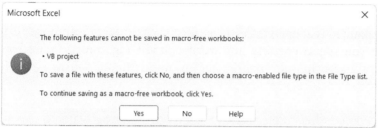

FIGURE 1.1 When a workbook contains programming code, you must save it in a macro-enabled file type instead of a regular .XLSX workbook file.

Macro Security Settings

Because macros can contain malicious code designed to put a virus on a user's computer, it is important to understand different security settings that are available in Excel. It is also critical that you run up-to-date antivirus software on your computer. Antivirus software installed on your computer will scan the workbook file you are attempting to open if the file contains macros. The default macro security setting is to disable all macros with notification, as shown in Figure 1.2.

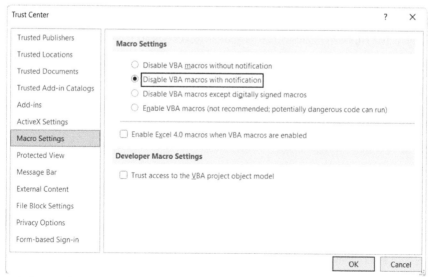

FIGURE 1.2 The Macro Settings options in the Trust Center allow you to control how Excel should deal with macros when they are present in an open workbook. To open Trust Center's Macro Settings, choose File | Options | Trust Center | Trust Center Settings and click the Macro Settings link.

Note that VBA macros are the macros you create using the Excel built-in language—VBA. You will be working with these macros throughout this book. Excel 4.0 macros are legacy Excel macros. Introduced in 1992, they are commonly referred to as XLM 4.0 macros. They are still in Excel for backward compatibility reasons. Using these macros is discouraged as they can hide malicious code in Excel formulas.

If VBA macros are present in a workbook you are trying to open, you will receive a security warning message just under the Ribbon, as shown in Figure 1.3.

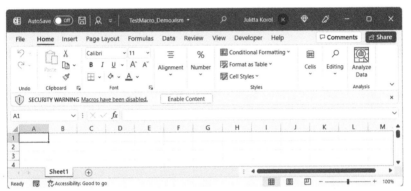

FIGURE 1.3 Upon opening a workbook with VBA macros, Excel brings up a security warning message.

To use the disabled components, you should click the Enable Content button on the message bar. This will add the workbook to the Trusted Documents list in your registry. The next time you open this workbook you will not be alerted to macros. If you need more information before enabling content, you can click the message text displayed in the security message bar to activate the Backstage View, where you will find an explanation of the active content that has been disabled, as shown in Figure 1.4. Clicking the Enable Content button in the Backstage View presents two options:

- Enable All Content

  This option provides the same functionality as the Enable Content button in the security message bar. This will enable all the content and make it a trusted document.

- Advanced Options

  This option brings up the Microsoft Office Security Options dialog shown in Figure 1.5. This dialog provides options for enabling content for the current session only.

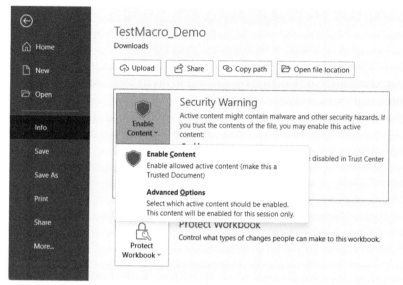

FIGURE 1.4 The Backstage View in Excel.

FIGURE 1.5 Disabled macros can be enabled for the current session in the Microsoft Office Security Options dialog.

ENABLING THE DEVELOPER TAB IN EXCEL

To make it easy to work with macro-enabled workbooks while working with this book's exercises, you will permanently trust your workbooks with recorded macros or VBA code by placing them in a folder on your local drive that you mark as trusted. Notice the Open the Trust Center hyperlink shown in Figure 1.5. This hyperlink will open the Trust Center dialog where you can set up a trusted folder. You can also activate the Trust Center by selecting File | Options.

Let's take a few minutes now to set up your Excel application so you can run VBA macros on your computer without security prompts.

NOTE	*Please note files for the "Hands-On" project may be found in the companion files.*

⊙   Hands-On 1.1   Setting Up Excel for Macro Development

1. Create a folder on your hard drive named **C:\VBAPrimerExcel2021_ByExample**.
2. Launch Excel and open a blank workbook.
3. Choose **File | Options**.
4. In the Excel Options dialog, click **Customize Ribbon**. In the Main Tabs listing on the right-hand side, select **Developer** as illustrated in Figure 1.6 and click **OK**. The Developer tab should now be visible in the Ribbon.
5. In the Code group of the Developer tab on the Ribbon, click the **Macro Security** button, as shown in Figure 1.7. The Trust Center dialog appears as depicted in Figure 1.2.
6. In the left pane of the Trust Center dialog, click **Trusted Locations**.
   The Trusted Locations dialog already shows several predefined trusted locations that were created when you installed Excel. For this book, we will add a custom location to this list.
7. Click the **Add new location** button.
8. In the Path text box, type the name of the folder you created in Step 1 of this Hands-On as shown in Figure 1.8.
9. Click **OK** to close the Microsoft Office Trusted Location dialog.
10. Notice that the Trusted Locations list in the Trust Center now includes the **C:\VBAPrimerExcel2021_ByExample** folder as a trusted location. Files placed in a trusted location can be opened without being checked by the Trust Center security feature.
11. Click **OK** to close the Trust Center dialog box.

Your Excel application is now set up for easy macro development as well as opening files containing macros. You should save all the files created in the book's Hands-On exercises into your trusted C:\VBAPrimerExcel2021_ByExample folder.

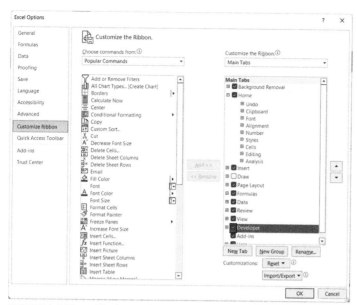

FIGURE 1.6 To enable the Developer tab on the Ribbon, use the Excel Options dialog and select Customize Ribbon.

FIGURE 1.7 Use the Macro Security button in the Code group on the Developer tab to customize the macro security settings.

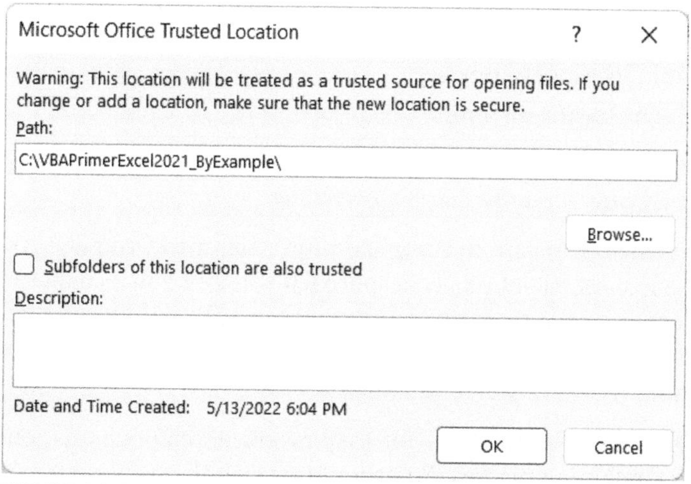

Microsoft Office Trusted Location ? ✕

Warning: This location will be treated as a trusted source for opening files. If you change or add a location, make sure that the new location is secure.

Path:

C:\VBAPrimerExcel2021_ByExample\

Browse...

☐ Subfolders of this location are also trusted

Description:

Date and Time Created: 5/13/2022 6:04 PM

OK   Cancel

FIGURE 1.8 Designating a Trusted Location folder for this book's programming examples.

USING THE BUILT-IN MACRO RECORDER

In this section, we will go through the process of recording several short macros that perform data entry and formatting tasks in an Excel worksheet. You will learn how to plan your macros, record your keystrokes, edit, and improve your recorded macro code, run your macros, and learn basic troubleshooting techniques that will get you back on track in case you encounter errors while running your macros. You will also learn how to save your macros, rename them, combine them, and print them.

Planning a Macro

Before you create a macro, take a few minutes to consider what you want to do. The easiest way to plan your macro is to manually perform all the actions that the macro needs to do. As you enter the keystrokes, write them down on a piece of paper exactly as they occur. Don't leave anything out. Like a voice recorder, Excel's macro recorder records every action you perform. If you do not plan your macro prior to recording, you may end up with unnecessary actions that will not only slow it down but also require more editing later to make it work as intended. Although it's easier to edit a macro than it is to erase unwanted passages from a voice recording, performing only the actions you want recorded will save you editing time and trouble later.

Suppose you are asked to programmatically create the worksheet depicted in Figure 1.9. No worries. Getting started is very easy with the macro recorder. Let's begin by identifying the tasks required to complete this worksheet.

Task 1	Insert a new sheet into a workbook and name it Employee Wages.
Task 2	Enter column headings into first row of the worksheet and apply required formatting (column size, font styles).
Task 3	Enter employee data (Full Name, Hourly Rate, Hours Worked).
Task 4 and 5	Enter formulas to fill in the employee First and Last Name columns.
Task 6	Enter formulas to calculate employee total wages.
Task 7	Apply formatting to the completed worksheet.

Instead of recording one macro to complete your assignment, you will create a separate macro for each task. This approach will give you a chance to learn how to combine code from several simpler macros and how to create a master macro. Let's get started.

	A	B	C	D	E	F	G
1	Employee Name ▾	First Name ▾	Last Name ▾	Hourly Rate ▾	Hours Worked ▾	Total Wages ▾	
2	James Rogers	James	Rogers	15	7	$105.00	
3	Martha Lambert	Martha	Lambert	13.4	6	$80.40	
4	Eugene Zelnik	Eugene	Zelnik	21.42	10	$214.20	
5	Enrique Martinez	Enrique	Martinez	16.5	11	$181.50	
6	Wanda Pasterniak	Wanda	Pasterniak	35	21	$735.00	
7	Bruce Smith	Bruce	Smith	28.33	14	$396.62	
8							

FIGURE 1.9 A sample worksheet to be created and formatted with the help of the Excel built-in macro recorder.

⊚ Hands-On 1.2   Getting Things Ready for Macro Recording

1. Open a new workbook and save it as **Chap01_ExcelPrimer.xlsm** in your trusted **VBAPrimerExcel2021_ByExample** folder. You must save the file in the macro-enabled file format (.xlsm) to allow for storing macros. Keep this file open as you will use it to record all the macros in this chapter.

Recording a Macro

Before you record a macro, you need to decide whether you want to record the positioning of the active cell. If you want the macro to always start in a specific location on the worksheet, turn on the macro recorder first and then select the cell you want to start in. If the location of the active cell does not matter, select a single cell first and then turn on the macro recorder.

⊚ Hands-On 1.3   Inserting and Naming a Worksheet (Macro Task 1)

1. Choose **Developer | Record Macro**.
2. In the Record Macro dialog box, enter the name **Insert_NewSheet** for the macro, as shown in Figure 1.10. Do not dismiss this dialog box until you are instructed to do so.

SIDEBAR *Naming Macros*

If you forget to enter a name for the macro, Excel assigns a default name, such as *Macro1, Macro2*, and so on. Macro names can contain letters, numbers, and the underscore character, but the first character must be a letter. For example, *Report1* is a correct macro name, while *1Report* is not. Spaces are not allowed. If you want a space between the words, use the underscore.

3. Select **This Workbook** in the **Store macro in** list box.

SIDEBAR *Storing Macros*

Excel allows you to store macros in three locations:

- Personal Macro Workbook—Macros stored in this location will be available each time you work with Excel. You can find the Personal Macro Workbook in the XLStart folder. If this workbook doesn't already exist, Excel creates it the first time you select this option.
- New Workbook—Excel will place the macro in a new workbook.
- This Workbook—The macro will be stored in the workbook you are currently using.

FIGURE 1.10 When you record a new macro, you must name it. In the Record Macro dialog box, you can also supply a shortcut key, a storage location, and a description for your macro.

4. In the Description box, enter the following text: **Insert and rename a worksheet**.
5. Choose **OK** to close the Record Macro dialog box.

   The Stop Recording button shown in Figure 1.11 appears in the status bar. Do not click this button until you are instructed to do so. When this button appears in the status bar, the workbook is in the recording mode.

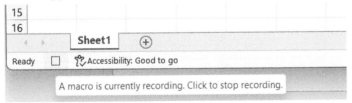

FIGURE 1.11 The Stop Recording button in the status bar indicates that the macro recording mode is active.

The Stop Recording button remains in the status bar while you record your macro. Only the actions finalized by pressing Enter or clicking OK are recorded. If you press the Esc key or click Cancel before completing the entry, the macro recorder does not record that action.

6. Add a new sheet to the current workbook. You can do this by either right clicking the Sheet1 tab and choosing **Insert | Worksheet | OK**, or simply clicking the plus button to the right of the Sheet1 tab.

7. Rename the new sheet **Employee Wages**.

8. Click the **Stop Recording** button in the status bar as shown in Figure 1.11 or choose **View | Macros | Stop Recording**. When you stop the macro recorder, the status bar displays a button that allows you to record another macro (see Figure 1.12).

FIGURE 1.12 Excel status bar with the macro recording button turned off.

You have now recorded your first macro. Excel has written all the necessary statements to execute the actions you performed. Let's continue recording all the remaining actions to complete the tasks that we defined earlier. After that you will have a chance to review the recorded macro code and try out your macros.

Hands-On 1.4   Inserting Column Headings and Applying Formatting (Macro Task 2)

1. Choose **View | Macros | Record Macro** (or you may click the **Begin recording** button located in the status bar).

2. Enter **Insert_Headings** as the name for your macro.

3. Ensure that **This Workbook** is selected in the **Store macro in** list box.

4. Click **OK**.
   Excel turns on the macro recorder. All your Excel actions from now on are being recorded.

5. Select **cell A1** and enter the first heading: **Employee Name**.

6. Move to cell **B1** and enter: **First Name**.

7. Enter the remaining headings in cells **C1: F1** (**Last Name, Hourly Rate, Hours Worked, Total Wage**s).

8. Select **A1:F1** and apply the bold formatting to the selection by pressing the **B** button in the Font group of the Ribbon's Home tab.

9. With the range **A1:F1** still selected, choose **Home | Cells | Format | Autofit Column Width**.

10. Click the **Stop Recording** button in the status bar as shown in Figure 1.11 or choose **View | Macros | Stop Recording**.

You have just recorded your second macro. The Employee Wages worksheet should now have the required headings in Row 1.

SIDEBAR **Using Relative or Absolute References in Macros**

The Excel macro recorder can record your actions using absolute or relative cell references (see Figure 1.13).

- To have your macro execute the recorded action in a specific cell, no matter what cell is selected during the execution of the macro, use absolute cell addressing. Absolute cell references have the following form: $A$1, $C$5, etc. By default, the Excel macro recorder uses absolute references. Before you begin to record a new macro, make sure the Use Relative References option is not selected when you click the Macros button as shown in Figure 1.13.

- To have your macro perform the action in any cell, be sure to select the Use Relative References option before you choose the Record Macro option. Relative cell references have the following form: A1, C5, etc. The Excel macro recorder will continue to use relative cell references until you exit Microsoft Excel or click the Use Relative References option again.

- During the process of recording your macro, you may use both methods of cell addressing. For example, you may select a specific cell (e.g., $A$4), perform an action, and then choose another cell relative to the selected cell (e.g., C9, which is located five rows down and two columns to the right of the currently active cell $A$4). Relative references automatically adjust when you copy them, and absolute references don't.

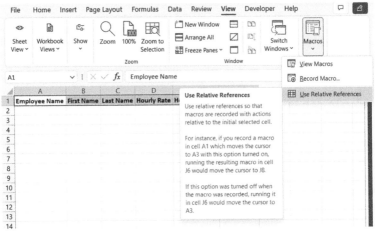

FIGURE 1.13 Excel macro recorder can record your actions using absolute or relative cell references. To make your selection, use the Macros drop-down on the Ribbon's View tab.

Hands-On 1.5   Entering Employee Data (Macro Task 3)

1. Choose **View | Macros | Record Macro** (or you may click the **Begin recording** button located in the status bar).
2. Enter **Insert_EmployeeData** as the name for your macro.
3. Ensure that **This Workbook** is selected in the **Store macro in** list box.
4. Click **OK**.

   Excel turns on the macro recorder. All your Excel actions from now on are being recorded.
5. Enter employee data in columns **A**, **D**, and **E** as shown in Figure 1.9. Leave the First Name, Last Name, and Total Wages columns blank as they will be filled in later.
6. Click the **Stop Recording** button in the status bar as shown in Figure 1.11 or choose **View | Macros | Stop Recording**.

   You have just recorded the third macro. The static data entry has been completed. We will now proceed to record macros that use formulas to fill the remaining columns of the worksheet.

Hands-On 1.6   Entering Formulas to Fill in Employee First Name (Macro Task 4)

1. Choose **View | Macros | Record Macro** (or you may click the **Begin recording** button, located in the status bar).
2. Enter **Get_FirstName** as the name for your macro.
3. Ensure that **This Workbook** is selected in the **Store macro in** list box.
4. Click **OK**.

   Excel turns on the macro recorder. All your Excel actions from now on are being recorded.
5. Enter the following formula in cell B2:

   ```
   =LEFT(A2,FIND(" ", A2)-1)
   ```

6. Copy the formula down to cells B3:B7 by dragging the selection handle in the bottom right corner of cell B2.

   Excel fills in the first names of all employees.
7. Click the **Stop Recording** button in the status bar as shown in Figure 1.11 or choose **View | Macros | Stop Recording**.

   You have just recorded a macro that makes use of a formula to retrieve employee first names from their full name. The next macro will populate the last name column using another formula.

Hands-On 1.7   Entering Formulas to Fill in Employee Last Name (Macro Task 5)

1. Choose **View | Macros | Record Macro** (or you may click the **Begin recording** button located in the status bar).

2. Enter **Get_LastName** as the name for your macro.
3. Ensure that **This Workbook** is selected in the **Store macro in** list box.
4. Click **OK**.

   Excel turns on the macro recorder. All your Excel actions from now on are being recorded.
5. Enter the following formula in cell **C2**:

   ```
   =RIGHT(A2,LEN(A2)-FIND(" ", A2))
   ```

6. Copy the formula down to cells **C3:C7** by dragging the selection handle in the bottom right corner of cell C2.

   Excel fills in the last names of all employees.
7. Click the **Stop Recording** button in the status bar as shown in Figure 1.11 or choose **View | Macros | Stop Recording**.

   You have just recorded a macro that makes use of a formula to retrieve employee last names from their full name. We have one more column to fill in before we can apply the final formatting to this worksheet.

⊙ Hands-On 1.8   Entering Formulas to Calculate Employee Total Wages (Macro Task 6)

1. Choose **View | Macros | Record Macro** (or you may click the **Begin recording** button located in the status bar).
2. Enter **CalculateWages** as the name for your macro.
3. Ensure that **This Workbook** is selected in the **Store macro in** list box.
4. Click **OK**.

   Excel turns on the macro recorder. All your Excel actions from now on are being recorded.
5. Select cells **F2:F7** and type the formula shown here. Press **Ctrl+Enter** to ensure that formula is entered into the selected range F2:F7.

   ```
   =D2*E2
   ```

6. Apply Currency format to cells **F2:F7**.
7. Click the **Stop Recording** button in the status bar as shown in Figure 1.11 or choose **View | Macros | Stop Recording**.

   In the next macro you will complete the worksheet by applying desired formatting.

⊙ Hands-On 1.9   Applying Table Format (Macro Task 7)

1. Choose **View | Macros | Record Macro** (or you may click the **Begin recording** button located in the status bar).
2. Enter **FormatTable** as the name for your macro.
3. Ensure that **This Workbook** is selected in the **Store macro in** list box.
4. Click **OK**.

Excel turns on the macro recorder. All your Excel actions from now on are being recorded.

5. Select all data in the Employee Wages worksheet and choose **Home | Styles | Format as a Table**. Select any of the predefined table styles from the drop-down.

6. Select cell **A1**.

7. Click the **Stop Recording** button in the status bar as shown in Figure 1.11 or choose **View | Macros | Stop Recording**.

You have now completed recording a set of macros that create and format a worksheet. Now that Excel has given us some code to work with, let's locate and examine it.

Editing Recorded Macros

Before you can modify your macro, you must find the location where the macro recorder placed its code. As you recall, when you turned on the macro recorder, you selected `ThisWorkbook` for the location. To find the location of your macros, you will use the Macro dialog box as instructed in Hands-On 1.10.

Hands-On 1.10   Examining the Macro Code

1. Choose **View | Macros | View Macros**.

You should see all seven macros you recorded earlier (see Figure 1.14).

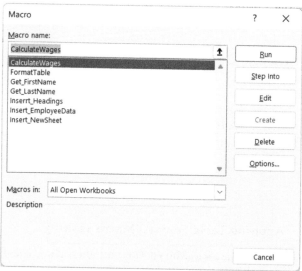

FIGURE 1.14 In the Macro dialog box, you can select a macro to run, debug (Step Into), edit, or delete. You can also set macro options.

2. Select the **Insert_NewSheet** macro name and click the **Edit** button.

   Excel opens a special window called Visual Basic Editor (also known as VBE), as shown in Figure 1.15. This window is your VBA programming environment. Using the keyboard shortcut Alt+F11, you can quickly switch between the Microsoft Excel application window and the Visual Basic Editor window. Now take a moment and try switching between both windows. When you are done, ensure that you are back in the VBE window.

3. Close the Visual Basic Editor window by using the key combination **Alt+Q** or choosing **File | Close and Return to Microsoft Excel**.

   Don't worry if the Visual Basic Editor window seems a bit confusing right now. As you work with the recorded macros and start writing your own VBA procedures from scratch, you will become familiar with all the elements of this screen.

4. In the Microsoft Excel application window, choose **Developer | Visual Basic** to switch again to the programming environment.

FIGURE 1.15 The Visual Basic Editor window is used for editing macros as well as writing new procedures in the Visual Basic for Applications language.

Notice the menu bar and toolbar in the Visual Basic Editor window look different from those in the Microsoft Excel window. As you can see, there is no Ribbon interface. The Visual Basic Editor uses the old Excel style menu bar and toolbar, which provide tools required for programming and testing your recorded macros as well as VBA procedures that you can write from scratch. As you work through the individual chapters of this book, you will feel very comfortable in using these tools.

The main part of the Visual Basic Editor window is a docking surface for various windows that you will find extremely useful while creating and testing your VBA procedures.

In Figure 1.15 you can see three windows that are docked in the Visual Basic Editor window: the Project Explorer window, the Properties window, and the Code window.

The Project Explorer window that appears in the left panel shows an open Modules folder. Excel records your macro actions in special work-sheets called Module1, Module2, and so on. These modules are stored in the Modules folder. Later in this book, you will also use modules to write the code of your own VBA procedures from scratch. A module resembles a blank document in Microsoft Word.

The Properties window displays the properties of the object that is currently selected in the Project Explorer window. In Figure 1.15, the Module1 object is selected in the Project - VBAProject window, and therefore the Properties - Module1 window displays the properties of Module1. Notice that the only available property for the module is the Name property. You can use this property to change the name of Module1 to a more meaningful name.

SIDEBAR *Macro or Procedure?*

A macro is a series of commands or functions recorded with the help of a built-in macro recorder or entered manually in a Visual Basic module. The term "macro" is often replaced with the broader term "procedure." Although the words can be used interchangeably, many programmers prefer "procedure." While macros allow you to mimic keyboard actions, true procedures can also execute actions that cannot be performed using the mouse, keyboard, or menu options. In other words, procedures are more complex macros that incorporate language structures found in the traditional programming languages. You will learn about these structures later in this book.

The Module1 (Code) window displays the code of all macros you recorded earlier. Note that the following code may not exactly match the code in your Code window. Excel records all actions while the recorder is on, so you may see more, or fewer statements recorded.

```
Sub Insert_NewSheet()
'
' Insert_NewSheet Macro
```

```vba
' Insert and rename a worksheet
'


    Sheets.Add After:=ActiveSheet
    Sheets("Sheet2").Select
    Sheets("Sheet2").Name = "Employee Wages"
End Sub
Sub Insert_Headings()
'
' Insert_Headings Macro
'


    Range("A1").Select
    ActiveCell.FormulaR1C1 = "Employee Name"
    Range("B1").Select
    ActiveCell.FormulaR1C1 = "First Name"
    Range("C1").Select
    ActiveCell.FormulaR1C1 = "Last Name"
    Range("D1").Select
    ActiveCell.FormulaR1C1 = "Hourly Rate"
    Range("E1").Select
    ActiveCell.FormulaR1C1 = "Hours Worked"
    Range("F1").Select
    ActiveCell.FormulaR1C1 = "Total Wages"
    Range("A1:F1").Select
    Selection.Font.Bold = True
    Selection.Columns.AutoFit
End Sub
Sub Insert_EmployeeData()
'
' Insert_EmployeeData Macro
'


    Range("A2").Select
    ActiveCell.FormulaR1C1 = "James Rogers"
    Range("D2").Select
    ActiveCell.FormulaR1C1 = "15"
    Range("E2").Select
    ActiveCell.FormulaR1C1 = "7"
    Range("A3").Select
    ActiveCell.FormulaR1C1 = "Martha Lambert"
    Range("D3").Select
    ActiveCell.FormulaR1C1 = "13.4"
    Range("E3").Select
    ActiveCell.FormulaR1C1 = "6"
    Range("A4").Select
    ActiveCell.FormulaR1C1 = "Eugene Zelnik"
    Range("D4").Select
```

```
    ActiveCell.FormulaR1C1 = "21.42"
    Range("E4").Select
    ActiveCell.FormulaR1C1 = "10"
    Range("A5").Select
    ActiveCell.FormulaR1C1 = «Enrique Martinez»
    Range(«D5»).Select
    ActiveCell.FormulaR1C1 = "16.5"
    Range("E5").Select
    ActiveCell.FormulaR1C1 = "11"
    Range("A6").Select
    ActiveCell.FormulaR1C1 = "Wanda Pasterniak"
    Range("D6").Select
    ActiveCell.FormulaR1C1 = "35"
    Range("E6").Select
    ActiveCell.FormulaR1C1 = "21"
    Range("A7").Select
    ActiveCell.FormulaR1C1 = "Bruce Smith"
    Range("D7").Select
    ActiveCell.FormulaR1C1 = "28.33"
    Range("E7").Select
    ActiveCell.FormulaR1C1 = "14"
    Range("A8").Select
End Sub
Sub Get_FirstName()
'
' Get_FirstName Macro
'

'

    Range("B2").Select
    ActiveCell.FormulaR1C1 = "=LEFT(RC[-1],FIND("" "", RC[-1])-
1)"
    Range("B2").Select
    Selection.Copy
    Range("B3:B7").Select
    ActiveSheet.Paste
    Application.CutCopyMode = False
End Sub
Sub Get_LastName()
'
' Get_LastName Macro
'

'

    Range("C2").Select
    ActiveCell.FormulaR1C1 = "=RIGHT(RC[-2],
        LEN(RC[-2])-FIND("" "", RC[-2]))"
    Range("C2").Select
    Selection.Copy
    Range("C3:C7").Select
    ActiveSheet.Paste
```

```
        Application.CutCopyMode = False
End Sub
Sub CalculateWages()
'
' CalculateWages Macro
'


'
    Range("F2").Select
    Application.CutCopyMode = False
    ActiveCell.FormulaR1C1 = "=RC[-2]*RC[-1]"
    Range("F2").Select
    Selection.AutoFill Destination:=Range("F2:F7"),
        Type:=xlFillDefault
    Range("F2:F7").Select
    Selection.NumberFormat = "$#,##0.00"
End Sub
Sub FormatTable()
'
' FormatTable Macro
'


'
Range("A1:F7").Select
Application.CutCopyMode = False
ActiveSheet.ListObjects.Add(xlSrcRange,-
Range("$A$1:$F$7"), , xlYes).Name = "Table1"
Range("Table1[#All]").Select
ActiveSheet.ListObjects("Table1").TableStyle="TableStyleLight14"
Range("Table1[[#Headers],[Employee Name]]").Select
End Sub
```

For now, let's focus on finding answers to two questions:

- How do you read the macro code?
- How can you edit macros?

Notice that each macro code you recorded is located between the Sub and End Sub. These words are known as keywords. You read the code line by line from top to bottom. You can edit the recorded macros by deleting or modifying existing code or typing new instructions in the Code window.

Macro Comments

Look at the recorded macro code. The lines that begin with a single quote denote comments. By default, comments appear in green. When the macro code is executed, Visual Basic ignores the comment lines. Comments are often placed within the macro code to document the meaning of certain lines that aren't obvious. Comments can also be used to temporarily disable certain blocks of code that you don't want to execute. This is often done while testing and troubleshooting your macros.

Let's add some comments to the CalculateWages macro to make the code easier to understand.

(●) Hands-On 1.11   Adding Comments to the Macro Code

1. Make sure that the Visual Basic Editor screen shows the Code window with the CalculateWages macro.
2. Click after the `Range("F2:F7").Select` and press **Enter**.
3. In the empty line you just created, type the following comment. Be sure to start with a single quote.

   ```
   ' Apply Currency Format
   ```

4. Press **Ctrl+S** to save the changes in Chap01_ExcelPrimer.xlsm, or choose **File | Save Chap01_ExcelPrimer.xlsm**.

All macro procedures begin with the keyword `Sub` and end with the keywords `End Sub`. The `Sub` keyword is followed by the macro name and a set of parentheses. Between the keywords `Sub` and `End Sub` are statements that Visual Basic executes each time you run your macro. Visual Basic reads the lines from top to bottom, ignoring the statements preceded with a single quote (see the information about comments) and stops when it reaches the keywords `End Sub`. Notice that the recorded macro contains many periods. The periods appear in almost every line of code and are used to join various elements of the Visual Basic for Applications language. How do you read the instructions written in this language? They are read from the right side of the last period to the left. Here are a few statements from the Insert_Headings macro and a description of what they mean:

Code Segment	Description
`Range("A1:F1").Select`	Select cells A1 to F1.
`Selection.Columns.AutoFit`	Extend the column width so that all entries fit.
`ActiveCell.FormulaR1C1 = "Hourly Rate"`	Let the formula of the active cell be "Hourly Rate."
`Selection.Font.Bold = True`	Applies bold format to all selected cells.

Cleaning Up the Macro Code

As you review and analyze your macro code line by line, you may notice that Excel recorded a lot of information that you didn't intend to include. For example, if you used the Font dialog box to apply bold formatting to the heading cells in your Insert_Headings macro, in addition to setting the font style to bold, Excel also recorded the current state of other options on the Font tab—strikethrough, superscript, subscript, outline font, shadow, underline, theme color, tint and shade, and theme font as shown in the following:

```
With Selection.Font
      .Name = "Calibri Light"
      .FontStyle = "Bold"
      .Size = 9
      .Strikethrough = False
      .Superscript = False
      .Subscript = False
      .OutlineFont = False
      .Shadow = False
      .Underline = xlUnderlineStyleNone
      .ThemeColor = xlThemeColorLight1
      .TintAndShade = 0
      .ThemeFont = xlThemeFontMajor
End With
```

When you use dialog boxes, Excel always records all the settings. These additional instructions make your macro code longer and more difficult to understand. Therefore, when you finish recording your macro, it is a good idea to go over the recorded statements and delete the unnecessary lines of code. In the previous code snippet, different font settings are applied to the selection of cells. This is done with the special block of code that begins with the keyword With and ends with the keyword End With. Assume you just wanted to change the font name, style, and size of the selected cells. In this case you can simply delete all the other settings that were recorded, and you are left with the following code:

```
With Selection.Font
      .Name = "Calibri Light"
      .FontStyle = "Bold"
      .Size = 9
End With
```

This makes your macro code easier to understand as only the settings you selected are shown.

Notice that each setting in the With...End With block begins with a period. If you wanted to list each setting separately you would write them as:

```
Selection.Font.Name = "Calibri Light"
Selection.Font.FontStyle = "Bold"
   Selection.Font.Size = 9
```

Using the With...End With block, you simply write the repeating code once. Simply move the repeating code Selection.Font to the right of the With keyword and end the entire block with End With.

As you work more with Excel macro recorder and learn more about VBA statements you will be able to make your recorded macros much cleaner.

Running a Macro

You can run your macros from either the Microsoft Excel window or the Visual Basic Editor window. When you execute a macro from the VBE screen, Visual Basic executes the macro behind the scenes. You can't see when Visual Basic performed a specific action. To watch Visual Basic at work, you must run your macro from the Macro dialog box or arrange your screen in such a way that the Microsoft Excel and Visual Basic windows can be viewed at the same time. Two monitors attached to your computer will help you greatly in the development work when you need to observe actions performed by your code.

After you create a macro, you should run it at least once to make sure it works correctly. Later in this chapter you will learn other ways to run macros, but for now, let's use the Macro dialog box.

◉ Hands-On 1.12   Running a Macro Using the Macro Dialog Box

1. Make sure that the Chap01_ExcelPrimer.xlsm workbook is open.
2. Delete the **Employee Wages** worksheet so we can start from scratch.
3. Choose **View | Macros | View Macros**.
4. In the Macro dialog box, click the **Insert_NewSheet** macro name.
5. Click **Run** to execute the macro.
   The Insert_NewSheet macro inserts a blank worksheet and renames it Employee Wages.

   Now, let's proceed to run the remaining macros. All macros should be run in the order they were recorded.
6. Choose **View | Macros | View Macros**.
7. In the Macro dialog box, click the **Insert_Headings** macro name.
8. Click **Run** to execute the macro.
9. Run the remaining macros: **Insert_EmployeeData, Get_FirstName, Get_LastName, CalculateWages**, and **FormatTable**.

After running all macros, you should see the completed and formatted Employee Wages worksheet.

Quite often, you will notice that your macro does not perform as expected the first time you run it. Perhaps during the macro recording you selected the wrong font or forgot to change the cell color or maybe you just realized it would be better to include an additional step. Don't panic. Excel makes it possible to modify the macro without forcing you to go through the tedious process of recording your keystrokes again.

Testing and Debugging a Macro

When you modify a recorded macro, it is quite possible that you will introduce some errors. For example, you may delete an important line of code, or you may inadvertently remove or omit a necessary period. To make sure that your macro continues to work correctly after your modifications, you need to run it again.

⊙ **Hands-On 1.13   Running a Macro from the VBE Screen**

1. In the Excel window, with the Employee Wages worksheet active, choose **Developer | Visual Basic**.
2. In the Visual Basic Editor Code window, place the pointer in any line of the **Insert_NewSheet** macro code (except for a comment line), and choose **Run | Run Sub/UserForm**.
   You should see the Microsoft Visual Basic error message dialog: *Run-time error '9' Subscript out of range* (see Figure 1.16). Visual Basic cannot find Sheet2 that the macro references, so it displays an error.

   Before you run macros, you must make sure that your macro can run in the worksheet that is currently selected. Click the **End** button in the error dialog box, and make sure that you select the correct worksheet before you try to run the macro again. In this case, you should either delete the Employee Wages worksheet, or insert a new workbook and rerun the macro.
3. When running a macro from a VBE screen, to see the result of your macro, you must switch to the Microsoft Excel window. To do this, press **Alt+F11**. Various errors can pop up during your macro execution. For example, if your macro code had a With...End With block and you happened to omit the period in With Selection.Font, Visual Basic will generate the "*Run time error '424' — Object required*" message when running this line of code. Instead of pressing the **End** button to end your macro, you can use the **Debug** button in the message box, so you can correct your macro code right away. When you press Debug, you will be placed in the Code window. At this time, Visual Basic will activate break mode and will use the yellow highlighter to indicate the line it had trouble executing. As soon as you correct your error, Visual Basic may announce, "*This action will reset your project, proceed anyway?*" Click **OK** to this message. Although you can edit code in break mode, some edits prevent continuing execution. After correcting the error, run the macro again, as there may be more errors to be fixed before the macro can run smoothly.
4. Switch back to the Visual Basic Editor screen by pressing **Alt+F11**.

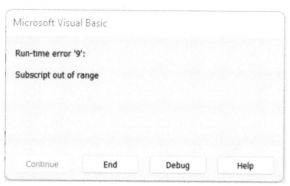

Microsoft Visual Basic

Run-time error '9':

Subscript out of range

| Continue | End | Debug | Help |

FIGURE 1.16 The Visual Basic Editor displays an error message when it encounters an error while executing a macro. The error may be caused by an incorrect statement or incorrect setup of worksheet environment prior to running a macro.

Saving and Renaming a Macro

The macros you recorded in this chapter are in a Microsoft Excel workbook. All macros are automatically saved when you save the workbook.

Hands-On 1.14 Saving Macros and Running Macros from Another Workbook

1. Close the **Chap01_ExcelPrimer.xlsm** workbook.
2. Open a brand-new workbook and press **Alt+F8** to open the Macro dialog box.

   Notice that there is no trace of your macros in the Macro dialog box. If you'd like to run the macros you recorded earlier in this chapter in another workbook, you need to open the file that stores these macros.
3. Close the Macro dialog box and save the open workbook file as **Chap01_ExcelPrimer2.xlsx** in your trusted **C:\VBAPrimerExcel2021_ByExample** folder. You will not have any macros in this workbook, so saving it in Excel's default file format will work just fine.
4. Open the **C:\VBAPrimerExcel2021_ByExample\Chap01_ExcelPrimer .xlsm** workbook file.
5. Activate **Sheet1** in the **Chap01_ExcelPrimer2.xlsx** workbook.
6. Press **Alt+F8** to activate the Macro dialog box. Notice that Excel displays macros in all open workbooks.
7. Run each of the macros listed in this dialog box in the order you have recorded them.

   Your macros go to work again. You should end up with the Employee Wages worksheet formatted to your liking.
8. Close the **Chap01_ExcelPrimer2.xlsx** workbook file. Do not save the changes. Do not close the Chap01_ExcelPrimer.xlsm workbook file. We will work with it in the next section.

When you add additional actions to your macro, you may want to change the macro name to better indicate its purpose. The name of the macro should communicate its function as clearly as possible. To change the macro name, you don't need to press a specific key. In the Code window, simply delete the old macro name and enter the new name following the Sub keyword.

Printing Macro Code

If you want to document your macro or perhaps study the macro code when you are away from the computer, you can print your macros. You can print the entire module sheet where your macro is stored or indicate a selection of lines to print. Let's print the entire module sheet that contains your macros.

⊙ **Hands-On 1.15   Printing Macro Code**

1. Switch to the Visual Basic Editor window and double-click **Module1** in the Project Explorer window to activate the module containing your macros.
2. Choose **File | Print**.
3. In the Print - VBAProject dialog box, the Current Module option button should be selected.
4. Click **OK** to print the entire module sheet.
   If you'd like to print only a certain block of programming code, perform the following steps:
1. In the module sheet, highlight the code you want to print.
2. Choose **File | Print**.
3. In the Print - VBAProject dialog box, the Selection option button should be selected.
4. Click **OK** to print the highlighted code.

IMPROVING YOUR RECORDED MACROS

After you record your macro, you may realize that you'd like the macro to perform additional tasks. Adding new instructions to the macro code is not very difficult if you are already familiar with the Visual Basic language. In most situations, however, you can do this more efficiently when you delegate the extra tasks to the macro recorder. You may argue that Excel records more instructions than are necessary. However, one thing is for sure—the macro recorder does not make mistakes. If you want to add additional instructions to your macro using the macro recorder, you must record a new macro, copy the sections you want, and paste them into the correct location in your original macro. Note that Microsoft Excel places the newly recorded macro in a new module sheet.

At times you may need to modify your macro code by removing some statements. Before you start deleting unnecessary lines of code, think of how you can use the comment feature that you've recently learned. You can comment out the unwanted lines and run the macro with the commented code. If the Visual Basic Editor does not generate errors, you can safely delete the commented lines. By following this path, you will never find yourself recording the same keystrokes more than once. And, if the macro does not perform correctly, you can remove the comments from the lines that may be needed after all.

When you create macros with the macro recorder, you can quickly learn the VBA equivalents for the Excel commands and dialog box settings. Then you can look up the meaning and the usage of these Visual Basic commands in the online help. It's obvious that the more instructions Visual Basic needs to read, the slower your macro will execute. Eliminating extraneous commands will speed up your macro. Learning the right word or expression in any language takes time. You'll learn about Visual Basic objects, properties, and methods in Chapter 3, "Excel VBA Fundamentals."

SIDEBAR *Including Additional Instructions*

To include additional instructions in the existing macro, add empty lines in the required places of the macro code by pressing Enter, and type in the necessary Visual Basic statements. If the additional instructions are keyboard actions or menu commands, you may use the macro recorder to generate the necessary code and then copy and paste these code lines into the original macro.

Want to add more improvements to your macro? How about a message to notify you when Visual Basic has finished executing the last macro line? This sort of action cannot be recorded, as Excel does not have a corresponding Ribbon command or shortcut menu option. However, using the Visual Basic for Applications language, you can add new instructions to your macro by hand. Let's see how this is done.

Hands-On 1.16   Adding Visual Basic Statements to the Recorded Macro Code

1. In the Code window containing the code of the **FormatTable** macro, click in front of the End Sub keywords and press **Enter**.
2. Place your cursor on the empty line and type the following statement:

```
MsgBox "Your worksheet is ready."
```

3. Press Ctrl+S to save the changes made in your macro code.
   When you run this macro next time around, you should see a message box with your programmed message text. You must click the OK button in the message box to discard this message. MsgBox is one of the most frequently used built-in VBA functions. You will learn more about its usage in Chapter 4, "Excel VBA Procedures."

CREATING A MASTER MACRO

In this chapter you recorded several macros that required that you execute them in the order they were recorded. Instead of running your macros one by one, it is more convenient to have one master macro that will perform all the required tasks in the correct order. Let's see how this is done in the next Hands-On.

(⦿) **Hands-On 1.17   Creating a Master Macro Procedure**

1. Switch to the Microsoft Visual Basic for Application window and select **VBAProject (Chap01_ExcelPrimer.xlsm)** in the Project Explorer window.
2. Choose **Insert | Module** to add a new module to the selected VBA project.
3. In the Properties window select **Module2** next to the (Name) property and rename it **MasterProcedure**.
4. In the Code window on your right, enter the following procedure:

```
Sub CreateEmployeeWorksheet()
    Insert_NewSheet
    Insert_Headings
    Insert_EmployeeData
    Get_FirstName
    Get_LastName
    CalculateWages
    FormatTable
End Sub
```

5. Press **Ctrl+S** to save the changes.
6. Choose **File | Close and Return to Microsoft Excel**.
7. In the Microsoft Excel window, choose **File | New | Blank workbook**.
8. Choose **View | Macros | View Macros** to display the Macro dialog box.
9. Select the **CreateEmployeeWorksheet** macro name and click **Run**.
   Excel runs your code and displays a message box that you added in the previous Hands-On.
10. Click **OK** to dismiss the message box.
11. Close the Excel workbook you just created without saving it.
    In this Hands-On you learned how easy it is to combine stand-alone macros into a master macro. All you need to do is list the macro names on separate lines between the Sub and End Sub keywords and name your macro. You could also copy all the code of the recorded macros into a new macro; however, this will make the macro code more difficult to troubleshoot. It is much easier to understand and work with shorter macros. When referencing macro names in other macros any misspelling of a macro name will cause a compile error *"Sub or Function not defined"* when you attempt to run your macro.

In Chapter 9 of this book, you will learn about different types of errors and techniques that will allow you to test your macros using Excel built-in tools.

VARIOUS METHODS OF RUNNING MACROS

So far in this chapter, you have learned a couple of methods of running macros. You already know that you can run a macro from the VBE screen or a Macro dialog box in the Microsoft Excel application window.

In the VBE screen you can run your macro / Visual Basic code in one of the following ways:

- Press F5 on the keyboard
- Choose Run | Run Sub/UserForm
- Choose Tools | Macros
- Click the Run Sub/UserForm (F5) button on the Standard toolbar as shown in Figure 1.17.

In this section, you will learn three cool methods of macro execution that will allow you to run your macros using a keyboard shortcut, toolbar button, or worksheet button. Let's get started.

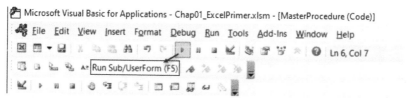

FIGURE 1.17 The Visual Basic code can also be run from the toolbar button.

Running the Macro Using a Keyboard Shortcut

A popular method to run a macro is by using an assigned keyboard shortcut. It is much faster to press Ctrl+Shift+I than it is to activate the macro from the Macro dialog box. Before you can use the keyboard shortcut, you must assign it to your macro. Let's learn how this is done.

(◉) **Hands-On 1.18   Assigning a Macro to a Keyboard Shortcut**

1. In the Excel application window, press **Alt+F8** to open the Macro dialog box.
2. In the list of macros, click the **CreateEmployeeWorksheet** macro, and then choose the **Options** button.

3. When the Macro Options dialog box appears, the cursor is in the Shortcut key text box.

4. Hold down the **Shift** key and press the letter **I** on the keyboard. Excel records the keyboard combination as Ctrl+Shift+I. The result is shown in Figure 1.18.

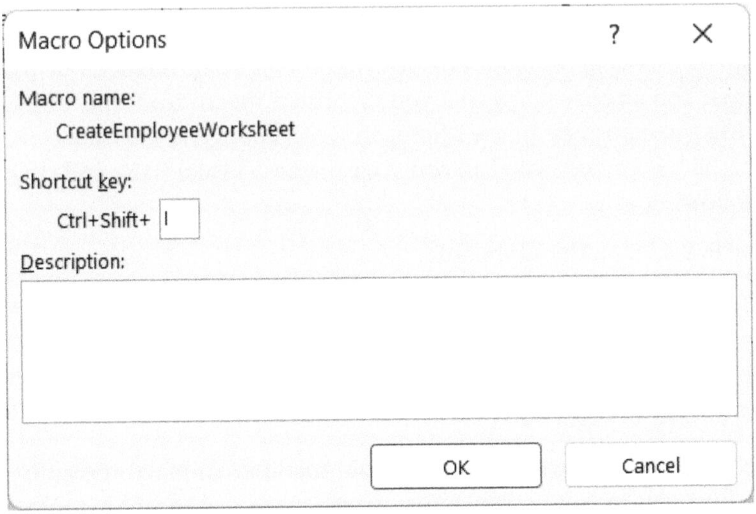

Macro Options	?	✕

Macro name:

    CreateEmployeeWorksheet

Shortcut key:

    Ctrl+Shift+ I

Description:

        OK   Cancel

FIGURE 1.18 Using the Macro Options dialog box, you can assign a keyboard shortcut for running a macro.

5. Click **OK** to close the Macro Options dialog box.
6. Click **Cancel** to close the Macro dialog box and return to the worksheet.
7. To run your macro using the newly assigned keyboard shortcut, open a new workbook and press **Ctrl+Shift+I**.
   Your macro goes to work, and your worksheet is ready to use.
8. Close the workbook with the employee worksheet you just created without saving it.

SIDEBAR *Avoid Shortcut Conflicts*

If you assign to your macro a keyboard shortcut that conflicts with a Microsoft Excel built-in shortcut, Excel will run your macro if the workbook containing the macro code is currently open.

Running the Macro from the Quick Access Toolbar

You can add your own buttons to the built-in Quick Access toolbar. Let's see how it is done to run a macro from Excel.

⊙ **Hands-On 1.19   Running a Macro from the Quick Access Toolbar**

1. In the Microsoft Excel window, click the **Customize Quick Access Toolbar** button (the downward-pointing arrow in the title bar) and choose **More Commands** as shown in Figure 1.19.

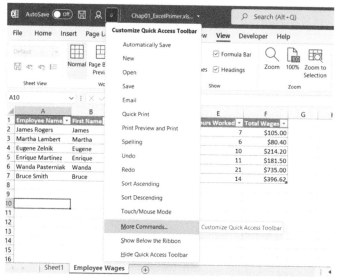

FIGURE 1.19 Adding a new button to the Quick Access toolbar (Step 1).

The Excel Options dialog box appears with the page titled Customize the Quick Access Toolbar.

2. In the Choose commands from drop-down list box, select **Macros**.
3. Select **CreateEmployeeWorksheet** in the list box on the left-hand side.
4. Click the **Add** button to move the CreateEmployeeWorksheet macro to the list box on the right-hand side.
   The current selections are shown in Figure 1.20.
5. To change the button image for your macro, click the **Modify** button.
6. In the button gallery, select any button you like and click **OK**.
7. After closing the gallery window, make sure that the image to the left of the macro name has changed.
8. Click **OK** to close the Excel Options dialog.
   You should now see a new button on the Quick Access toolbar as shown in Figure 1.21. This button will be available for any open workbook.
9. Click the macro button you've just added to run the macro assigned to it. Again, your macro goes to work; however, this time it runs into a problem. Recall that previously before you ran it you opened a new blank workbook. To run this macro from any workbook, you need to modify it.
10. Click the **End** button in the error dialog box.
11. Switch to the Visual Basic Editor screen and modify the **Insert_ NewSheet** macro as shown in Figure 1.22.

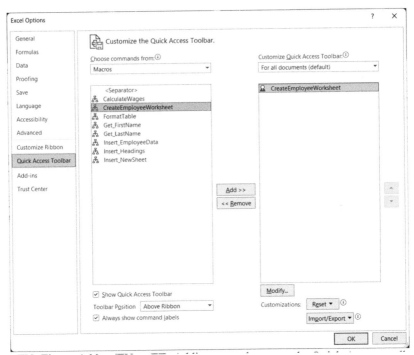

FIGURE 1.20 Adding a new button to the Quick Access toolbar (Step 2).

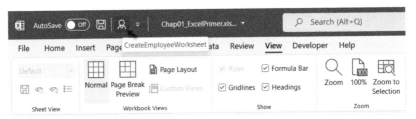

FIGURE 1.21 A custom button placed on the Quick Access toolbar will run the specified macro (Step 3).

```
Sub Insert_NewSheet()
'
' Insert_NewSheet Macro
' Insert and rename a worksheet
'

'
    Sheets.Add After:=ActiveSheet
    ActiveSheet.Name = Application.InputBox("Enter the name for your worksheet:", "Rename This Sheet")

End Sub
```

FIGURE 1.22 The recorded Insert_NewSheet macro was modified to correct issues encountered during its execution.

To allow the user to name the sheet during the macro execution you can use the Excel InputBox method discussed in detail in Chapter 4.

12. Save the workbook and return to the Microsoft Excel window.

13. Click the macro button on the Quick Access toolbar (see Figure 1.21). Excel adds a new worksheet to the active workbook and prompts you for the name of the worksheet.

14. Enter any name for the newly created worksheet and click **OK**.

NOTE	*If you clicked the Cancel button instead of typing in the name for the worksheet, Visual Basic will run into an issue and you will see the Application-defined or object-defined run time error 1004. Click End to close the error message and you will be returned to the Microsoft Excel application window. Manually delete the empty sheet that was added to the workbook and execute the macro again this time entering the name for the sheet when prompted. You will learn how to handle the Cancel button in Chapter 9.*

After you supply the worksheet name, the Visual Basic continues to execute the remaining macros in your master procedure. The execution fails again when the program reaches the FormatTable procedure. What's wrong with this macro code? It worked perfectly well when you recorded it. Oftentimes issues with recorded code arise with the named ranges. A line of the Format-Table procedure assigns the name 'Table1' to the table range. Because you are running the master procedure inside the workbook where the 'Table1' name already exists, the Visual Basic throws the error – "Select method of range class failed". Table names within the workbook must be unique. For your code to run correctly you must revise the FormatTable procedure.

15. Click the **Debug** button in the error message dialog and Visual Basic will highlight the line of code it cannot execute.

16. Exit the break mode by choosing **Run | Reset**.

17. Modify the **FormatTable** procedure as shown in Figure 1.23.

```
Sub FormatTable()
'
' FormatTable Revised Macro
'

'
Dim strTableName As String
strTableName = InputBox("Enter the name for your table:", "Name your table range")

    ActiveSheet.ListObjects.Add(xlSrcRange, Range("$A$1:$F$7"), , xlYes).Name = strTableName
    ActiveSheet.ListObjects(strTableName).TableStyle = "TableStyleLight14"
    Range("A1").Select
    MsgBox "Your worksheet is ready."
End Sub
```

FIGURE 1.23 The recorded macro FormatTable was modified to correct issues encountered during its execution.

The first line of code in the revised procedure declares *strTableName* variable to hold the name of the table supplied by the InputBox function on the next line. You will learn about variables and their types, declarations, and assignments in Chapter 3. The third line creates a new list object and assigns it a name stored in the *strTableName* variable. Every time you run the procedure and are prompted for a table name you must enter a unique name.

After adding and assigning a name to the table object, the macro again refers to the *strTableName* variable to assign a predefined formatting style to the table. The procedure then selects cell A1 in the active worksheet and displays a message to the user.

18. After making changes to the **FormatTable** procedure save your code and return to the Microsoft Excel application window.

19. Run the procedure again by clicking the button on the Quick Access toolbar.

The master procedure should now run as expected.

Running the Macro from a Worksheet Button

Sometimes it makes the most sense to place a macro button right on the worksheet, where it cannot be missed. Let's go over the steps that will attach the WhatsInACell macro to a worksheet button.

Hands-On 1.20   Running a Macro from a Button Placed on a Worksheet

1. Copy **Chap01_Supplement.xlsm** workbook from the companion files to your **C:\VBAPrimerExcel2021_ByExample** folder.
2. Open the copied workbook file in Excel.
3. Choose **Developer | Insert**. The Forms toolbar appears, as shown in Figure 1.24.

FIGURE 1.24 Adding a button to a worksheet.

4. In the Form Controls area, click the first image, which represents a button.
5. Click anywhere in the empty area of the worksheet. When the Assign Macro dialog box appears, choose the **WhatsInACell** macro and click **OK**.
6. Excel creates a button with the default label 'Button 1'. To change the button's label, click inside the button, delete the default text and type **Format Cells**. If the text does not fit, do not worry; you will resize the button in Step 7. When the button is selected, it looks like the one shown in Figure 1.25. If the selection handles are not displayed, right-click **Button 1** on the worksheet and choose **Edit Text** on the shortcut menu. Select the default text and enter the new label.

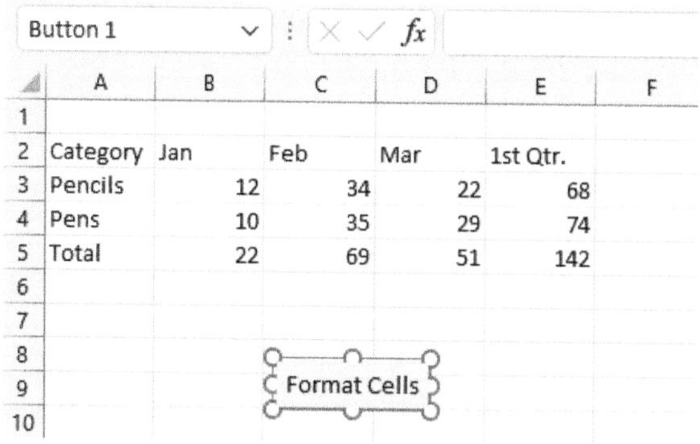

FIGURE 1.25 A button with an attached macro.

7. When you're done renaming the button, click outside the button to exit the edit mode.
   Because the text you entered is longer than the default button text, let's resize the button so that the entire text is visible.

8. Right-click the button you've just renamed to select it, point to one of the tiny circles that appear in the button's right edge, and drag right to expand the button until you see the complete entry, Format Cells.

NOTE	*If you left click the button inadvertently, there is nothing you can do to stop the macro from running. You can resize the button after the macro has run.*

9. When you're done resizing the button, click outside the button to exit the selection mode.

10. To run your macro, click the button you just created.
    Your macro goes to work, and your worksheet is now formatted as shown in Figure 1.26.

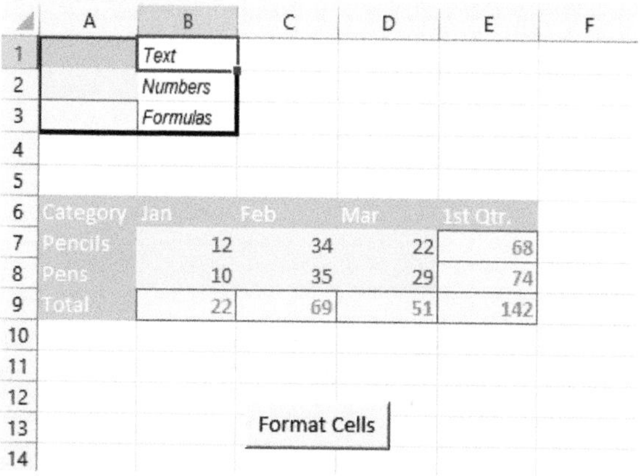

FIGURE 1.26 The worksheet was formatted with a macro attached to the Format Cells button.

Let's remove the formatting you just applied by running the RemoveFormats macro.

11. Press **Alt+F8** to open the Macro dialog box. Select the **RemoveFormats** macro and click the **Run** button.

12. On your own, create another button on this worksheet that will be used for running the RemoveFormats macro.

13. Save your workbook with a different file name so that the original workbook can be reused again in case you'd like to revisit the button creation process.

NOTE	*The code of WhatsInACell and RemoveFormat macros in this practice workbook was written by the built-in macro recorder while executing a series of commands via Excel menu / Ribbon options.*

You can also run macros from a hyperlink, or a button placed in the Ribbon. These techniques are not introduced in this book because they require the understanding of the advanced topic of Ribbon Customizations.

SUMMARY

In this chapter, you have learned how to create macros by recording your selections in the Microsoft Excel application window. You also learned how to view, read, and modify the recorded macros in the Visual Basic Editor window. In addition, you tried various methods of running macros. This chapter has also explained macro security issues that you should be aware of when opening workbooks containing macro code.

The next chapter focuses on using the Visual Basic Editor window.

Chapter 2

EXCEL PROGRAMMING ENVIRONMENT

A QUICK OVERVIEW OF ITS TOOLS AND FEATURES (VBE)

Now that you know how to record, run, and edit macros, let's spend some time in the Visual Basic Editor window (also known as VBE) and become familiar with its features. With the tools located in the VBE window, you can:

- Write your own VBA procedures.
- Create custom forms.
- View and modify object properties.
- Test VBA procedures and locate errors.

The Visual Basic Editor window can be accessed in the following ways:

- Choose Developer | Code | Visual Basic.
- Choose Developer | Controls | View Code.
- Press Alt+F11.

UNDERSTANDING THE PROJECT EXPLORER WINDOW

The Project Explorer window displays a hierarchical list of currently open projects and their elements. A VBA project can contain the following elements:

- Worksheets
- Charts
- ThisWorkbook—The workbook where the project is stored
- Modules—Special sheets where programming code is stored
- Classes—Special modules that allow you to create your own objects
- Forms
- References to the other projects

With the Project Explorer you can manage your projects and easily move between projects that are loaded into memory. You can activate the Project Explorer window in one of three ways:

- From the View menu by selecting Project Explorer.
- From the keyboard by pressing Ctrl+R.
- From the Standard toolbar by clicking the Project Explorer button as shown in Figure 2.1.

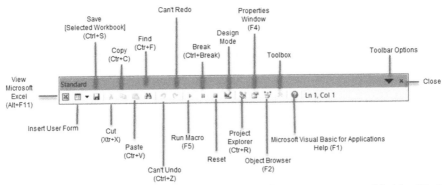

FIGURE 2.1 Buttons on the Standard toolbar provide a quick way to access many of the Visual Basic Editor features.

The Project Explorer window contains three buttons as shown in Figure 2.2. The first button from the left (View Code) displays the Code window for the selected module. The middle button (View Object) displays either the selected sheet in the Microsoft Excel Object folder or a form located in the Forms folder. The button on the right (Toggle Folders) hides and/or activates the display of folders in the Project Explorer window.

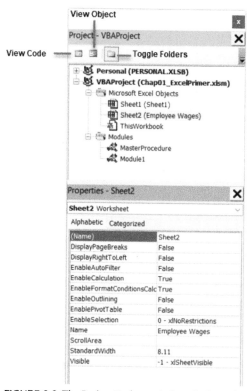

FIGURE 2.2 The Project Explorer window displays a list of currently open projects. The Properties window displays the settings for the object currently selected in the Project Explorer.

UNDERSTANDING THE PROPERTIES WINDOW

The Properties window allows you to review and set properties of various objects in your project. The name of the currently selected object is displayed in the Object box located just below the Properties window's title bar. For example, Figure 2.2 displays the properties of the Sheet1 object. Properties of the object can be viewed alphabetically or by category by clicking the appropriate tab.

- Alphabetic tab—Lists alphabetically all properties for the selected object. You can change the property setting by selecting the property name and typing or selecting the new setting.

- Categorized tab—Lists all properties for the selected object by category. You can collapse the list so that you see the categories, or you can expand a category to see the properties. The plus sign (+) icon to the left of the category name indicates that the category list can be expanded. The minus sign (–) indicates that the category is currently expanded.

The Properties window can be accessed in three ways:

- From the View menu by selecting Properties Window.
- From the keyboard by pressing F4.
- From the toolbar by clicking the Properties Window button.

UNDERSTANDING THE CODE WINDOW

The Code window is used for Visual Basic programming as well as viewing and modifying the code of recorded macros and existing VBA procedures. Each module can be opened in a separate Code window. There are several ways to activate the Code window:

- From the Project Explorer window, choose the appropriate UserForm or module, and click the View Code button.
- From the menu bar, choose View | Code.
- From the keyboard, press F7.

In Figure 2.3, you will notice at the top of the Code window two drop-down list boxes that allow you to move quickly within the Visual Basic code. In the Object box on the left side of the Code window, you can select the object whose code you want to view. The box on the right side of the Code window lets you quickly choose a procedure or event procedure to view. When you open this box, the names of all procedures located in a module are sorted alphabetically. If you select a procedure in the Procedures/Events box, the cursor will jump to the first line of this procedure.

By dragging the split bar shown in Figure 2.3 down to a selected position in the Code window, you can divide the Code window into two panes. You can then view different sections of a long procedure or a different procedure in each pane. This two-pane display in the Code window is often used for copying or cutting and pasting sections of code between procedures of the same module.

To return to the one-window display, simply drag the split bar all the way to the top of the Code window.

At the bottom left of the Code window, there are two icons. The Procedure View icon displays one procedure at a time in the Code window. To select another procedure, use the Procedures/Events box. The Full Module View icon displays all the procedures in the selected module. Use the vertical scrollbar to scroll through the module's code.

The margin indicator bar is used by Visual Basic Editor to display helpful indicators during editing and debugging. If you'd like to take a quick look at some of these indicators, skim through Chapter 9, "Excel Tools for Testing and Debugging."

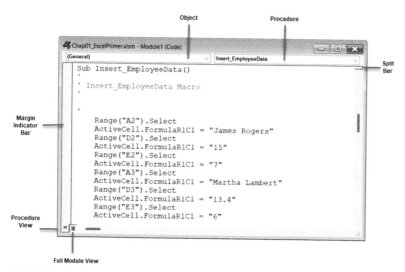

FIGURE 2.3 The Visual Basic Code window has several elements that make it easy to locate procedures and review the VBA code.

SETTING THE VBE OPTIONS

There are several other windows that are frequently used in the Visual Basic environment.

Figure 2.4 displays the list of windows that can be docked in the Visual Basic Editor window. You will learn how to use some of these windows in Chapter 3 (Object Browser, Immediate window) and Chapter 9 (Locals window, Watch window).

FIGURE 2.4 The Docking tab in the Tools | Options dialog box allows you to choose which windows you want to be dockable in the Visual Basic Editor screen.

SYNTAX AND PROGRAMMING ASSISTANCE

Figure 2.5 shows the Edit toolbar in the VBE window that contains several buttons that let you enter correctly formatted VBA instructions with speed and ease. If the Edit toolbar isn't currently docked in the Visual Basic Editor window, you can turn it on by choosing View | Toolbars | Edit.

Writing procedures in Visual Basic requires that you use hundreds of built-in instructions and functions. Because most people cannot memorize the correct syntax of all the instructions that are available in VBA, the IntelliSense® technology provides you with syntax and programming assistance on demand when entering instructions. You can have special windows pop up and guide you through the process of creating correct VBA code.

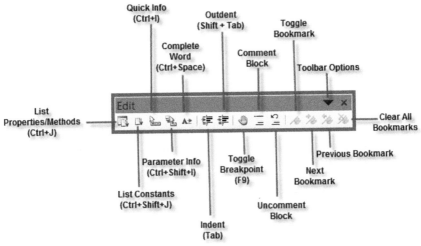

FIGURE 2.5 Buttons located on the Edit toolbar make it easy to write and format VBA instructions.

List Properties/Methods

Each object can contain several properties and methods. When you enter the name of the object and a period that separates the name of the object from its property or method in the Code window, a pop-up menu may appear. This menu lists the properties and methods available for the object that precedes the period as shown in Figure 2.6. To turn on this automated feature, choose Tools | Options. In the Options dialog box, click the Editor tab, and make sure the Auto List Members check box is selected.

To choose an item from the pop-up menu that appears, start typing the name of the property or method that you want to select. When Excel highlights the correct item name, press Enter to insert the item into your code and start a new line. Or, if you want to continue writing instructions on the same line, press the Tab key instead. You can also double-click the item to insert it in your code. To close the pop-up menu without inserting an item,

```
Sub InsertNewSheet()
    Worksheets.|
End Sub
```

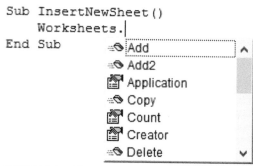

FIGURE 2.6 While you are entering the VBA instructions, Visual Basic suggests properties and methods that can be used with the object.

simply press Esc. When you press Esc to remove the pop-up menu, Visual Basic will not display it again for the same object. To display the Properties/Methods pop-up menu again, you can:

- Press Ctrl+J.
- Use the Backspace key to delete the period and type the period again.
- Right-click in the Code window and select List Properties/Methods from the shortcut menu.
- Choose Edit | List Properties/Methods.
- Click the List Properties/Methods button on the Edit toolbar.

List Constants

A *constant* is a value that indicates a specific state or result. Excel has many predefined, built-in constants. You will learn about constants, their types, and usage in Chapter 3.

Suppose you want your program to turn on the Page Break Preview of your worksheet. In the Microsoft Excel application window, the View tab lists four types of workbook views:

- The Normal View is the default view for most tasks in Excel.
- Page Layout View allows you to view the document as it will appear on the printed page.
- Page Break Preview allows you to see where pages will break when the document is printed.
- Custom Views allows you to save the set of display and print settings as a custom view.

The first three view options are represented by a built-in constant. Microsoft Excel constant names begin with the characters "xl." As soon as you enter in the Code window the instruction:

```
ActiveWindow.View =
```

a pop-up menu will appear with the names of valid constants for the property, as shown in Figure 2.7.

```
Sub PrintView()
    ActiveWindow.View =
End Sub
```

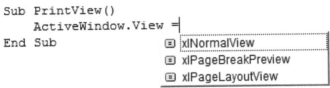

FIGURE 2.7 The List Constants pop-up menu displays a list of constants that are valid for the property entered.

To work with the List Constants pop-up menu, use the same techniques as for the List Properties/Methods pop-up menu outlined in the preceding section.

The List Constants pop-up menu can be activated by pressing Ctrl+Shift+J or clicking the List Constants button on the Edit toolbar.

Parameter Info

If you've had a chance to work with Excel worksheet functions, you already know that many functions require one or more arguments (or *parameters*). For example, here's the syntax for the most common worksheet function:

```
SUM(number1,number2, ...)
```

where `number1, number2, ...` are 1 to 30 arguments that you can add up.

Like functions, VBA methods may require one or more arguments. If a method requires an argument, you can see the names of required and optional arguments in a tooltip box that appears just below the cursor as soon as you type the beginning parenthesis as illustrated in Figure 2.8. In the tooltip, the current argument is displayed in bold. When you supply the first argument and enter the comma, Visual Basic displays the next argument in bold. Optional arguments are surrounded by square brackets [ ].

You can open the Parameter Info tooltip using the keyboard. To do this, enter the method or function name, follow it with the left parenthesis, and press Ctrl+Shift+I. You can also click the Parameter Info button on the Edit toolbar or choose Edit | Parameter Info.

```
Sub PrintView()
    ActiveWindow.View = xlPageBreakPreview
    ActiveWorkbook.SaveAs
End Sub    SaveAs([Filename], [FileFormat], [Password], [WriteResPassword], [ReadOnlyRecommended], [CreateBackup], [AccessMode As
           XlSaveAsAccessMode = xlNoChange], [ConflictResolution], [AddToMru], [TextCodepage], [TextVisualLayout], [Local])
```

FIGURE 2.8 A tooltip displays a list of arguments utilized by a VBA method.

The Parameter Info feature makes it easy for you to supply correct arguments to a VBA method. In addition, it reminds you of two other things that are very important for the method to work correctly: the order of the arguments and the required data type of each argument. You will learn about data types in Chapter 3.

Quick Info

When you select an instruction, function, method, procedure name, or constant in the Code window and then click the Quick Info button on the Edit toolbar (or press Ctrl+I), Visual Basic displays the syntax of the highlighted item, as well as the value of a constant, as depicted in Figure 2.9. The Quick Info feature can be turned on or off using the Options dialog box. To use the feature, click the Editor tab and choose the Auto Quick Info option.

```
Sub PrintView()
    ActiveWindow.View = xlPageBreakPreview
    ActiveWorkbook.SaveA xlPageBreakPreview = 2 el_ByExample\CopyChap02_ExcelPrimer.xlsm")
End Sub
```

FIGURE 2.9 The Quick Info feature displays a list of arguments required by a selected method or function, a value of a selected constant, or the type of the selected object or property.

Complete Word

Another way to increase the speed of writing VBA procedures in the Code window is with the Complete Word feature. As you enter the first few letters of a keyword and press Ctrl+Spacebar or click the Complete Word button on the Edit toolbar, Visual Basic will fill in the remaining letters by completing the keyword entry for you. For example, when you enter the first four letters of the keyword Application (Appl) in the Code window and press Ctrl+Spacebar, Visual Basic will complete the rest of the word, and in the place of "Appl," you will see the entire word "Application."

Indent/Outdent

If the Auto Indent option is turned on, you can automatically indent the selected lines of code by the number of characters specified in the Tab Width text box. The default entry for Auto Indent is four characters. You can easily change this setting via the Options dialog box (by selecting the Editor tab; see Figure 2.4).

Why would you want to use indentation in your code? When you indent certain lines in your VBA procedures, you make them more readable and easier to understand. Indenting is especially recommended for entering lines of code that make decisions or repeat actions. You will learn how to create these kinds of Visual Basic instructions in Chapters 5 and 6, "Adding Decisions to Excel VBA Programs" and "Adding Repeating Actions to Excel VBA Programs." Let's spend a few minutes learning how to apply the indent and outdent features to the lines of code in the WhatsInACell macro that you worked with in Chapter 1.

(⦿) Hands-On 2.1   Indenting/Outdenting Visual Basic Code

1. Open the **Chap01_Supplement.xlsm** workbook that you worked with in Chapter 1.

2. Press **Alt+F11** to switch to the VBE window.
3. Choose **View | Toolbars | Edit** to gain access to the Editing toolbar. If the toolbar pops up in the middle of the screen, double-click its title bar to get it docked at the top of the VBE window.
4. In the Project Explorer window, select the **Chap01_Supplement. xlsm**VBA project and activate the **Module1** that contains the code of the **WhatsInACell** macro.
5. Select the block of code located between the keyword `With` and `End With`.
6. Click the **Indent** button (see Figure 2.5) on the Edit toolbar or press **Tab** on the keyboard. The selected block of instructions will move four spaces to the right if you are using the default setting in the Tab Width box in the Options dialog box (Editor tab).
7. Click the **Outdent** button on the Edit toolbar or press **Shift+Tab** to return the selected lines of code to the previous location in the Code window.
8. Close the **Chap01_Supplement.xlsm** workbook.
   The Indent and Outdent options are also available from the Edit menu.

Comment Block/Uncomment Block

In Chapter 1, you learned that a single quote placed at the beginning of a line of code denotes a comment. Not only do comments make it easier to understand what the procedure does, but also, they are very useful in testing and troubleshooting VBA code.

For example, when you execute your code, it may not run as expected. Instead of deleting the lines that may be responsible for the problems you encounter, you may want to skip those lines of code for now and return to them later. By placing a single quote at the beginning of the line you want to avoid, you can continue checking the other parts of your procedure.

- To comment a few lines of code, simply select the lines and click the Comment Block button on the Edit toolbar (see Figure 2.5).
- To turn the commented code back into VBA instructions, select the lines and click the Uncomment Block button on the Edit toolbar (see Figure 2.5).

If you don't select text and click the Comment Block button, the single quote is added only to the line of code where the cursor is currently located.

USING THE OBJECT BROWSER

You can move easily through the myriad of VBA elements and features by examining the capabilities of the Object Browser. To access the Object Browser, use any of the following methods in the VBE window:

- Press F2.

- Choose View | Object Browser.
- Click the Object Browser button on the toolbar.

The Object Browser allows you to browse through the objects that are available to your VBA procedures, as well as view their properties, methods, and events. With the aid of the Object Browser, you can move quickly between procedures in your own VBA projects, as well as search for objects and methods across object type libraries.

The Object Browser window is divided into three sections as illustrated in Figure 2.10. The top of the window displays the Project/Library drop-down list box with the names of all libraries and projects that are available to the currently active VBA project. A library is a special file that contains information about the objects in an application. New libraries can be added via the References dialog box (Tools | References). The entry for <All Libraries> lists the objects of all libraries that are installed on your computer. When you select the library called Excel, you will see only the names of the objects that are exclusive to Microsoft Excel. In contrast to the Excel library, the VBA library lists the names of all the objects in Visual Basic for Applications.

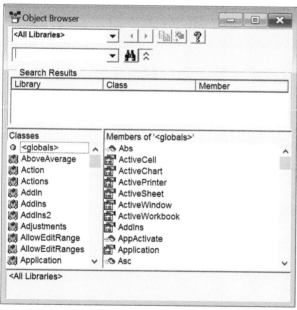

FIGURE 2.10 The Object Browser window allows you to browse through all the objects, properties, and methods available to the current VBA project.

Below the Project/Library drop-down list box is a Search text box that you'll use to quickly find information in a library. This field remembers the last four items for which you searched. To find only whole words, you can right-click anywhere in the Object Browser window and choose Find Whole Word Only from the shortcut menu.

The Search Results section of the Object Browser displays the library, class, and member elements that met the criteria entered in the Search text box as shown in Figure 2.11.

When you type the search text and click the Search button (the binoculars icon), Visual Basic expands the Object Browser dialog box to show the Search Results area. You can hide or show the Search Results by clicking the button located to the right of the Search button.

The Classes list box displays the available object classes in the selected library. If you select a VBA project, this list shows objects in the project. In Figure 2.11 the Application object class is selected. When you highlight a class, the list on the right-hand side (Members) shows the properties, methods, and events available for that class. By default, members are listed alphabetically. You can, however, organize the members list by group type (properties, methods, or events) using the Group Members command from the Object Browser shortcut menu.

If you select a VBA project in the Project/Library list box, the Members list box will list all the procedures available in this project. To examine the code of a procedure, simply double-click its name. If you select a VBA library, you will see a listing of Visual Basic built-in functions and constants. If you need more information on the selected class or a member, click the question mark button at the top of the Object Browser window.

FIGURE 2.11 Searching for answers in the Object Browser.

The bottom of the Object Browser window displays a code template area with the definition of the selected member. If you click the green hyperlink text in the code template, you can quickly jump to the selected member's class or library in the Object Browser window. Text displayed in the code template area can be copied to the Windows clipboard and then pasted to a Code window. If the Code window is visible while the Object Browser window is open, you can save time by dragging the highlighted code template and dropping it into the Code window.

You can easily adjust the size of the various sections of the Object Browser window by dragging the dividing horizontal and vertical lines.

Now that you've discovered the Object Browser, you may wonder how you can put it to use in VBA programming. Let's assume that you placed a text box in the middle of your worksheet. How can you make Excel move this text box so that it is positioned at the top left-hand corner of the sheet? Hands-On 2.2 should provide the answer to this question.

Hands-On 2.2   Writing a VBA Procedure to Move a Text Box on the Worksheet

1. Open a new workbook.
2. Choose **Insert | Text |Text Box**.
3. Now draw a box in the middle of the sheet and enter any text as shown in Figure 2.12.

FIGURE 2.12 Excel displays the name of the inserted object in the Name box above the worksheet.

4. Select any cell outside the text box area.
5. Press **Alt+F11** to activate the Visual Basic Editor window.
6. Choose **Insert | Module** to add a new module sheet.
7. In the Properties window, enter the new name for this module: **Manipulations**.
8. Choose **View | Object Browser** or press **F2**.
9. In the Project/Library list box, click the drop-down arrow and select the **Excel** library.

10. Enter **textbox** as the search text in the Search box as shown in Figure 2.13, and then click the **Search** button. Make sure you don't enter a space in the search string.

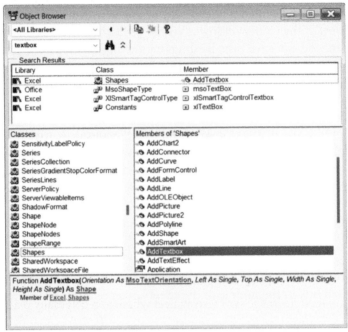

FIGURE 2.13 Using the Object Browser window, you can find the appropriate VBA instructions for writing your own procedures.

Visual Basic searches the Excel library and displays the search results. It appears that the Shapes object shown in Figure 2.13 is in control of our text box operations. Looking at the members list, you can quickly determine that the `AddTextbox` method is used for adding a new text box to a worksheet. The code template at the bottom of the Object Browser shows the correct syntax for using this method. If you select the `AddTextbox` method and press F1, you will see the Help window with more details on how to use this method. The Help window tells us that the Left and Top properties determine the position of the text box in a worksheet.

11. Close the Object Browser window and the Help window if they are open. Double-click the **Manipulations** module and enter the MoveTextBox procedure, as shown here:

```
Sub MoveTextBox()
    With ActiveSheet.Shapes("TextBox 1")
        .Select
        .Left = 0
        .Top = 0
    End With
End Sub
```

The MoveTextBox procedure selects TextBox 1 in the collection of Shapes. TextBox 1 is the default name of the first object placed in the worksheet. Each time you add a new object to your worksheet, Excel assigns a new number (index) to it. Instead of using the object name, you can refer to the member of a collection by its index. For example, instead of:

```
With ActiveSheet.Shapes("TextBox 1")
```

enter:

```
With ActiveSheet.Shapes(1)
```

12. Choose **Run | Run Sub/UserForm** to execute this procedure.
13. Press **Alt+F11** to switch to the Microsoft Excel application window. The text box should be positioned at the top left-hand corner of the worksheet.
14. Save the workbook file as **Chap02_ExcelPrimer.xlsm**. Keep this file open as you will continue to work with it in Hands-On 2.3.

Let's manipulate another object with Visual Basic.

Hands-On 2.3   Writing a VBA Procedure to Move a Circle on the Worksheet

1. Place a small circle in the same worksheet where you originally placed the text box in Hands-On 2.2. Use the **Oval** shape in the Basic Shapes area of the **Insert | Illustrations | Shapes** tool. Hold down the **Shift** key while drawing on the worksheet to create a perfect circle.
2. Click outside the circle to deselect it.
3. Press **Alt+F11** to activate the Visual Basic Editor screen.
4. In the Manipulations Module's Code window, write a VBA procedure that will place the circle inside the text box. Keep in mind that Excel numbers objects consecutively. The first object is assigned a number 1, the second object a number 2, and so on. The type of object—whether it is a text box, a circle, or a rectangle—does not matter.
5. The MoveCircle procedure shown here demonstrates how to move a circle to the top left-hand corner of the active worksheet:

```
Sub MoveCircle()
    With ActiveSheet.Shapes(2)
        .Select
        .Left = 0
        .Top = 0
    End With
End Sub
```

Moving a circle is like moving a text box or any other object placed in a worksheet. Notice that instead of referring to the circle by its name, Oval 2, the procedure uses the object's index.

6. Run the MoveCircle procedure.
7. Press **Alt+F11** to return to the Microsoft Excel window.
8. The circle should now appear on the top of the text box.

Locating Procedures with the Object Browser

In addition to locating objects, properties, and methods, the Object Browser is a handy tool for locating and accessing procedures written in various VBA projects. The Hands-On 2.4 exercise demonstrates how you can find quickly which procedures are stored in the selected project.

Hands-On 2.4   Using Object Browser to Locate VBA Procedures

1. In the Object Browser, select **VBAProject** from the Project/Library drop-down list as shown in Figure 2.14.
   The left side of the Object Browser displays the names of objects that are included in the selected project. The Members list box on the right shows the names of all the available procedures.

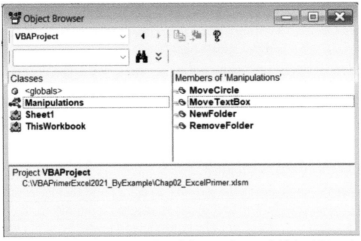

FIGURE 2.14 The Object Browser lists all the procedures available in a VBA project.

2. In the Members list, double-click the **MoveCircle** procedure.
3. Excel locates the selected procedure in the Code window.

USING THE VBA OBJECT LIBRARY

In the previous examples, you used the properties of objects that are members of the Shapes collection in the Excel object library. While the Excel library contains objects specific to using Microsoft Excel, the VBA object library provides access to many built-in VBA functions that are general in nature. They allow you to manage files, set the date and time, interact with users, convert data types, deal with text strings, or perform mathematical calculations. In the following Hands-On 2.5 exercise, you will use one of the built-in VBA functions to create a new Windows subfolder without leaving Excel.

Hands-On 2.5   Writing a VBA Procedure to Create a Folder in Windows

1. Press **Alt+F11** to return to the Manipulations module, where you entered the MoveTextBox and MoveCircle procedures.
2. On a new line, type the name of the new procedure: **Sub NewFolder()**.
3. Press **Enter**. Visual Basic will enter the ending keywords `End Sub`.
4. Press **F2** to activate the Object Browser.
5. Click the drop-down arrow in the Project/Library list box and select **VBA**.
6. Enter **file** as the search text in the Search box and press the **Search** button.
7. Scroll down in the Members list box and highlight the **MkDir** method as shown in Figure 2.15.

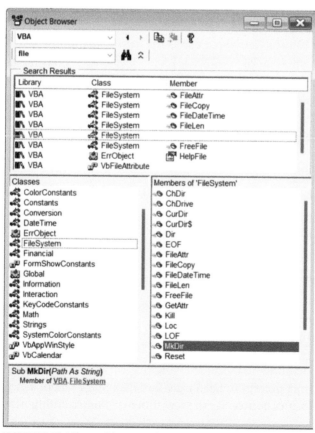

FIGURE 2.15 When writing procedures from scratch, consult the Object Browser for names of the built-in VBA functions.

8. Click the **Copy** button (the middle button in the top row) in the Object Browser window to copy the selected method name to the Windows clipboard.

9. Return to the Manipulations Code window and paste the copied instruction inside the procedure NewFolder.

10. Enter a space, followed by **"C:\Study"**. Be sure to enter the name of the entire path in quotes. The NewFolder procedure should look like this:

```
Sub NewFolder()
    MkDir "C:\Study"
End Sub
```

11. Position the insertion point within the code of the NewFolder procedure and choose **Run | Run Sub/UserForm** to execute the NewFolder procedure. When you run the NewFolder procedure, Visual Basic creates a new folder on drive C. To see the folder, activate Windows Explorer.

    After creating a new folder, you may realize that you don't need it after all. Although you could easily delete the folder while in Windows Explorer, how about getting rid of it programmatically? The Object Browser displays many other methods that are useful for working with folders and files. The RmDir method is just as simple to use as the MkDir method.

12. To remove the Study folder from your hard drive, you could replace the MkDir method with the RmDir method, and then rerun the NewFolder procedure. However, let's write a new procedure called RemoveFolder in the Manipulations Code window, as shown here:

```
Sub RemoveFolder()
    RmDir "C:\Study"
End Sub
```

    The RmDir method allows you to remove unwanted folders from your hard disk.

13. Position the insertion point within the code of the RemoveFolder procedure and choose **Run | Run Sub/UserForm** to execute the RemoveFolder procedure.
    Check Windows Explorer to see that the Study folder is gone.

USING THE IMMEDIATE WINDOW

The Immediate window is used for trying out various instructions, functions, and operators present in the Visual Basic language before using them in your own VBA procedures. It is a great tool for experimenting with your new language.

The Immediate window allows you to type VBA statements and test their results immediately without having to write a procedure. The Immediate window is like a scratch pad. Use it to try out your statements. If the statement produces the expected result, you can copy the statement from the Immediate window into your procedure (or you can drag it right onto the Code window if it is visible).

The Immediate window can be moved anywhere on the Visual Basic Editor screen, or it can be docked so that it always appears in the same area of the screen. The docking setting can be turned on and off on the Docking tab in the Options dialog box (Tools | Options).

- To quickly access the Immediate window, simply press Ctrl+G while in the Visual Basic Editor screen.

- To close the Immediate window, click the Close button in the top right-hand corner of the window.

Before you start creating full-fledged VBA procedures (this awaits you in the next chapter!), begin with some warm-up exercises to build up your VBA vocabulary. How can you do this quickly and painlessly? How can you try out some of the newly learned VBA statements? Here is a short, interactive language exercise: Enter a simple VBA instruction and Excel will check it out and display the result in the next line. Let's begin by setting up your exercise screen.

Hands-On 2.6   Entering and Executing VBA Statements in the Immediate Window

1. In the Visual Basic Editor window, choose **View | Immediate Window**.
2. Arrange the screen so that both the Microsoft Excel window and the Visual Basic window are placed side by side as presented in Figure 2.16 or use a setup with two monitors displaying Excel windows on separate screens.

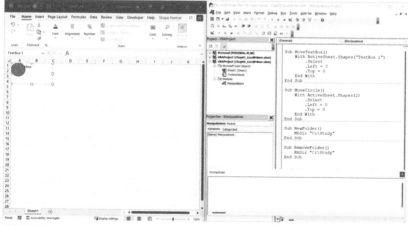

FIGURE 2.16 By positioning the Microsoft Excel and Visual Basic windows side by side you can watch the execution of the instructions entered in the Immediate window.

3. In the VBE screen, press Ctrl+G to activate the Immediate window.
4. In the Immediate window, type the following instruction and press **Enter**:

```
Worksheets.Add
```

When you press the Enter key, Visual Basic gets to work. If you entered the foregoing VBA statement correctly, VBA adds a new sheet in the current workbook. The Sheet2 tab at the bottom of the workbook should now be highlighted.

5. In the Immediate window, type another VBA statement and be sure to press **Enter** when you're done:

```
Range("A1:A4").Select
```

As soon as you press **Enter**, Visual Basic highlights the cells A1, A2, A3, and A4 in the active worksheet.

6. Enter the following instruction in the Immediate window:

```
[A1:A4].Value = 55
```

When you press **Enter**, Visual Basic places the number 55 in every cell of the specified range, A1:A4. This statement is an abbreviated way of referring to the Range object. The full syntax is more readable:

```
Range("A1:A4").Value = 55
```

7. Enter the following instruction in the Immediate window:

```
Selection.ClearContents
```

When you press **Enter**, VBA deletes the results of the previous statement from the selected cells. Cells A1:A4 are now empty.

8. Enter the following instruction in the Immediate window:

```
ActiveCell.Select
```

When you press **Enter**, Visual Basic makes cell A1 active.

Figure 2.17 shows all the instructions entered in the Immediate window in this exercise. Every time you pressed the Enter key, Excel executed the statement on the line where the cursor was located. If you want to execute the same instruction again, click anywhere in the line containing the instruction and press Enter.

```
Immediate
─────────────────────────
Worksheets.Add
Range("A1:A4").Select
[A1:A4].Value = 55
Selection.ClearContents
ActiveCell.Select


───
```

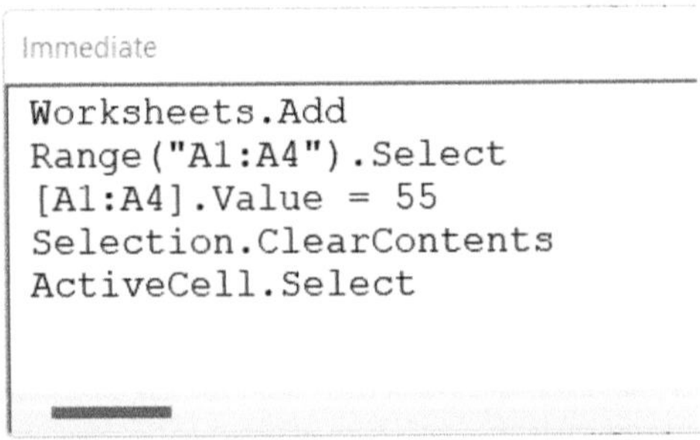

FIGURE 2.17 Instructions entered in the Immediate window are executed as soon as you press the Enter key.

For more practice you may want to rerun the statements shown in Figure 2.17. Execute the instructions one by one by clicking in the appropriate line and pressing the Enter key.

Obtaining Information in the Immediate Window

So far you have used the Immediate window to perform actions. These actions could have been performed manually by clicking the mouse in various areas of the worksheet and entering data.

Instead of simply performing actions, the Immediate window also allows you to ask questions. Suppose you want to find out which cells are currently selected, the value of the active cell, the name of the active sheet, or the number of the current window. When working in the Immediate window, you can easily get answers to these and other questions.

In the preceding exercise, you entered several instructions. Let's return to the Immediate window to ask some questions. Excel remembers the instructions entered in the Immediate window even after you close this window. Note that the contents of the Immediate window are automatically deleted when you exit Microsoft Excel.

Hands-On 2.7   Obtaining Information in the Immediate Window

1. Click the mouse in the second line of the Immediate window where you previously entered the instruction `Range("A1:A4").Select`.
2. Press **Enter** to have Excel reselect cells A1:A4.
3. Click in the new line of the Immediate window, enter the following question, and press **Enter**:

```
?Selection.Address
```

When you press Enter, Excel will not select anything in the worksheet. Instead, it will display the result of the instruction on a separate line in the Immediate window. In this case, Excel returns the absolute address of the cells that are currently selected ($A$1:$A$4).

The question mark (?) tells Excel to display the result of the instruction in the Immediate window. Instead of the question mark, you can use the Print keyword, as shown in the next step.

4. In a new line in the Immediate window, enter the following statement and press **Enter**:

```
Print ActiveWorkbook.Name
```

Excel enters the name of the active workbook on a new line in the Immediate window.

How about finding the name of the application?

5. In a new line in the Immediate window, enter the following statement and press **Enter**:

```
?Application.Name
```

Excel will reveal its full name: Microsoft Excel.

The Immediate window can also be used for a quick calculation.

6. In a new line in the Immediate window, enter the following statement and press **Enter**:

```
?12/3
```

Excel shows the result of the division on the next line. But what if you want to know right away the result of 3+2 and 12*8?

Instead of entering these instructions on separate lines, you can enter them on one line, as in the following example:

```
?3+2:?12*8
```

Notice the colon separating the two blocks of instructions. When you press the Enter key, Excel displays the results 5, 96 on separate lines in the Immediate window.

The following lists all the instructions you entered in the Immediate window, including Excel's answers to your questions:

```
Worksheets.Add
Range("A1:A4").Select
[A1:A4].Value = 55
Selection.ClearContents
ActiveCell.Select
?Selection.Address
$A$1:$A$4
Print ActiveWorkbook.Name
Book2
?Application.Name
Microsoft Excel
?12/3
 4
?3+2:?12*8
 5
 96
```

To delete the instructions from the Immediate window, make sure that the selection point is in the Immediate window, press Ctrl+A to highlight all the lines, and then press Delete.

WORKING WITH WORKSHEET CELLS AND RANGES

When you are ready to write your own VBA procedure to automate a spreadsheet task, you will most likely begin searching for instructions that allow you to manipulate worksheet cells. You will need to know how to select cells, how to enter data in cells, how to assign range names, how to format cells, and how to move, copy, and delete cells. Although these tasks can be easily performed with the mouse or keyboard, mastering these techniques in Visual Basic for Applications requires a little practice. You must use the Range object to refer to a single cell, a range of cells, a row, or a column. There are three properties that allow you to access the Range object: the Range property, the Cells property, and the Offset property.

Using the Range Property

The Range property returns a cell or a range of cells. The reference to the range must be in an A1-style and in quotation marks (for example, "A1"). The reference can include the range operator, which is a colon (for example, "A1:B2"), or the union operator, which is a comma (for example, "A5", "B12").

Hands-On 2.8 Using the Range Property to Select Worksheet Cells

To render this into VBA:	Enter this in the Immediate window:
Select a single cell (e.g., A5).	`Range("A5").Select`
Select a range of cells (e.g., A6:A10).	`Range("A6:A10").Select`
Select several nonadjacent cells (e.g., A1, B6, C8).	`Range("A1, B6, C8").Select`
Select several nonadjacent cells and cell ranges (e.g., A11:D11, C12, D3).	`Range("A11:D11, C12, D3").Select`

Using the Cells Property

You can use the Cells property to return a single cell. When selecting a single cell, this property requires two arguments. The first argument indicates the row number and the second one is the column number. Arguments are entered in parentheses. When you omit arguments, Excel selects all the cells in the active worksheet. Let's try out a couple of statements in Hands-On 2.9.

Hands-On 2.9 Using the Cells Property to Select Worksheet Cells (Part I)

To render this into VBA:	Enter this in the Immediate window:
Select a single cell (e.g., A5).	`Cells(5, 1).Select`
Select a range of cells (e.g., A6:A10).	`Range(Cells(6, 1), Cells(10, 1)).Select`
Select all cells in a worksheet.	`Cells.Select`

Notice how you can combine the Range property and the Cells property:

```
Range(Cells(6, 1), Cells(10, 1)).Select
```

In this example, the first Cells property returns cell A6, while the second one returns cell A10. The cells returned by the Cells properties are then used as a reference for the Range object. As a result, Excel will select the range of cells where the top cell is specified by the result of the first Cells property and the bottom cell is defined by the result of the second Cells property.

A worksheet is a collection of cells. You can also use the Cells property with a single argument that identifies a cell's position in the collection of a worksheet's cells. Excel numbers the cells in the following way: Cell A1 is the first cell in a worksheet, cell B1 is the second one, cell C1 is the third one, and so on. Cell 16384 is the last cell in the first worksheet row. Now let's write some practice statements in Hands-On 2.10.

Hands-On 2.10   Using the Cells Property to Select Worksheet Cells (Part II)

To render this into VBA:	Enter this in the Immediate window:

Select cell A1.	`Cells(1).Select`
	or
	`Cells.Item(1).Select`

Select cell C1.	`Cells(3).Select`
	or
	`Cells.Item(3).Select`

Select cell XFD.	`Cells(16384).Select`
	or
	`Cells.Item(16384).Select`

Notice that the word Item is a property that returns a single member of a collection. Because Item is the default member for a collection, you can refer to a worksheet cell without explicitly using the Item property.

Now that you've discovered two ways to select cells (Range property and Cells property), you may wonder why you should bother using the more complicated Cells property. It's obvious that the Range property is more readable; after all, you used the Range references in Excel formulas and functions long before you decided to learn about VBA. Using the Cells property is more convenient, however, when it comes to working with cells as a collection. Use this property to access all the cells or a single cell from a collection.

Using the Offset Property

Another very flexible way to refer to a worksheet cell is with the Offset property. Quite often when automating worksheet tasks, you may not know exactly where a specific cell is located. How can you select a cell whose address you don't know? The answer: Have Excel select a cell based on an existing selection.

The Offset property calculates a new range by shifting the starting selection down or up a specified number of rows. You can also shift the selection to the right or left a specified number of columns. In calculating the position of a new range, the Offset property uses two arguments. The first argument indicates the row offset and the second one is the column offset. Let's try out some examples in Hands-On 2.11.

(◉) Hands-On 2.11 Selecting Cells Using the Offset Property

To render this into VBA:	Enter this in the Immediate window:
Select a cell located one row down and three columns to the right of cell A1.	```Range("A1").Offset(1, 3).Select```
Select a cell located two rows above and one column to the left of cell D15.	```Range("D15").Offset(-2, -1).Select```
Select a cell located one row above the active cell. If the active cell is in the first row, you will get an error message.	```ActiveCell.Offset(-1, 0).Select```

In the first example, Excel selects cell D2. As soon as you enter the second example, Excel chooses cell C13.

If cells A1 and D15 are already selected, you can rewrite the first two statements in the following way:

```
Selection.Offset(1, 3).Select
Selection.Offset(-2, -1).Select
```

Notice that the third example in the practice table displays zero (0) in the position of the second argument. Zero entered as a first or second argument of the Offset property indicates a current row or column. The instruction `ActiveCell.Offset(-1, 0).Select` will cause an error if the active cell is located in the first row.

Using the Resize Property

When working with the Offset property, you may occasionally need to change the size of a selection of cells. Suppose that the starting selection is A5:A10. How about shifting the selection two rows down and two columns to the right and then changing the size of the new selection? Let's say the new selection should highlight cells C7:C8. The Offset property can take care of only the first part of this task. The second part requires another property. Excel has a special Resize property. You can combine the Offset property with the Resize property to answer the foregoing question. Before you combine these two properties, let's proceed to Hands-On 2.12 to learn how you can use them separately.

⊙ **Hands-On 2.12   Writing a VBA Statement to Resize a
Selection of Cells**

1. Arrange the screen so that the Microsoft Excel window and the Visual Basic window are side by side.
2. Activate the Immediate window and enter the following instructions:

```
Range("A5:A10").Select
Selection.Offset(2, 2).Select
Selection.Resize(2, 4).Select
```

The first instruction selects range A5:A10. Cell A5 is the active cell. The second instruction shifts the current selection to cells C7:C12. Cell C7 is located two rows below the active cell A5 and two columns to the right of A5. Now the active cell is C7.

The last instruction resizes the current selection. Instead of range C7:C12, cells C7:F8 are selected.

Like the Offset property, the Resize property takes two arguments. The first argument is the number of rows you intend to include in the selection, and the second argument specifies the number of columns. Hence, the instruction `Selection.Resize(2, 4).Select` resizes the current selection to two rows and four columns.

The last two instructions can be combined in the following way:

```
Selection.Offset(2, 2).Resize(2, 4).Select
```

In this statement, the Offset property calculates the beginning of a new range, the Resize property determines the new size of the range, and the Select method selects the specified range of cells.

SIDEBAR *Recording a Selection of Cells*

By default, the macro recorder selects cells using the Range property. If you turn on the macro recorder and select cell A2, enter any text, and select cell A5, you will see the following lines of code in the Visual Basic Editor window:

```
Range("A2").Select
ActiveCell.FormulaR1C1 = "text"
Range("A5").Select
```

You can have the macro recorder use the Offset property if you tell it to use relative references. To do this, click View | Macros | Use Relative References, and then choose Record Macro. The macro recorder produces the following lines of code:

```
ActiveCell.Offset(-1, 0).Range("A1").Select
ActiveCell.FormulaR1C1 = "text"
ActiveCell.Offset(3, 0).Range("A1").Select
```

When you record a procedure using the relative references, the procedure will always select a cell relative to the active cell. The first and third lines in this set of instructions reference cell A1, even though nothing was said about cell A1. As you remember from Chapter 1, the macro recorder has its own way of getting things done. To make things simpler, you can delete the reference to `Range("A1")`:

```
ActiveCell.Offset(-1, 0).Select
ActiveCell.FormulaR1C1 = "text"
ActiveCell.Offset(3, 0).Select
```

After recording a procedure using the relative reference, make sure Use Relative References is not selected if your next macro does not require the use of relative addressing.

Using the End Property

If you often must quickly access certain remote cells in your worksheet, you may already be familiar with the following keyboard shortcuts: End+up arrow, End+down arrow, End+left arrow, and End+right arrow. In VBA, you can use the End property to quickly move to remote cells. Let's move around the worksheet by writing statements listed in Hands-On 2.13.

Hands-On 2.13 Selecting Cells Using the End Property

To render this into VBA:	Enter this in the Immediate window:
Select the last cell in any row.	`ActiveCell.End(xlToRight).Select`
Select the last cell in any column.	`ActiveCell.End(xlDown).Select`
Select the first cell in any row.	`ActiveCell.End(xlToLeft).Select`
Select the first cell in any column.	`ActiveCell.End(xlUp).Select`

Notice that the End property requires an argument that indicates the direction you want to move. Use the following Excel built-in Direction Enumeration constants to jump in the specified direction: `xlToRight`, `xlToLeft`, `xlUp`, `xlDown`.

Moving, Copying, and Deleting Cells

In the process of developing a new worksheet model, you often find yourself moving and copying cells and deleting cell contents. Visual Basic allows you to automate these worksheet editing tasks with three simple-to-use methods: Cut, Copy, and Clear. And now let's do some hands-on exercises to get some practice in the most frequently used worksheet operations.

⊙ Hands-On 2.14   Moving, Copying, and Deleting Cells

To render this into VBA:	Enter this in the Immediate window:
Move the contents of cell A5 to cell A4.	`Range("A5").Cut` `Destination:=Range("A4")`
Copy a formula from cell A3 to cells D5:F5.	`Range("A3").Copy` `Destination:=Range("D5:F5")`

Delete the contents of cell A4.	`Range("A4").Clear`
	or
	`Range("A4").Cut`

Notice that the first two methods in the table require a special argument called `Destination`. This argument specifies the address of a cell or a range of cells where you want to place the cut or copied data. In the last example, the `Cut` method is used without the `Destination` argument to remove data from the specified cell.

The `Clear` method deletes everything from the specified cell or range, including any applied formats and cell comments. If you want to be specific about what you delete, use the following methods:

- `ClearContents`—Clears only data from a cell or range of cells
- `ClearFormats`—Clears only applied formats
- `ClearComments`—Clears all cell comments from the specified range
- `ClearNotes`—Clears notes and sound notes from all the cells in the specified range
- `ClearHyperlinks`—Removes all hyperlinks from the specified range
- `ClearOutline`—Clears the outline for the specified range

WORKING WITH ROWS AND COLUMNS

Excel uses the EntireRow and EntireColumn properties to select the entire row or column. Let's now write the statements in Hands-On 2.15 to quickly select entire rows and columns.

⊙ Hands-On 2.15   Selecting Entire Rows and Columns

To render this into VBA:	Enter this in the Immediate window:
Select an entire row where the active cell is located.	`Selection.EntireRow.Select`
Select an entire column where the active cell is located.	`Selection.EntireColumn.Select`

When you select a range of cells you may want to find out how many rows or columns are included in the selection. Let's have Excel count rows and columns in `Range("A1:D15")`.

1. Type the following VBA statement in the Immediate window and press **Enter**:

```
Range("A1:D15").Select
```

If the Microsoft Excel window is visible, Visual Basic will highlight the range A1:D15 when you press Enter.

2. To find out how many rows are in the selected range, enter the following statement:

```
?Selection.Rows.Count
```

As soon as you press **Enter**, Visual Basic displays the answer on the next line. Your selection includes 15 rows.

3. To find out the number of columns in the selected range, enter the following statement:

```
?Selection.Columns.Count
```

As soon as you press **Enter**, Visual Basic tells you that the selected `Range("A1:D15")` occupies the width of four columns.

4. In the Immediate window, position the cursor anywhere within the word Rows or Columns and press **F1** to find out more information about these useful properties.

Obtaining Information about the Worksheet

How big is an Excel worksheet? How many columns and rows does it contain? If you ever forget the details, use the Count property as shown in Hands-On 2.16.

(⊙) Hands-On 2.16 Counting Rows and Columns

To render this into VBA:	Enter this in the Immediate window:
Find out the total number of rows in an Excel worksheet.	`?Rows.Count`
Find out the total number of columns in an Excel worksheet.	`?Columns.Count`

A Microsoft Excel worksheet has 1,048,576 rows and 16,384 columns.

ENTERING DATA AND FORMATTING CELLS

The information entered in a worksheet can be text, numbers, or formulas. To enter data in a cell or range of cells, you can use either the Value property or the Formula property of the Range object.

- Using the Value property:

```
ActiveSheet.Range("A1:C4").Value = "=4 * 25"
```

- Using the Formula property:

```
ActiveSheet.Range("A1:C4").Formula = "=4 * 25"
```

In both examples, cells A1:C4 display 100—the result of the multiplication 4 * 25. Let's proceed to some practice in Hands-On 2.17.

Hands-On 2.17   Using VBA Statements to Enter Data in a Worksheet

To render this into VBA:	Enter this in the Immediate window:
Enter in cell A5 the following text: Amount Due	`Range("A5").Formula = "Amount Due"`
Enter the number 123 in cell D21.	`Range("D21").Formula = 123` or `Range("D21").Value = 123`
Enter in cell B4 the following formula: = D21 * 3	`Range("B4").Formula = "=D21 * 3"`

Returning Information Entered in a Worksheet

In some Visual Basic procedures, you will undoubtedly need to return the contents of a cell or a range of cells. Although you can use either the Value or Formula property, this time the two Range object's properties are not interchangeable.

- The Value property displays the result of a formula entered in a specified cell. If, for example, cell A1 contains a formula = 4 * 25, then the instruction

```
?Range("A1").Value
```

  will return the value of 100.

- If you want to display the formula instead of its result, you must use the Formula property:

```
?Range("A1").Formula
```

Excel will display the formula (= 4 * 25) instead of its result (100).

Finding Out about Cell Formatting

A frequent spreadsheet task is applying formatting to a selected cell or a range. Your VBA procedure may need to find out the type of formatting applied to a worksheet cell. To retrieve the cell formatting, use the Number-Format property:

```
?Range("A1").NumberFormat
```

Upon entering the foregoing statement in the Immediate window, Excel displays the word "General," which indicates that no special formatting was applied to the selected cell. To change the format of a cell to dollars and cents using VBA, enter the following instruction:

```
Range("A1").NumberFormat = "$#,##0.00"
```

If you enter 125 in cell A1 after it has been formatted using this code, cell A1 will display $125.00. You can look up the available format codes in the Format Cells dialog box in the Microsoft Excel application window as shown in Figure 2.18.

FIGURE 2.18 You can apply different formatting to selected cells and ranges using format codes, as displayed in the Custom category in the Format Cells dialog box. To quickly bring up this dialog box, press the Alt, H, F, and M keys one at a time.

WORKING WITH WORKBOOKS AND WORKSHEETS

Now that you've got your feet wet working with worksheet cells and ranges, it's time to move up one level and learn how you can control a single workbook, as well as an entire collection of workbooks. You cannot prepare a new worksheet if you don't know how to open a new workbook. You cannot remove a workbook from the screen if you don't know how to close a workbook. You cannot work with an existing workbook if you don't know how to open it. These important tasks are handled by the following VBA methods: Add, Open, and Close. The next series of drills in Hands-On 2.18 and 2.19 will give you the language skills necessary for dealing with workbooks and worksheets.

(⊙) Hands-On 2.18   Working with Workbooks

To render this into VBA:	Enter this in the Immediate window:
Open a new workbook.	`Workbooks.Add`
Find out the name of the first workbook.	`?Workbooks(1).Name`
Find out the number of open workbooks.	`?Workbooks.Count`
Activate the second open workbook.	`Workbooks(2).Activate`
Close the Chap01_ExcelPrimer.xlsm workbook and save the changes.	`Workbooks("Chap01_ExcelPrimer.` `xlsm").Close SaveChanges:=True`

Open the Chap01_ExcelPrimer.xlsm workbook. Type the correct path to the file location on your computer.	`Workbooks.Open "C:\VBAEx-`
	`cel2021Primer_ByExample\`
	`Chap01_ExcelPrimer.xlsm"`

Activate the Chap01_ExcelPrimer.xlsm workbook.	`Workbooks("Chap01_ExcelPrimer.` `xlsm").Activate`
Save the active workbook as NewChap.xlsm.	`ActiveWorkbook.SaveAs` `Filename:= "NewChap.xlsm"`
Close the first workbook.	`Workbooks(1).Close`
Close the active workbook without saving recent changes to it.	`ActiveWorkbook.Close` `SaveChanges:=False`
Close all open workbooks.	`Workbooks.Close`

If you worked through the last example in Hands-On 2.18, all workbooks are now closed. Before you experiment with worksheets, make sure you have opened a new workbook.

When you deal with individual worksheets, you must know how to add a new worksheet to a workbook, select a worksheet or a group of worksheets, name a worksheet, and copy, move, and delete worksheets. In Visual Basic, each of these tasks is handled by a special method or property.

(⊙) Hands-On 2.19   Working with Worksheets

To render this into VBA:	Enter this in the Immediate window:
Add a new worksheet.	`Worksheets.Add`
Find out the name of the first worksheet.	`?Worksheets(1).Name`
Select a sheet named Sheet3.	`Worksheets(3).Select`
Select sheets 1, 3, and 4.	`Worksheets(Array(1,3,4)).Select`
Activate a sheet named Sheet1.	`Worksheets("Sheet1").Activate`
Move Sheet2 before Sheet1.	`Worksheets("Sheet2").Move` `Before:=Worksheets("Sheet1")`
Rename worksheet Sheet2 to Expenses.	`Worksheets("Sheet2").Name =` `"Expenses"`
Find out the number of worksheets in the active workbook.	`?Worksheets.Count`

To render this into VBA:	Enter this in the Immediate window:
Remove the worksheet named Expenses from the active workbook.	`Worksheets("Expenses").Delete`

Notice the difference between the `Select` and `Activate` methods:

- The `Select` and `Activate` methods can be used interchangeably if only one worksheet is selected.
- If you select a group of worksheets, the `Activate` method allows you to decide which one of the selected worksheets is active. As you know, only one worksheet can be active at a time.

SIDEBAR *Sheets Other than Worksheets*

In addition to worksheets, the collection of workbooks contains chart sheets. To add a new chart sheet to your workbook, use the `Add` method:

```
Charts.Add
```

To count the chart sheets, use:

```
?Charts.Count
```

WORKING WITH WINDOWS

When you work with several Excel workbooks and need to compare or consolidate data or you want to see different parts of the same worksheet, you are bound to use the options available from the Microsoft Excel Window menu: New Window and Arrange.

In Hands-On 2.20 you will learn how to work with Windows using VBA.

(⊙) Hands-On 2.20   Working with Windows

To render this into VBA:	Enter this in the Immediate window:
Show the active workbook in a new window.	`ActiveWorkbook.NewWindow`
Display on screen all open workbooks.	`Windows.Arrange`
Activate the second window.	`Windows(2).Activate`
Find out the title of the active window.	`?ActiveWindow.Caption`
Change the active window's title to My Window.	`ActiveWindow.Caption = "My Window"`

When you display windows on screen, you can decide how to arrange them. The `Arrange` method has many arguments, as shown in Table 2.1. The argument that allows you to control the way the windows are positioned on your screen is called `ArrangeStyle`. If you omit the `ArrangeStyle` argument, all windows are tiled.

TABLE 2.1 Arguments of the `Arrange` method of the Windows object.

Constant	Value	Description
`xlArrangeStyleTiled`	1	Windows are tiled (the default value).
`xlArrangeStyleCascade`	7	Windows are cascaded.
`xlArrangeStyleHorizontal`	2	Windows are arranged horizontally.
`xlArrangeStyleVertical`	3	Windows are arranged vertically.

Instead of the names of constants, you can use the value equivalents shown in Table 2.1.

To cascade all windows, use the following VBA instruction:

```
Windows.Arrange ArrangeStyle:=xlArrangeStyleCascade
```

or simply:

```
Windows.Arrange ArrangeStyle:=7
```

WORKING WITH THE EXCEL APPLICATION

The Application object represents the Excel application itself. By controlling the Application object, you can perform many tasks, such as saving the way your screen looks at the end of a day's work or quitting the application. As you know, Excel allows you to save the screen settings by using the Save Workspace button on the View tab. The task of saving the workspace can be easily performed with VBA:

```
Application.SaveWorkspace "Project"
```

This instruction saves the screen settings in the workspace file named Project. The next time you need to work with the same files and arrangement of windows, simply open the Project.xlwx file so Excel will bring up the correct files and restore your screen with those settings. And now let's write some statements that use the Application object.

⊙ Hands-On 2.21   Working with the Excel Application

To render this into VBA:	Enter this in the Immediate window:
Check the name of the active application.	`?Application.Name`
Change the title of the Excel application to My Application.	`Application.Caption = "My Application"`
Change the title of the Excel application back to Microsoft Excel.	`Application.Caption = "Microsoft Excel"`
Find out what operating system you are using.	`?Application.OperatingSystem`
Find out the name of a person or firm to whom the application is registered.	`?Application.OrganizationName`

To render this into VBA:	Enter this in the Immediate window:
Find out the name of the folder where the Excel executable file (Excel.exe) resides.	`?Application.Path`
Quit working with Microsoft Excel.	`Application.Quit`

SUMMARY

This chapter has given you an overview of the Visual Basic Editor window. You learned many basic VBA terms and practiced them by executing single statements in the Immediate window.

In the next chapter, you will learn how the data can be stored for later use in variables. You will also explore VBA data types and constants.

Chapter 3

EXCEL VBA FUNDAMENTALS

A QUICK REFERENCE TO WRITING VBA CODE

In programming, just as in life, certain things need to be done at once while others can be put off until later. When you postpone a task, you may enter it in your mental or paper "to-do" list and classify it by its type or importance. When you delegate the task or finally get around to doing it yourself, you cross it off the list. This chapter shows you how your VBA procedures can memorize important pieces of information for use in later statements or calculations. You will learn how a procedure can keep a "to-do" entry in a variable, how variables are declared, and how they relate to data types and constants.

EXCEL OBJECTS, PROPERTIES, AND METHODS

You can create procedures that control many features of Microsoft Excel using Visual Basic for Applications. You can also control many other applications. The power of Visual Basic comes from its ability to control and manage various objects. But what is an object?

An *object* is a thing you can control with VBA. Workbooks, a worksheet, a range in a worksheet, a chart, and a toolbar are just a few examples of the objects you may want to control while working in Excel. Excel contains a multitude of objects that you can manipulate in different ways. All these objects are organized in a hierarchy. Some objects may contain other objects. For example, Microsoft Excel is an Application object. The Application object contains other objects, such as workbooks or command bars. The Workbook object may contain other objects, such as worksheets or charts. In this chapter, you will learn how to control the following Excel objects: Range, Window, Worksheet, Workbook, and Application. You begin by learning about the Range object. You can't do much work in spreadsheets unless you know how to manipulate ranges of cells.

Certain objects look alike. For example, if you open a new workbook and examine its worksheets, you won't see any differences. A group of like objects is called a *collection*. A Worksheets collection includes all worksheets in a workbook. Collections are also objects. In Microsoft Excel, the most frequently used collections are:

- Workbooks collection—represents all currently open workbooks.

- Worksheets collection—represents all the Worksheet objects in the specified or active workbook. Each Worksheet object represents a worksheet.

- Sheets collection—represents all the sheets in the specified or active workbook. The Sheets collection can contain Chart or Worksheet objects.

- Windows collection—represents all the Window objects in Microsoft Excel. The Windows collection for the Application object contains all the windows in the application, whereas the Windows collection for the Workbook object contains only the windows in the specified workbook.

When you work with collections, you can perform the same action on all the objects in the collection.

Each object has some characteristics that allow you to describe the object. In Visual Basic, the object's characteristics are called *properties*. For example, a Workbook object has a Name property, and the Range object has such properties as Column, Font, Formula, Name, Row, Style, and Value. The object properties can be set. When you set an object's property, you control its appearance or its position. Object properties can take on only one specific value at any one time. For example, the active workbook can't be called two different names at the same time.

The most difficult part of Visual Basic is to understand the fact that some properties can also be objects. Let's consider the Range object. You can change the appearance of the selected range of cells by setting the Font property. But the font can have a different name (Times New Roman, Arial, …), different size (10, 12, 14, …), and different style (bold, italic, underline, …). These are font properties. If the font has properties, then the font is also an object.

Properties are great. They let you change the look of the object, but how can you control the actions? Before you can make Excel carry out some tasks, you need to know another term. Objects have methods. Each action you want the object to perform is called a *method*. The most important Visual Basic method is the `Add` method, which you can use to add a new workbook or worksheet. Objects can use various methods. For example, the Range object has special methods that allow you to clear the cell contents (`ClearContents` method), clear just formats (`ClearFormats` method), and clear both contents and formats (`Clear` method). Other methods allow objects to be selected, copied, or moved.

Methods can have optional parameters that specify how the method is to be carried out. For example, the Workbook object has a method called `Close`. You can close any open workbook using this method. If there are changes to the workbook, Microsoft Excel will display a message prompting you to save the changes. You can use the `Close` method with the `SaveChanges` parameter set to False to close the workbook and discard any changes that have been made to it, as in the following example:

```
Workbooks("Chap01_Excel.xlsm").Close SaveChanges:=False
```

MICROSOFT EXCEL OBJECT MODEL

When you learn new things, theory can give you the necessary background, but how do you really know what's where? All the available Excel objects as well as their properties and methods can be looked up in the online Excel Object Model Reference that you can access by choosing Help | Microsoft Visual Basic for Applications Help in the Visual Basic Editor window. Figure 3.1 illustrates the Excel Object Model Reference in the online help. This page can be accessed via the following link:

https://docs.microsoft.com/en-us/office/vba/api/overview/Excel/object-model

Objects are listed alphabetically for easy perusal, and when you click the object, you will see object subcategories that list the object's properties, methods, and events. Reading the object model reference is a great way to learn about Excel objects and collections of objects. The time you spend here will pay big dividends later when you need to write complex VBA procedures from scratch. A good way to get started is to always look up objects that you come across in Excel programming texts or example procedures. Now take a few minutes to familiarize yourself with the main Excel object— Application. This object allows you to specify application-level properties and execute application-level methods. You saw several examples of working with the Application object in Chapter 2.

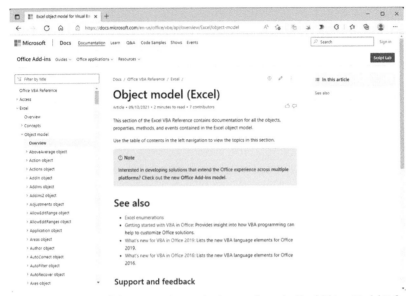

FIGURE 3.1 In your VBA programming work, always refer to the Excel Object Model Reference that contains documentation for all the objects, properties, methods, and events contained in the Excel object model.

WRITING SIMPLE AND COMPLEX VBA STATEMENTS

Now that you know the basic elements of VBA (objects, properties, and methods), it's time to start using them. But how do you combine objects, properties, and methods into correct language structures? Every language has grammar rules that people follow to make themselves understood. Whether you communicate in English, Spanish, French, or another language, you apply certain rules to your writing and speech. In programming, we use the term *syntax* to specify language rules. You can look up the syntax of each object, property, or method in the online help or in the Object Browser window.

To make sure Excel always understands what you mean, just stick to the following rules:

Rule #1: Referring to the property of an object
If the property does not have arguments, the syntax is as follows:

```
Object.Property
```

Object is a placeholder. It is where you should place the name of the actual object that you are trying to access. Property is also a placeholder. Here you place the name of the object's characteristics. For example, to refer to the value entered in cell A4 on your worksheet, you can write the following instruction:

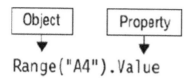

```
Range("A4").Value
```

Notice that there is a period between the name of the object and its property.

When you need to access the property of an object that is contained within several other objects, you must include the names of all objects in turn, separated by the dot operator, as shown here:

```
ActiveSheet.Shapes(2).Line.Weight
```

This example references the Weight property of the Line object and refers to the second object in the collection of Shapes located in the active worksheet.

Some properties require one or more arguments. For example, when using the Offset property, you can select a cell relative to the active cell. The Offset property requires two arguments. The first argument indicates the row number (rowOffset), and the second one determines the column number (columnOffset).

```
ActiveCell.Offset(3, 2)
```

In this example, assuming the active cell is A1, Offset(3, 2) will reference the cell located three rows down and two columns to the right of cell A1. In other words, cell C4 is referenced. Because the arguments placed within parentheses are often difficult to understand, it's common practice to precede the value of the argument with its name, as in the following example:

```
ActiveCell.Offset(rowOffset:=3, columnOffset:=2)
```

Notice that a colon and an equal sign must always follow the named arguments. When you use the named arguments, you can list them in any order. The foregoing instruction can also be written as follows:

```
ActiveCell.Offset(columnOffset:=2, rowOffset:=3)
```

The revised instruction does not change the meaning; you are still referencing cell C4 assuming that A1 is the active cell. However, if you transpose the arguments in a statement that does not use named arguments, you will end up referencing another cell. For example, the statement ActiveCell.Offset(2, 3) will reference cell D3 instead of C4.

Rule #2: Changing the property of an object

```
Object.Property = Value
```

Value is a new value that you want to assign to the property of the object. The value can be:

- A number. The following instruction enters the number 25 in cell A4.

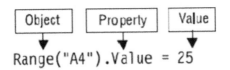

```
Range("A4").Value = 25
```

- Text entered in quotes. The following instruction changes the font of the active cell to Times New Roman.

```
ActiveCell.Font.Name = "Times New Roman"
```

- A logical value (True or False). The following instruction applies bold formatting to the active cell.

```
ActiveCell.Font.Bold = True
```

Rule #3: Returning the current value of the object property

```
Variable = Object.Property
```

Variable is the name of the storage location where Visual Basic is going to store the property setting. You will learn about variables later in this chapter.

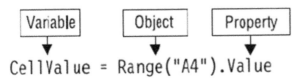

```
CellValue = Range("A4").Value
```

This instruction saves the current value of cell A4 in the variable named `CellValue`.

Rule #4: Referring to the object's method
If the method does not have arguments, the syntax is as follows:

```
Object.Method
```

Object is a placeholder. It is where you should place the name of the actual object that you are trying to access. Method is also a placeholder. Here you place the name of the action you want to perform on the object. For example, to clear the contents in cell A4, use the following instruction:

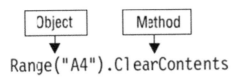

```
Range("A4").ClearContents
```

If the method requires arguments, the syntax is as follows:

```
Object.Method (argument1, argument2, ... argumentN)
```

For example, using the `GoTo` method, you can quickly select any range in a workbook. The syntax of the `GoTo` method is shown here:

```
Object.GoTo(Reference, Scroll)
```

The `Reference` argument is the destination cell or range. The `Scroll` argument can be set to True to scroll through the window or to False to not scroll through the window. For example, the following VBA statement selects cell P100 in Sheet1 and scrolls through the window:

```
Application.GoTo _
    Reference:=Worksheets("Sheet1").Range("P100"), _
    Scroll:=True
```

The foregoing instruction did not fit on one line, so it was broken into sections using the special line continuation character (the underscore), described in the next section.

Suppose you want to delete the contents of cell A4. To do this manually, you would select cell A4 and press the Delete key on your keyboard. To perform the same operation using Visual Basic, you first need to find out how to make Excel select an appropriate cell. Cell A4, like any other worksheet cell, is represented by the Range object. Visual Basic does not have a Delete method for deleting contents of cells. Instead, you should use the `Clear-Contents` method, as in the following example:

```
Range("A4").ClearContents
```

Notice the dot operator between the name of the object and its method. This instruction removes the contents of cell A4. However, how do you make Excel delete the contents of cell A4 located in the first sheet of the Chap03_ExcelPrimer.xlsm workbook? Let's also assume that there are several workbooks open. If you don't want to end up deleting the contents of cell A4 from the wrong workbook or worksheet, you must write a detailed instruction so that Visual Basic knows where to locate the necessary cell:

```
Application.Workbooks("Chap03_ExcelPrimer.xlsm")
.Worksheets("Sheet1").Range("A4").ClearContents
```

The foregoing instruction should be written on one line and read from right to left as follows: Clear the contents of cell A4, which is part of a range located in a worksheet named Sheet1 contained in a workbook named Chap03_ExcelPrimer.xlsm, which in turn is part of the Excel application. Be sure to include the letter "s" at the end of the collection names: Workbooks and Worksheets. All references to the names of workbooks, worksheets, and cells must be enclosed in quotation marks.

Breaking Up Long VBA Statements

When you start writing complete VBA procedures from scratch, you will need to know how to break up a long VBA statement into two or more lines to make your procedure more readable. Visual Basic has a special line continuation character that can be used at the end of a line to indicate that the next line is a continuation of the previous one, as in the following example:

```
Selection.PasteSpecial _
    Paste:=xlValues, _
    Operation:=xlMultiply, _
    SkipBlanks: =False, _
    Transpose:=False
```

The line continuation character is the underscore (_). You must precede the underscore with a space.

You can use the line continuation character in your code before or after:

- Operators; for example: &, +, Like, NOT, AND
- A comma
- An equal sign
- An assignment operator (:=)

You cannot use the line continuation character between a colon and an equal's sign. For example, the following use of the continuation character is not recognized by Visual Basic:

```
Selection.PasteSpecial Paste: _
    =xlValues, Operation: _
    =xlMultiply, SkipBlanks: _
    =False, Transpose: _
    =False
```

Also, you may not use the line continuation character within text enclosed in quotes. For example, the following usage of the underscore is invalid:

```
MsgBox "To continue the long instruction, use the _
    line continuation character."
```

Instead, break it up as follows:

```
MsgBox "To continue the long instruction, use the " & _
    "line continuation character."
```

SAVING RESULTS OF VBA STATEMENTS

In Chapter 2, while working in the Immediate window, you tried several Visual Basic instructions that returned some information. For example, when you entered ?Rows.Count, you found out that there are 1,048,576 rows in a worksheet. However, when you write Visual Basic procedures outside of the Immediate window, you can't use the question mark. If you want to know the result after executing an instruction, you must tell Visual Basic to memorize it. In programming, results returned by Visual Basic instructions can be written to variables. Since variables can hold various types of data, the next section focuses on introducing you to VBA data types. Once you understand the basics of data types, it will be easy to tackle the variable part.

INTRODUCING DATA TYPES

When you create Visual Basic procedures, you have a purpose in mind: You want to manipulate data. Because your procedures will handle different kinds of information, you should understand how Visual Basic stores data. The *data type* determines how the data is stored in the computer's memory. For example, data can be stored as a number, text, date, object, and so on. If you forget to tell Visual Basic the type of your data, it assigns the Variant data type. The Variant type can figure out on its own what kind of data is being manipulated and then take on that type.

The Visual Basic data types are shown in Table 3.1. In addition to the built-in data types, you can define your own data types. Because data types take up different amounts of space in the computer's memory, some of them are more expensive than others. Therefore, to conserve memory and make your procedure run faster, you should select the data type that uses the least number of bytes and, at the same time, can handle the data that your procedure has to manipulate.

TABLE 3.1 VBA data types.

Data Type (Name)	Size (Bytes)	Description
Boolean	2	Stores a value of True (0) or False (–1).
Byte	1	A number in the range of 0 to 255.
Integer	2	A number in the range of –32,768 to 32,767. The type declaration character for Integer is the percent sign (%).
Long (Long integer)	4	A number in the range of –2,147,483,648 to 2,147,483,647. The type declaration character for Long is the ampersand (&).
LongLong (LongLong integer)	8	Stored as a signed 64-bit (8-byte) number ranging in value from –9,223,372,036,854,775,808 to 9,223,372,036,854,775,807. The type declaration character for LongLong is the caret (^). LongLong is a valid declared type only on 64-bit platforms.

(Contd.)

Data Type (Name)	Size (Bytes)	Description
LongPtr (Long integer on 32-bit systems; LongLong integer on 64-bit systems)	4 on 32-bit 8 on 64-bit	Numbers ranging in value from –2,147,483,648 to 2,147,483,647 on 32-bit systems; –9,223,372,036,854,775,808 to 9,223,372,036,854,775,807 on 64-bit systems. Using LongPtr enables writing code that can run in both 32-bit and 64-bit environments.
Single (single-precision floating-point)	4	Single-precision floating-point real number ranging in value from –3.402823E38 to –1.401298E–45 for negative values and from 1.401298E–45 to 3.402823E38 for positive values. The type declaration character for Single is the exclamation point (!).
Double (double-precision floating-point)	8	Double-precision floating-point real number in the range of –1.79769313486231E308 to –4.94065645841247E–324 for negative values and 4.94065645841247E–324 to 1.79769313486231E308 for positive values. The type declaration character for Double is the number sign (#).
Currency (scaled integer)	8	(scaled integer) Monetary values used in fixed-point calculations: –922,337,203,685,477.5808 to 922,337,203,685,477.5807. The type declaration character for Currency is the at sign (@).
Decimal	14	96-bit (12-byte) signed integer scaled by a variable power of 10. The power of 10 scaling factor specifies the number of digits to the right of the decimal point, and ranges from 0 to 28. With no decimal point (scale of 0), the largest value is +/–79,228,162,514,264,337,593,543,950,335. With 28 decimal places, the largest value is +/–7.9228162514264337593543950335. The smallest nonzero value is +/–0.0000000000000000000000000001. You cannot declare a variable to be of type Decimal. You must use the Variant data type. Use the CDec function to convert a value to a decimal number: ```Dim numDecimal As Variant\nnumDecimal = CDec(0.02 * 15.75 *\n0.0006)```
Date	8	Date from January 1, 100, to December 31, 9999, and times from 0:00:00 to 23:59:59. Date literals must be enclosed within number signs (#)—for example: #January 1, 2022#
String (variable-length)	10 bytes + string length	A variable-length string can contain up to approximately 2 billion characters. The type declaration character for String is the dollar sign ($).
String (fixed-length)	Length of string	A fixed-length string can contain 1 to approximately 65,400 characters.

Data Type (Name)	Size (Bytes)	Description
Object	4	Object variable used to refer to any Excel object. Use the Set statement to declare a variable as an Object.
Variant (with numbers)	16	Any numeric value up to the size of a Double.
Variant (with characters)	22 bytes + string length	Any valid nonnumeric data type in the same range as for a variable-length string.

User-Defined (using Type)	One or more elements	A data type you define using the Type statement. User-defined data types can contain one or more elements of a data type, an array, or a previously defined user-defined type—for example:
		
		`Type custInfo`
		`   custFullName as String`
		`   custTitle as String`
		`   custBusinessName as String`
		`   custFirstOrderDate as Date`
		`End Type`

NOTE	*For more information about data types see the online help at: https://docs.microsoft.com/en-us/office/vba/language/reference/user-interface-help/data-type-summary*

USING VARIABLES

A *variable* is simply a name that is used to refer to an item of data. Each time you want to remember a result of a VBA instruction, think of a name that will represent it. For example, if the number 1,048,576 must remind you of the total number of rows in a worksheet (a very important piece of information when you want to bring external data into Excel), you can make up a name such as AllRows, NumOfRows, or TotalRows, and so on. The names of variables can contain characters, numbers, and some punctuation marks, except for the following:

, # $ % & @ !

The name of a variable cannot begin with a number or contain a space. If you want the name of the variable to include more than one word, use the underscore (_) as a separator. Although the name of a variable can contain as many as 254 characters, it's best to use short and simple variable names. Using short names will save you typing time when you need to refer to the variable in your Visual Basic procedure. Visual Basic doesn't care whether you use uppercase or lowercase letters in variable names, but most programmers use lowercase letters. For variable names that are made up of one or more words, you may want to use title case, as in the names NumOfRows and First_Name.

SIDEBAR *Reserved Words Can't Be Used for Variable Names*

You can use any label you want for a variable name, except for the reserved words that VBA uses. Visual Basic statements and certain other words that have a special meaning in VBA cannot be used as names of variables. For example, words such as Name, Len, Empty, Local, Currency, or Exit will generate an error message if used as a variable name.

SIDEBAR *Meaningful Variable Names*

Give variables names that can help you remember their roles. Some programmers use a prefix to identify the type of a variable. A variable name that begins with "str" (for example, strName) can be quickly recognized within the code of your procedure as the one holding the text string.

How to Create Variables

You can create a variable by declaring it with a special command or by just using it in a statement. When you declare your variable, you make Visual Basic aware of the variable's name and data type. This is called *explicit variable declaration*. There are several advantages to explicit variable declaration:

- Explicit variable declaration speeds up the execution of your procedure. Because Visual Basic knows the data type, it reserves only as much memory as is necessary to store the data.

- Explicit variable declaration makes your code easier to read and understand because all the variables are listed at the very beginning of the procedure.

- Explicit variable declaration helps prevent errors caused by misspelled variable names. Visual Basic automatically corrects the variable name based on the spelling used in the variable declaration.

If you don't let Visual Basic know about the variable prior to using it, you are implicitly telling VBA that you want to create this variable. Variables declared implicitly are automatically assigned the Variant data type (see Table 3.1 in the previous section). Although implicit variable declaration is convenient (it allows you to create variables on the fly and assign values without knowing in advance the data type of the values being assigned), it can cause several problems, as outlined here:

- If you misspell a variable name in your procedure, Visual Basic may display a runtime error or create a new variable. You are guaranteed to waste some time troubleshooting problems that could have been easily avoided had you declared your variable at the beginning of the procedure.

- Because Visual Basic does not know what type of data your variable will store, it assigns it a Variant data type. This causes your procedure to run slower because Visual Basic must check the data type every time it deals with your variable. Because a Variant can store any type of data, Visual Basic must reserve more memory to store your data.

How to Declare Variables

You declare a variable with the Dim keyword. Dim stands for dimension. The Dim keyword is followed by the name of the variable and then the variable type.

Suppose you want the procedure to display the age of an employee. Before you can calculate the age, you must tell the procedure the employee's date of birth. To do this, you declare a variable called DateOfBirth, as follows:

```
Dim DateOfBirth As Date
```

Notice that the Dim keyword is followed by the name of the variable (DateOfBirth). This name can be anything you choose, if it is not one of the VBA keywords. Specify the data type the variable will hold by placing the As keyword after its name, followed by one of the data types from Table 4.1. The Date data type tells Visual Basic that the variable DateOfBirth will store a date. To store the employee's age, declare the age variable as follows:

```
Dim age As Integer
```

The age variable will store the number of years between today's date and the employee's date of birth. Because age is displayed as a whole number, this variable has been assigned the Integer data type.

You may also want your procedure to keep track of the employee's name, so you declare another variable to hold the employee's first and last name:

```
Dim FullName As String
```

Because the word "Name" is on the VBA list of reserved words, using it in your VBA procedure would guarantee an error. To hold the employee's full name, call the variable FullName and declare it as the String data type, because the data it will hold is text.

Declaring variables is regarded as a good programming practice because it makes programs easier to read and helps prevent certain types of errors.

Informal Variables

Variables that are not explicitly declared with `Dim` statements are said to be implicitly declared. These variables are automatically assigned a data type called Variant. They can hold numbers, strings, and other types of information. You can create a variable by simply assigning some value to a variable name anywhere in your VBA procedure. For example, you will implicitly declare a variable in the following way:

```
DaysLeft = 100
```

Now that you know how to declare your variables, let's look at a procedure that uses them:

```
Sub AgeCalc()
    ' variable declaration
    Dim FullName As String
    Dim DateOfBirth As Date
    Dim age As Integer

    ' assign values to variables
    FullName = "John Smith"
    DateOfBirth = #01/03/1981#

    ' calculate age
    age = Year(Now())-Year(DateOfBirth)

    ' print results to the Immediate window
    Debug.Print FullName & " is " & age & " years old."
End Sub
```

The variables are declared at the beginning of the procedure in which they are going to be used. In this procedure, the variables are declared on separate lines. If you want, you can declare several variables on the same line, separating each variable name with a comma, as shown here:

```
Dim FullName As String, DateOfBirth As Date, age As Integer
```

Notice that the `Dim` keyword appears only once at the beginning of the variable declaration line.

When Visual Basic executes the variable declaration statements, it creates the variables with the specified names and reserves memory space to store their values. Then specific values are assigned to these variables.

To assign a value to a variable, begin with a variable name followed by an equal sign. The value entered to the right of the equals sign is the data you want to store in the variable. The data you enter here must be of the type determined by the variable declaration. Text data should be surrounded by quotation marks, and dates by the # characters.

Using the data supplied by the DateOfBirth variable, Visual Basic calculates the age of an employee and stores the result of the calculation in the age variable. Then the full name of the employee as well as the age is printed to the Immediate window using the instruction Debug.Print. When the Visual Basic procedure has executed, you must view the Immediate window to see the results.

Let's see what happens when you declare a variable with the incorrect data type. The purpose of the following procedure is to calculate the total number of rows in a worksheet and then display the results in a dialog box.

```
Sub HowManyRows()
    Dim NumOfRows As Integer

    NumOfRows = Rows.Count

    MsgBox "The worksheet has " & NumOfRows & " rows."
End Sub
```

A wrong data type can cause an error. In the foregoing procedure, when Visual Basic attempts to write the result of the Rows.Count statement to the variable NumOfRows, the procedure fails, and Excel displays the message "*Run-time error 6—Overflow.*" This error results from selecting an invalid data type for that variable. The number of rows in a spreadsheet does not fit the Integer data range. To correct the problem, you should choose a data type that can accommodate a larger number:

```
Sub HowManyRows2()
    Dim NumOfRows As Long

    NumOfRows = Rows.Count
    MsgBox "The worksheet has " & NumOfRows & " rows."
End Sub
```

You can also correct the problem caused by the assignment of the wrong data type in the first example by deleting the variable type (As Integer). When you rerun the procedure, Visual Basic will assign to your variable the Variant data type. Although Variants use up more memory than any other variable type and slow down the speed at which your procedures run (because Visual Basic must do extra work to check the Variant's context), when it comes to short procedures, the cost of using Variants is barely noticeable.

SIDEBAR *What Is the Variable Type?*

You can quickly find out the type of a variable used in your procedure by right clicking the variable name and selecting Quick Info from the shortcut menu.

SideBar *Concatenation*

You can combine two or more strings to form a new string. The joining operation is called *concatenation*. You have seen examples of concatenated strings in the foregoing AgeCalc and HowManyRows2 procedures. Concatenation is represented by an ampersand character (&). For instance, `"His name is "` & `FirstName` will produce the following string: His name is John. The name of the person is determined by the contents of the `FirstName` variable. Notice that there is an extra space between "is" and the ending quote: "His name is ."

Concatenation of strings also can be represented by a plus sign (+). However, many programmers prefer to restrict the plus sign to operations on numbers to eliminate ambiguity.

Specifying the Data Type of a Variable

If you don't specify the variable's data type in the `Dim` statement, you end up with an untyped variable. Untyped variables in VBA are always Variant data types. It's highly recommended that you create typed variables. When you declare a variable of a certain data type, your VBA procedure runs faster because Visual Basic does not have to stop to analyze the Variant variable to determine its type.

Visual Basic can work with many types of numeric variables. Integer variables can hold only whole numbers from −32,768 to 32,767. Other types of numeric variables are Long, Single, Double, and Currency. Long variables can hold whole numbers in the range −2,147,483,648 to 2,147,483,647. Unlike the Integer and Long variables, the Single and Double variables can hold decimals. String variables are used to refer to text. When you declare a variable of String data type, you can tell Visual Basic how long the string should be—for instance:

```
Dim extension As String * 3
```

declares a fixed-length String variable named `extension` that is three characters long. If you don't assign a specific length, the String variable will be dynamic. This means that Visual Basic will make enough space in computer memory to handle whatever amount of text is assigned to it.

After you declare a variable, you can store only the type of information in it that you determined in the declaration statement. Assigning string values to numeric variables or numeric values to string variables results in the error message "Type mismatch" or causes Visual Basic to modify the value. For example, if your variable was declared to hold whole numbers and your data uses decimals, Visual Basic will disregard the decimals and use only the whole part of the number. When you run the MyNumber procedure shown here, Visual Basic modifies the data to fit the variable's data type (Integer), and instead of 23.11 the variable ends up holding a value of 23.

```
Sub MyNumber()
      Dim myNum As Integer
   myNum = 23.11
   MsgBox myNum
End Sub
```

If you don't declare a variable with a Dim statement, you can still designate a type for it by using a special character at the end of the variable name. To declare the FirstName variable as String, you can append the dollar sign to the variable name:

```
Dim FirstName$
```

This declaration is the same as Dim FirstName As String. The type declaration characters are shown in Table 3.2.

TABLE 3.2 Type declaration characters.

Data Type	Character
Integer	%
Long	&
Single	!
Double	#
Currency	@
String	$

Notice that the type declaration characters can be used only with six data types. To use the type declaration character, append the character to the end of the variable name.

In the AgeCalc2 procedure here we use two type declaration characters shown in Table 3.2.

```
Sub AgeCalc2()
   ' variable declaration
   Dim FullName$
   Dim DateOfBirth As Date
   Dim age%

   ' assign values to variables
   FullName$ = "John Smith"
   DateOfBirth = #1/3/1981#

   ' calculate age
   age% = Year(Now()) - Year(DateOfBirth)

   ' print results to the Immediate window
   Debug.Print FullName$ & " is " & age% & " years old."
End Sub
```

SideBar *Declaring Typed Variables*

The variable type can be indicated by the As keyword or a type symbol. If you don't add the symbol type or the As command, the variable will be the default data type Variant.

Assigning Values to Variables

Now that you know how to name and declare variables and have seen examples of using variables in complete procedures, let's gain experience using them. In Hands-On 3.1 we will begin by creating a variable and assigning it a specific value.

NOTE	*Please note files for the "Hands-On" project may be found in the companion files.*

Hands-On 3.1   Writing a VBA Procedure with Variables

1. Open a new workbook and save it as **C:\VBAPrimerExcel2021_ ByExample\Chap03_ExcelPrimer.xlsm**.
2. Activate the Visual Basic Editor window.
3. In the Project Explorer window, select the new project VBAProject (Chap03_ExcelPrimer.xlsm) and in the Properties window change its name to **Chapter3**.
4. Choose **Insert | Module** to add a new module to the **Chapter3 (Chap03_ ExcelPrimer.xlsm)** VBA project.
5. While the Module1 is selected, use the Properties window to change its name to **Variables**.
6. In the Code window, enter the CalcCost procedure shown here:

```
Sub CalcCost()
    slsPrice = 35
    slsTax = 0.085

    Range("A1").Formula = "The cost of calculator"
    Range("A4").Formula = "Price"
    Range("B4").Formula = slsPrice
    Range("A5").Formula = "Sales Tax"
    Range("A6").Formula = "Cost"
    Range("B5").Formula = slsPrice * slsTax
    cost = slsPrice + (slsPrice * slsTax)

    With Range("B6")
       .Formula = cost
       .NumberFormat = "0.00"
    End With

    strMsg = "The calculator total is $" & cost & "."
    Range("A8").Formula = strMsg
End Sub
```

The foregoing procedure calculates the cost of purchasing a calculator using the following assumptions: The price of a calculator is $35 and the sales tax equals 8.5%.

The procedure uses four variables: `slsPrice`, `slsTax`, `cost`, and `strMsg`. Because none of these variables have been explicitly declared, they all have the same data type—Variant. The variables `slsPrice` and `slsTax` were created by assigning some values to variable names at the beginning of the procedure. The `cost` variable was assigned a value that is a result of a calculation: `slsPrice + (slsPrice * slsTax)`. The cost calculation uses the values supplied by the `slsPrice` and `slsTax` variables. The `strMsg` variable puts together a text message to the user. This message is then entered as a complete sentence in a worksheet cell. When you assign values to variables, place an equal sign after the name of the variable. After the equals sign, you should enter the value of the variable. This can be a number, a formula, or text surrounded by quotation marks. While the values assigned to the variables `slsPrice`, `slsTax`, and `cost` are easily understood, the value stored in the `strMsg` variable is a little more involved. Let's examine the contents of the `strMsg` variable.

```
strMsg = "The calculator total is $ " & cost & "."
```

- The string `"The calculator total is "` is surrounded by quotation marks. Notice that there is an extra space before the ending quotation marks.
- The dollar sign inside the quotes is used to denote the Currency data type. Because the dollar symbol is a character, it is surrounded by the quotes.
- The & character allows another string or the contents of a variable to be appended to the string. The & character must be used every time you want to append a new piece of information to the previous string.
- The `cost` variable is a placeholder. The actual cost of the calculator will be displayed here when the procedure runs.
- The & character attaches yet another string.
- The period is surrounded by quotes. When you require a period at the end of a sentence, you must attach it separately when it follows the name of the variable.

SIDEBAR *Variable Initialization*

When Visual Basic creates a new variable, it initializes the variable. Variables assume their default value. Numerical variables are set to zero (0), Boolean variables are initialized to False, String variables are set to the empty string (""), and Date variables are set to December 30, 1899.

Now let's execute the CalcCost procedure.

7. Position the cursor anywhere within the CalcCost procedure and choose **Run | Run Sub/UserForm**.

When you run this procedure, Visual Basic may display the following message: "Compile error: Variable not defined." If this happens, click **OK** to close the message box. Visual Basic will select the slsPrice variable and highlight the name of the CalcCost procedure. The title bar displays "Microsoft Visual Basic – Chap03_ExcelPrimer.xlsm [break]." The Visual Basic break mode allows you to correct the problem before you continue. Later in this book, you will learn how to fix problems in break mode. For now, exit this mode by choosing **Run | Reset**. Now go to the top of the Code window and delete the statement Option Explicit that appears on the first line. The Option Explicit statement means that all variables used within this module must be formally declared. You will learn about this statement in the next section. When the Option Explicit statement is removed from the Code window, choose **Run | Run Sub/UserForm** to rerun the procedure. This time, Visual Basic goes to work with no objections.

8. After the procedure has finished executing, press **Alt+F11** to switch to Microsoft Excel.

The result of the procedure should match Figure 3.2.

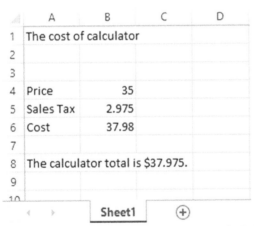

FIGURE 3.2 The VBA procedure can enter data and calculate results in a worksheet.

Cell A8 displays the contents of the strMsg variable. Notice that the cost entered in cell B6 has two decimal places, while the cost in strMsg displays three decimals. To display the cost of a calculator with two decimal places in cell A8, you must apply the required format not to the cell but to the cost variable itself.

VBA has special functions that allow you to change the format of data. To change the format of the `cost` variable, you will now use the `Format` function. This function has the following syntax:

```
Format(expression, format)
```

where `expression` is a value or variable that you want to format, and `format` is the type of format you want to apply.

9. In the VBE window, select the entire code of the CalcCost procedure and copy and paste it below the current procedure on the first empty line. Add some spacing between the two procedures by pressing Enter two times after the first procedure End Sub keywords.
10. Change the name of the copied procedure to CalcCost_Modified.
11. Change the calculation of the `cost` variable in the CalcCost procedure:

```
cost = Format(slsPrice + (slsPrice * slsTax), "0.00")
```

12. Replace the `With...End With` block of instructions with the following:

```
Range("B6").Formula = cost
```

13. Replace the statement `Range("B5").Formula = slsPrice * slsTax` with the following instruction:

```
Range("B5").Formula = Format((slsPrice * slsTax), "0.00")
```

14. Rerun the modified procedure.
   After running the procedure, the text displayed in cell A8 shows the cost of the calculator formatted with two decimal places.

After trying out the CalcCost procedure, you may wonder why you should bother declaring variables if Visual Basic can handle undeclared variables so well. The CalcCost procedure is very short, so you don't need to worry about how many bytes of memory will be consumed each time Visual Basic uses the Variant variable. In short procedures, however, it is not the memory that matters but the mistakes you are bound to make when typing variable names. What will happen if the second time you use the `cost` variable you omit the "o" and refer to it as `cst`?

```
Range("B6").Formula = cst
```

What will you end up with if instead of `slsTax` you use the word `Tax` in the formula?

```
Cost = Format(slsPrice + (slsPrice * Tax), "0.00")
```

The result of the CalcCost procedure after introducing these two mistakes is shown in Figure 3.3.

	A	B	C
1	The cost of calculator		
2			
3			
4	Price	35	
5	Sales Tax	2.98	
6	Cost		
7			
8	The calculator total is $35.00.		
9			

FIGURE 3.3 Misspelling variable names will produce incorrect results.

Notice that in Figure 3.3 cell B6 does not show a value because Visual Basic does not find the assignment statement for the cst variable. Because Visual Basic does not know the sales tax, it displays the price of the calculator (see cell A8) as the total cost. Visual Basic does not guess. It simply does what you tell it to do. This brings us to the next section, which explains how to make sure this kind of error doesn't occur.

NOTE	If you have made changes in the variable names as described earlier, be sure to replace the names of the variables cst and tax with cost and slsTax in the appropriate lines of the VBA code before you continue.

Forcing Declaration of Variables

Visual Basic has the Option Explicit statement that automatically reminds you to formally declare all your variables. This statement must be entered at the top of each of your modules. The Option Explicit statement will cause Visual Basic to generate an error message when you try to run a procedure that contains undeclared variables as demonstrated in Hands-On 3.2.

Hands-On 3.2   Writing a VBA Procedure with Explicitly Declared Variables

This Hands-On requires prior completion of Hands-On 3.1.

1. Return to the Code window where you entered the CalcCost procedure.
2. At the top of the module window (in the first line), type **Option Explicit** and press **Enter**. Excel will display the statement in blue.
3. Run the CalcCost procedure. Visual Basic displays the error message "*Compile error: Variable not defined.*"
4. Click **OK** to exit the message box.

Visual Basic highlights the name of the variable slsPrice. Now you must formally declare this variable. When you declare the slsPrice variable and rerun your procedure, Visual Basic will generate the same error as soon as it encounters another variable name that was not declared.

5. Choose **Run | Reset** to reset the VBA project.

6. Enter the following declarations at the beginning of the CalcCost procedure:

```
' declaration of variables
Dim slsPrice As Currency
Dim slsTax As Single
Dim cost As Currency
Dim strMsg As String
```

The revised CalcCost procedure is shown here:

```
Sub CalcCost()
   ' declaration of variables
   Dim slsPrice As Currency
   Dim slsTax As Single
   Dim cost As Currency
   Dim strMsg As String

   slsPrice = 35
   slsTax = 0.085
   Range("A1").Formula = "The cost of calculator"
   Range("A4").Formula = "Price"
   Range("B4").Formula = slsPrice
   Range("A5").Formula = "Sales Tax"
   Range("A6").Formula = "Cost"
   Range("B5").Formula = Format((slsPrice * slsTax), "0.00")
   cost = Format(slsPrice + (slsPrice * slsTax), "0.00")

   Range("B6").Formula = cost
   strMsg = "The calculator total is $" & cost & "."
   Range("A8").Formula = strMsg
End Sub
```

7. Rerun the procedure to ensure that Excel no longer displays the error.

SIDEBAR *Option Explicit in Every Module*

To automatically include Option Explicit in every new module you create, follow these steps:

- Choose **Tools | Options**.
- Make sure that the **Require Variable Declaration** check box is selected in the **Options** dialog box (Editor tab).
- Choose **OK** to close the Options dialog box.

From now on, every new module will be added with the `Option Explicit` statement in line 1. If you want to require variables to be explicitly declared in a previously created module, you must enter the `Option Explicit` statement manually by editing the module yourself.

`Option Explicit` forces formal (explicit) declaration of all variables in a module. One big advantage of using `Option Explicit` is that any mistyping of the variable name will be detected at compile time (when Visual Basic attempts to translate the source code to executable code). If included, the `Option Explicit` statement must appear in a module before any procedures.

Understanding the Scope of Variables

Variables can have different ranges of influence in a VBA procedure. The term *scope* defines the availability of a variable to the same procedure, other procedures, and other VBA projects.

Variables can have the following three levels of scope in Visual Basic for Applications:

- Procedure-level scope
- Module-level scope
- Project-level scope

Procedure-Level (Local) Variables

From this chapter, you already know how to declare a variable by using the `Dim` keyword. The position of the `Dim` keyword in the module sheet determines the scope of a variable. Variables declared with the `Dim` keyword placed within a VBA procedure have a *procedure-level scope*.

Procedure-level variables are frequently referred to as *local variables*. Local variables can be used only in the procedure in which they were declared. Undeclared variables always have a procedure-level scope. A variable's name must be unique within its scope. This means that you cannot declare two variables with the same name in the same procedure. However, you can use the same variable name in different procedures. In other words, the CalcCost procedure can have the `slsTax` variable, and the ExpenseRep procedure in the same module can have its own variable called `slsTax`. Both variables are independent of each other.

Module-Level Variables

Local variables help save computer memory. As soon as the procedure ends, the variable dies and Visual Basic returns the memory space used by the variable to the computer. In programming, however, you often want the variable to be available to other VBA procedures after the procedure in which the variable was declared has finished running. This situation requires that you change the scope of a variable. Instead of a procedure-level variable, you want to declare a module-level variable. To declare a module-level variable, you must place the Dim keyword at the top of the module sheet before any procedures (just below the Option Explicit keyword). For instance, to make the slsTax variable available to any other procedure in the Variables module, declare the slsTax variable in the following way:

```
Option Explicit
Dim slsTax As Single

Sub CalcCost()
...Instructions of the procedure...
End Sub
```

In the foregoing example, the Dim keyword is located at the top of the module, below the Option Explicit statement. Before you can see how this works, you need another procedure that uses the slsTax variable. In Hands-On 3.3 we will write a new VBA procedure named ExpenseRep.

Hands-On 3.3   Writing a VBA Procedure with a Module-Level Variable

1. In the Code window, cut the declaration line **Dim slsTax As Single** in the Variables module from the CalcCost procedure and paste it at the top of the module sheet below the Option Explicit statement.
2. In the same module where the CalcCost procedure is located, enter the code of the ExpenseRep procedure as shown here:

```
Sub ExpenseRep()
    Dim slsPrice As Currency
    Dim cost As Currency

    slsPrice = 55.99

    cost = slsPrice + (slsPrice * slsTax)
    MsgBox slsTax
    MsgBox cost
End Sub
```

The ExpenseRep procedure declares two Currency type variables: slsPrice and cost. The slsPrice variable is then assigned a value of 55.99. The slsPrice variable is independent of the slsPrice variable that is declared within the CalcCost procedure.

The ExpenseRep procedure calculates the cost of a purchase. The cost includes the sales tax stored in the slsTax variable. Because the sales tax is the same as the one used in the CalcCost procedure, the slsTax variable has been declared at the module level.

3. Run the **ExpenseRep** procedure.

Because you have not yet run the CalcCost procedure, Visual Basic does not know the value of the slsTax variable, so it displays zero in the first message box.

4. Run the **CalcCost** procedure.

After Visual Basic executes the CalcCost procedure that you revised in Hands-On 3.2, the contents of the slsTax variable equals 0.085. If slsTax were a local variable, the contents of this variable would be empty upon the termination of the CalcCost procedure.

When you run the CalcCost procedure, Visual Basic erases the contents of all the variables except for the slsTax variable, which was declared at a module level.

5. Run the **ExpenseRep** procedure again.

As soon as you attempt to calculate the cost by running the ExpenseRep procedure, Visual Basic retrieves the value of the slsTax variable and uses it in the calculation.

SIDEBAR *Private Variables*

When you declare variables at a module level, you can use the Private keyword instead of the Dim keyword—for instance:

```
Private slsTax As Single
```

Private variables are available only to the procedures that are part of the module where they were declared. Private variables are always declared at the top of the module after the Option Explicit statement.

Project-Level Variables

Module-level variables that are declared with the Public keyword (instead of Dim) have project-level scope. This means that they can be used in any Visual Basic for Applications module. When you want to work with a variable in all the procedures in all the open VBA projects, you must declare it with the Public keyword—for instance:

```
Option Explicit
Public slsTax As Single

Sub CalcCost()
    ...procedure statements...
    End Sub
```

Notice that the slsTax variable declared at the top of the module with the Public keyword will now be available to any other procedure in the VBA project.

Keeping the Project-Level Variable Private

To prevent a project-level variable's contents from being referenced outside its project, you can use the `Option Private Module` statement at the top of the module sheet, just below the `Option Explicit` statement and before the declaration line—for example:

```
Option Explicit
Option Private Module
Public slsTax As Single

Sub CalcCost()
... procedure statements...
End Sub
```

Lifetime of Variables

In addition to scope, variables have a lifetime. The *lifetime* of a variable determines how long a variable retains its value. Module-level and project-level variables preserve their values as long as the project is open. Visual Basic, however, can reinitialize these variables if required by the program's logic. Local variables declared with the Dim statement lose their values when a procedure has finished. Local variables have a lifetime while a procedure is running, and they are reinitialized every time the program is run. Visual Basic allows you to extend the lifetime of a local variable by changing the way it is declared.

Finding a Variable Definition

When you find an instruction in a VBA procedure that assigns a value to a variable, you can quickly locate the definition of the variable by selecting the variable name and pressing Shift+F2 or choosing View | Definition. Visual Basic will jump to the variable declaration line. Press Ctrl+Shift+F2 or choose View | Last Position to return your mouse pointer to its previous position.

Determining a Data Type of a Variable

You can find out the type of a variable by using one of the VBA built-in functions. The `VarType` function returns an integer indicating the type of a variable. Figure 3.4 displays the `VarType` function's syntax and the values it returns. Let's try using the `VarType` function in the Immediate window.

(•) Hands-On 3.4   Using the Built-In VarType Function

1. In the Visual Basic Editor window, choose **View | Immediate Window**.
2. Type the following statements that assign values to variables:

```
age = 18
```

```
birthdate = #1/1/1981#
firstName = "John"
```

3. Now ask Visual Basic what type of data each of the variables holds:

```
?VarType(age)
```

When you press **Enter**, Visual Basic returns 2. As shown in Figure 3.4, the number 2 represents the Integer data type. If you type:

```
?VarType(birthdate)
```

Visual Basic returns 7 for Date. If you make a mistake in the variable name (let's say you type birthday, instead of birthdate), Visual Basic returns zero (0). If you type:

```
?VarType(firstName)
```

Visual Basic tells you that the value stored in the variable firstName is a String type (8).

VarType(*varname*)

The required *varname* argument is a Variant containing any variable except a variable of a user-defined type.

Return values

Either one of the following constants or the summation of a number of them is returned.

Constant	Value	Description
vbEmpty	0	Empty (uninitialized)
vbNull	1	Null (no valid data)
vbInteger	2	Integer
vbLong	3	Long integer
vbSingle	4	Single-precision floating-point number
vbDouble	5	Double-precision floating-point number
vbCurrency	6	Currency value
vbDate	7	Date value
vbString	8	String
vbObject	9	Object
vbError	10	Error value
vbBoolean	11	Boolean value
vbVariant	12	Variant (used only with arrays of variants)
vbDataObject	13	A data access object
vbDecimal	14	Decimal value
vbByte	17	Byte value
vbLongLong	20	LongLong integer (valid on 64-bit platforms only)
vbUserDefinedType	36	Variants that contain user-defined types
vbArray	8192	Array (always added to another constant when returned by this function)

FIGURE 3.4 With the built-in VarType function, you can learn the data type the variable holds.
Source: *https://docs.microsoft.com/en-us/office/vba/Language/Reference/user-interface-help/vartype-function*

USING CONSTANTS

The contents of a variable can change while your procedure is executing. If your procedure needs to refer to unchanged values repeatedly, you should use constants. A *constant* is like a named variable that always refers to the same value. Visual Basic requires that you declare constants before you use them. Declare constants by using the `Const` statement, as in the following examples:

```
Const dialogName = "Enter Data" As String
Const slsTax = 8.5
Const ColorIdx = 3
```

A constant, like a variable, has a scope. To make a constant available within a single procedure, declare it at the procedure level, just below the name of the procedure—for instance:

```
Sub WedAnniv()
   Const Age As Integer = 25
   MsgBox (Age)
End Sub
```

If you want to use a constant in all the procedures of a module, use the `Private` keyword in front of the `Const` statement—for instance:

```
Private Const driveLetter As String = "C:"
```

The `Private` constant has to be declared at the top of the module, just before the first `Sub` statement. If you want to make a constant available to all modules in the workbook, use the `Public` keyword in front of the `Const` statement—for instance:

```
Public Const NumOfChars As Integer = 255
```

The `Public` constant must be declared at the top of the module, just before the first `Sub` statement. When declaring a constant, you can use any one of the following data types: Boolean, Byte, Integer, Long, Currency, Single, Double, Date, String, or Variant.

Like variables, several constants can be declared on one line if separated by commas—for instance:

```
Const Age As Integer = 25, City As String = "Denver"
```

Using constants makes your VBA procedures more readable and easier to maintain. For example, if you refer to a certain value several times in your procedure, use a constant instead of the value. This way, if the value changes (for example, the sales tax goes up), you can simply change the value in the declaration of the `Const` statement instead of tracking down every occurrence of that value.

Built-In Constants

Both Microsoft Excel and Visual Basic for Applications have a long list of predefined constants that do not need to be declared. These built-in constants can be looked up using the Object Browser window. Let's proceed to Hands-On 3.5, where we open the Object Browser to look at the list of Excel constants.

Hands-On 3.5   Viewing Excel Constants in the Object Browser

1. In the Visual Basic Editor window, choose **View | Object Browser**.
2. In the Project/Library list box, click the drop-down arrow and select **Excel**.
3. Enter **constants** as the search text in the Search box and press **Enter** or click the **Search** button. Visual Basic shows the result of the search in the Search Results area.
4. Scroll down in the Classes list box to locate and then select **Constants** as shown in Figure 3.5. The right side of the Object Browser window displays a list of all built-in constants that are available in the Microsoft Excel object library. Notice that the names of all the constants begin with the prefix "xl."
5. To look up VBA constants, choose **VBA** in the Project/Library list box (see Figure 3.6). Notice that the names of the VBA built-in constants begin with the prefix "vb."

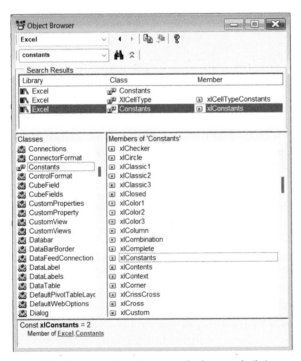

FIGURE 3.5 Use the Object Browser to look up any built-in constant.

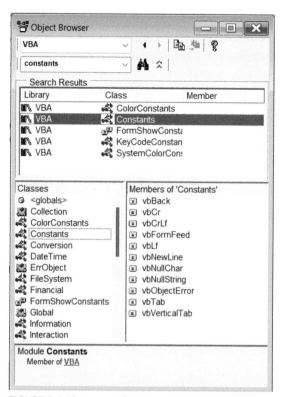

FIGURE 3.6 The names of VBA constants begin with the "vb" prefix.

CONVERTING BETWEEN DATA TYPES

While VBA handles a lot of data type conversion automatically in the background, it also provides several data conversion functions (see Table 3.3) that allow you to convert one data type to another. These functions should be used in situations where you want to show the result of an operation as a specific data type rather than the default data type. For example, instead of showing the result of your calculation as an integer or single-precision or double-precision number, you may want to use the CCur function to force currency arithmetic, as in the following example procedure:

```vba
Sub ShowMoney()
    'declare variables of two different types
    Dim myAmount As Single
    Dim myMoneyAmount As Currency

    myAmount = 345.34

    myMoneyAmount = CCur(myAmount)
    Debug.Print "Amount = $" & myMoneyAmount
End Sub
```

When using the CCur function, currency options are recognized depending on the locale setting of your computer. The same holds true for the CDate function. By using this function, you can ensure that the date is formatted according to the locale setting of your system. Use the IsDate function to determine whether a return value can be converted to date or time.

```
Sub ConvertToDate()
    'assume you have entered  Jan 1 2021 in cell A1
    Dim myEntry As String
    Dim myRangeValue As Date

    myEntry = Sheet2.Range("A1").Value
    If IsDate(myEntry) Then
        myRangeValue = CDate(myEntry)
    End If
    Debug.Print myRangeValue
End Sub
```

In cases where you need to round the value to the nearest even number, you will find the CInt and CLng functions quite handy, as demonstrated in the following procedure:

```
Sub ShowInteger()
    'declare variables of two different types
    Dim myAmount As Single
    Dim myIntAmount As Integer

    myAmount = 345.64

    myIntAmount = CInt(myAmount)
    Debug.Print "Original Amount = " & myAmount
    Debug.Print "New Amount = " & myIntAmount
End Sub
```

As you can see in the code of the foregoing procedures, the syntax for the VBA conversion functions is as follows:

```
conversionFunctionName(variablename)
```

where variablename is the name of a variable, a constant, or an expression (like x + y) that evaluates to a specific data type.

TABLE 3.3 VBA data type conversion functions.

Conversion Function	Return Type	Description
CBool	Boolean	Any valid string or numeric expression
CByte	Byte	0 to 255
CCur	Currency	–922,337,203,685,477.5808 to 922,337,203,685,477.5807
CDate	Date	Any valid date expression

Conversion Function	Return Type	Description
CDbl	Double	−1.79769313486231E308 to −−4.94065645841247E-324 for negative values; 4.94065645841247E-324 to 1.79769313486232E308 for positive values.
CDec	Decimal	+/−79,228,162,514,264,337,593,543,950,335 for zero-scaled numbers—that is, numbers with no decimal places. For numbers with 28 decimal places, the range is +/−7.9228162514264337593543950335. The smallest possible nonzero number is 0.0000000000000000000000000001.
CInt	Integer	−32,768 to 32,767; fractions are rounded.
CLng	Long	−2,147,483,648 to 2,147,483,647; fractions are rounded.
CLngLng	LongLong	−9,223,372,036,854,775,808 to 9,223,372,036,854,775,807; fractions are rounded. (Valid on 64-bit platforms only.)
CLngPtr	LongPtr	−2,147,483,648 to 2,147,483,647 on 32-bit systems; −9,223,372,036,854,775,808 to 9,223,372,036,854,775,807 on 64-bit systems. Fractions are rounded for 32-bit and 64-bit systems.
CSng	Single	−3.402823E38 to −1.401298E-45 for negative values; 1.401298E-45 to 3.402823E38 for positive values.
CStr	String	Returns for CStr depend on the expression argument. If Expression Is CStr returns Boolean A string containing True or False Date A string containing a date in the short date format of your system Null A runtime error Empty A zero-length string ("") Error A string containing the word "Error" followed by the error number Other numeric A string containing the number
Cvar	Variant	Same range as Double for numerics. Same range as String for nonnumeric.

⊚ Hands-On 3.6   Using Data Type Conversion Functions in VBA

1. Select **Insert | Module** to insert a new module into the Chapter3 (**Chap03_ ExcelPrimer.xslm**) project.
2. Use the Properties window to rename the module to **DataTypeConversion**.
3. Enter the code of the procedures introduced in this section: **ShowMoney, ConvertToDate**, and **ShowInteger**.
4. Insert a new worksheet into current workbook and enter **Jan 1 2021** in cell **A1**.
5. Run each procedure and check the results in the Immediate window.

USING STATIC VARIABLES IN VBA PROCEDURES

A variable declared with the `Static` keyword is a special type of local variable. Static variables are declared at the procedure level. Unlike local variables declared with the `Dim` keyword, static variables do not lose their contents when the program is not in their procedure. For example, when a VBA procedure with a static variable calls another procedure, after Visual Basic executes the statements of the called procedure and returns to the calling procedure, the static variable still retains the original value. The CostOfPurchase procedure shown in Hands-On 3.7 demonstrates the use of the static variable named `allPurchase`. Notice how this variable keeps track of the running total.

⊚ Hands-On 3.7   Writing a VBA Procedure with a Static Variable

1. In the Code window of the Variables module, write the following procedure:

```
Sub CostOfPurchase()
   ' declare variables
   Static allPurchase
   Dim newPurchase As String
   Dim purchCost As Single

   newPurchase = InputBox("Enter the cost of a purchase:")
   purchCost = CSng(newPurchase)
   allPurchase = allPurchase + purchCost

   ' display results
   MsgBox "The cost of a new purchase is: " & newPurchase
   MsgBox "The running cost is: " & allPurchase
End Sub
```

The foregoing procedure begins with declaring a static variable named `allPurchase` and two other local variables: `newPurchase` and `purchCost`. The `InputBox` function used in this procedure displays a dialog box and waits for the user to enter the value. As soon as you input the value and click OK, Visual Basic assigns this value to the variable `newPurchase`.

The `InputBox` function is discussed in detail in Chapter 4. Because the result of the `InputBox` function is always a string, the `newPurchase` variable was declared as the String data type. You can't, however, use strings in mathematical calculations. That's why the next instruction uses a type conversion function (`CSng`) to translate the text value into a numeric variable of the Single data type. The `CSng` function requires one argument—the value you want to translate. To find out more about the `CSng` function, position the insertion point anywhere within the word `CSng` and press F1. The number obtained as the result of the `CSng` function is then stored in the variable `purchCost`.

The next instruction, `allPurchase = allPurchase + purchCost`, adds to the current purchase value the new value supplied by the `InputBox` function.

2. Position the cursor anywhere within the `CostOfPurchase` procedure and press **F5**. When the dialog box appears, enter a number. For example, enter **100** and click **OK** or press **Enter**. Visual Basic displays the message "The cost of a new purchase is: 100." Click **OK** in the message box. Visual Basic displays the second message "The running cost is: 100."

3. When you run this procedure for the first time, the content of the `allPurchase` variable is the same as the content of the `purchCost` variable.

4. Rerun the same procedure. When the input dialog appears, enter another number. For example, enter **50** and click **OK** or press **Enter**. Visual Basic displays the message "The cost of a new purchase is: 50." Click **OK** in the message box. Visual Basic displays the second message "The running cost is: 150."

5. When you run the procedure the second time, the value of the static variable is increased by the new value supplied in the dialog box. You can run the `CostOfPurchase` procedure as many times as you want. The `allPurchase` variable will keep the running total for as long as the project is open.

USING OBJECT VARIABLES IN VBA PROCEDURES

The variables that you've learned in the preceding sections are used to store data. Storing data is the main reason for using "normal" variables in your procedures. In addition to the normal variables that store data, there are special variables that refer to the Visual Basic objects. These variables are called *object variables*. In Chapter 2, you worked with several objects in the Immediate window. Now you will learn how you can represent an object with the object variable.

Object variables don't store data; instead, they tell where the data is located. For example, with the object variable you can tell Visual Basic that the data is in cell E10 of a worksheet. Object variables make it easy to locate data. When writing Visual Basic procedures, you often need to write long instructions, such as:

```
Worksheets("Sheet2").Range(Cells(1, 1), Cells(10, 5).Select
```

Instead of using long references to the object, you can declare an object variable that will tell Visual Basic where the data is located. Object variables are declared similarly to the variables you already know. The only difference is that after the As keyword, you enter the word Object as the data type—for instance:

```
Dim myRange As Object
```

The foregoing statement declares the object variable named myRange.

Well, it's not enough to declare the object variable. You also must assign a specific value to the object variable before you can use this variable in your procedure. Assign a value to the object variable by using the Set keyword. The Set keyword must be followed by the equals sign and the value that the variable will refer to—for example:

```
Set myRange = Worksheets("Sheet2").Range(Cells(1, 1),
Cells(10, 5))
```

This statement assigns a value to the object variable myRange. This value refers to cells A1:E10 in Sheet1. If you omit the word Set, Visual Basic will respond with an error message—"*Run-time error 91: Object variable or With block variable not set.*"

Again, it's time to see a practical example.

⊙ **Hands-On 3.8   Writing a VBA Procedure with Object Variables**

1. In the Code window of the Variables module, write the following procedure:

```
Sub UseObjVariable()
 Dim myRange As Object
 Sheets.Add
 Set myRange = Worksheets("Sheet2").Range(Cells(1, 1), _
     Cells(10, 5))
 myRange.BorderAround Weight:=xlMedium

 With myRange.Interior
     .ColorIndex = 6
     .Pattern = xlSolid
 End With

 Set myRange = Worksheets("Sheet2").Range(Cells(12, 5), _
     Cells(12, 10))
```

```
    myRange.Value = 54

    Debug.Print IsObject(myRange)
End Sub
```

Let's examine the code of the UseObjVariable procedure line by line. The procedure begins with the declaration of the object variable `myRange`. The next statement sets the object variable `myRange` to the range A1:E10 on Sheet2. From now on, every time you want to reference this range, instead of using the entire object's address, you'll use the shortcut—the name of the object variable. The purpose of this procedure is to create a border around the range A1:E10. Instead of writing a long instruction:

```
Worksheets("Sheet2").Range(Cells(1, 1), _
        Cells(10, 5)).BorderAround Weight:=xlMedium
```

you can take a shortcut by using the name of the object variable:

```
myRange.BorderAround Weight:=xlMedium
```

The next series of statements changes the color of the selected range of cells (A1:E10). Again, you don't need to write the long instruction to reference the object that you want to manipulate. Instead of the full object name, you can use the `myRange` object variable. The next statement assigns a new reference to the object variable `myRange`. Visual Basic forgets the old reference, and the next time you use `myRange`, it refers to another range (E12:J12).

After the number 54 is entered in the new range (E12:J12), the procedure shows you how you can make sure that a specific variable is of the Object type. The instruction `Debug.Print IsObject(myRange)` will enter True in the Immediate window if `myRange` is an object variable. `IsObject` is a VBA function that indicates whether a specific value represents an object variable.

2. Position the cursor anywhere within the UseObjVariable procedure and press **F5**.

SIDEBAR *The Advantages of Using Object Variables*

- They can be used instead of the actual object.
- They are shorter and easier to remember than the actual values to which they point.
- You can change their meaning while your procedure is running.

Using Specific Object Variables

The object variable can refer to any type of object. Because Visual Basic has many types of objects, it's a good idea to create object variables that refer to a specific object to make your programs more readable and faster. For instance, in the UseObjVariable procedure (see the previous section), instead of the generic object variable (`Object`), you can declare the `myRange` object variable as a Range object:

```
Dim myRange As Range
```

If you want to refer to a specific worksheet, then you can declare the Worksheet object:

```
Dim mySheet As Worksheet
Set mySheet = Worksheets("Marketing")
```

When the object variable is no longer needed, you can assign Nothing to it. This frees up memory and system resources:

```
Set mySheet = Nothing
```

SUMMARY

This chapter introduced several new VBA concepts, such as data types, variables, and constants. You learned how to declare various types of variables and define their types. You also saw the difference between a variable and a constant. Now that you know what variables are and how to use them, you can create VBA procedures that allow you to manipulate data in more meaningful ways than you saw in previous chapters.

In the next chapter, you will expand your VBA knowledge by learning how to write custom function procedures. In addition, you will learn about built-in functions that will allow your VBA procedure to interact with users.

Chapter 4

Excel VBA Procedures

A QUICK GUIDE TO WRITING FUNCTION PROCEDURES

Earlier in this book you learned that a procedure is a group of instructions that allows you to accomplish specific tasks when your program runs. In this book you get acquainted with the following types of VBA procedures:

- **Subroutine procedures** (*subroutines*) perform some useful tasks but don't return any values. They begin with the keyword `Sub` and end with the keywords `End Sub`. Subroutines can be recorded with the macro recorder or written from scratch in the Visual Basic Editor window. In Chapter 1, you learned various ways to execute this type of procedure.

- **Function procedures** (*functions*) perform specific tasks that return values. They begin with the keyword `Function` and end with the keywords `End Function`. In this chapter, you will create your first function procedure. Function procedures can be executed from a subroutine or accessed from a worksheet just like any Excel built-in function.

- **Property procedures** are used with custom objects. Use them to set and get the value of an object's property or set a reference to an object. Property procedures are advanced features of VBA and are not covered in this primer book.

In this chapter, you will learn how to create and execute custom functions. In addition, you find out how variables are used in passing values to subroutines and functions. Later in the chapter, you will take a thorough look at the two most useful VBA built-in functions: `MsgBox` and `InputBox`.

UNDERSTANDING FUNCTION PROCEDURES

With the hundreds of built-in Excel functions, you can perform a wide variety of calculations automatically. However, there will be times when you may require a custom calculation. With VBA programming, you can quickly fulfill this special need by creating a function procedure. You can build any functions that are not supplied with Excel. Among the reasons for creating custom VBA functions are the following:

- analyze data and perform calculations
- modify data and report information
- take a specific action based on supplied or calculated data

Creating a Function Procedure

Like Excel functions, function procedures perform calculations and return values. The best way to learn about functions is to create one, so let's get started. After setting up a new VBA project, you will create a simple function procedure that sums two values.

NOTE	Please note files for the "Hands-On" project may be found in the companion files.

⦿ **Hands-On 4.1   Writing a Simple Function Procedure**

1. Open a new Excel workbook and save it as **C:\ VBAPrimerExcel_ByExample\Chap04_ExcelPrimer.xlsm**.
2. Switch to the Visual Basic Editor window and select **VBAProject (Chap04_ExcelPrimer.xlsm)**.
3. In the Properties window, change the name of the project name to **ProcAndFunctions**.
4. Select the **ProcAndFunctions (Chap04_ExcelPrimer.xlsm)** project in the Project Explorer window and choose **Insert | Module**.
5. In the Properties window, change the Module1 name to **Sample1**.
6. In the Project Explorer window, highlight **Sample1** and click anywhere in the Code window. Choose **Insert | Procedure**. The Add Procedure dialog box appears.
7. In the Add Procedure dialog box, make the entries shown in Figure 4.1:
   Name: **SumItUp**
   Type: **Function**
   Scope: **Public**

FIGURE 4.1 When you use the Add Procedure dialog box, Visual Basic automatically creates the procedure type you choose.

8. Click **OK** to close the Add Procedure dialog box. Visual Basic enters an empty function procedure that looks like this:

```
Public Function SumItUp()

End Function
```

9. Modify the function declaration as follows:

```
Public Function SumItUp(m, n)

End Function
```

The purpose of this function is to add two values. Instead of passing the actual values to the function, you can make the function more flexible by providing it with the arguments in the form of variables. By doing this, your custom function will be able to add any two numbers that you specify. Each of the passed-in variables (m, n) represents a value. You will supply the values for each of these variables when you run this function.

10. Type the following statement between the `Public  Function` and `End Function` statements:

```
SumItUp = m + n
```

This statement instructs Visual Basic to add the value stored in the n variable to the value stored in the m variable and return the result to the SumItUp function. To specify the value that you want the function to return, type the function name followed by the equals sign and the value you want it to return. In the foregoing statement, set the name of the function equal to the total of m + n. The completed custom function procedure is shown here:

```
Public Function SumItUp(m,n)
    SumItUp = m + n
End Function
```

The first statement declares the name of the function procedure. The `Public` keyword indicates that the function is accessible to all other procedures in all other modules. The `Public` keyword is optional. Notice the keyword `Function` followed by the name of the function (`SumItUp`) and a pair of parentheses. In the parentheses, you will list the data items that the function will use in the calculation. Every function procedure ends with the `End Function` statement.

SIDEBAR *About Function Names*

Function names should suggest the role that the function performs and must conform to the rules for naming variables (see Chapter 3).

SIDEBAR *Scoping VBA Procedures*

In the previous chapter, you learned that the variable's scope determines which modules and procedures it can be used in. Like variables, VBA procedures have scope. A procedure scope determines whether it can be called by procedures in other modules. By default, all VBA procedures are public. This means they can be called by other procedures in any module. Because procedures are public by default, you can skip the `Public` keyword if you want. And if you replace the `Public` keyword with the `Private` keyword, your procedure will be available only to other procedures in the same module, not to procedures in other modules.

VARIOUS METHODS OF RUNNING FUNCTION PROCEDURES

Unlike a subroutine, a function procedure can be executed in just two ways: You can use it in a worksheet formula, or you can call it from another procedure. In the following sections, you will learn special techniques for executing functions.

Running a Function Procedure from a Worksheet

A custom function procedure is like an Excel built-in function. If you don't know the exact name of the function or its arguments, you can use the Formula palette to help enter the required function in a worksheet as shown in Hands-On 4.2.

Hands-On 4.2   Executing a Function Procedure from within an Excel Worksheet

1. Switch to the Microsoft Excel window and select any cell.
2. Click the **Insert Function** (*fx*) button on the Formula bar. Excel displays the Insert Function dialog box. The lower portion of the dialog box displays an alphabetical listing of all the functions in the selected category.
3. In the category drop-down box, select **User Defined**. In the function name box, locate and select the **SumItUp** function that was created in Hands-On 4.1. When you highlight the name of the function in the function name box (Figure 4.2), the bottom part of the dialog box displays the function's syntax: SumItUp(m,n).

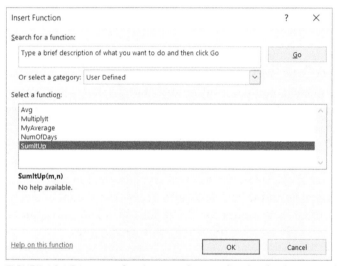

FIGURE 4.2 VBA custom function procedures are listed under the User Defined category in the Insert Function dialog box. They also appear in the list of all Excel built-in functions when you select All in the category drop-down.

4. Click **OK** to begin writing a formula. The Function Arguments dialog
   box appears, as shown in Figure 4.3. This dialog displays the name of the
   function and each of its arguments: m and n.

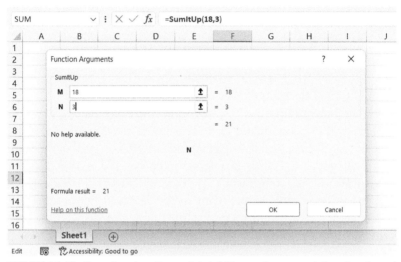

FIGURE 4.3 The Formula palette feature is helpful in entering any worksheet function, whether
built-in or custom-made with VBA programming.

5. Enter the values for the arguments as shown in Figure 4.3 or enter your own
   values. As you type the values in the argument text boxes, Excel displays
   the values you entered and the current result of the function. Because both
   arguments (m and n) are required, the function will return an error if you
   skip either one of the arguments.
6. Click **OK** to exit the Function Arguments dialog.
   Excel enters the SumItUp function in the selected cell and displays its result.
7. To edit the function, select the cell that displays the function's result and
   click the **Insert Function** (*fx*) button to access the Function Arguments
   dialog box. Enter new values for the function's m and n arguments and
   click **OK**.

NOTE	*To edit the arguments' values directly in the cell, double-click the cell containing the function and make the necessary changes. You may also set up the SumItUp function to perform calculations based on the values entered in cells. To do this, in the Function Arguments dialog box shown in Figure 4.3, simply enter cell references instead of values. For example, enter C1 for the m argument and C2 for the n argument. When you click OK, Excel will display zero (0) as the result of the function. On the worksheet, enter the values in cells C1 and C2 and your custom function will recalculate the result just like any other built-in Excel function.*

Running a Function Procedure from Another VBA Procedure

To execute a custom function, write a VBA subroutine and call the function when you need it. The following procedure calls the SumItUp function and prints the result of the calculation to the Immediate window.

(•) **Hands-On 4.3   Executing a Function from a VBA Procedure**

1. In the same module where you entered the code of the SumItUp function procedure, enter the RunSumItUp procedure.

```
Sub RunSumItUp()
  Dim m As Single, n As Single
  m = 37
  n = 3459.77

  Debug.Print SumItUp(m,n)
  MsgBox "Open the Immediate Window to see the result."
End Sub
```

Notice how the foregoing subroutine uses one Dim statement to declare the m and n variables. These variables will be used to feed the data to the function. The next two statements assign the values to those variables. Next, Visual Basic calls the SumItUp function and passes the values stored in the m and n variables to it. When the function procedure statement SumItUp = m + n is executed, Visual Basic returns to the RunSumItUp subroutine and uses the Debug.Print statement to print the function's result to the Immediate window. Finally, the MsgBox function informs the user where to look for the result. You can find more information about using the MsgBox function later in this chapter.

2. Place the mouse pointer anywhere within the **RunSumItUp** procedure and press **F5** to run it.

ENSURING AVAILABILITY OF YOUR CUSTOM FUNCTIONS

Your custom VBA function is available only while the workbook where the function is stored is open. If you close the workbook, the function is no longer available. To make sure that your custom VBA functions are available every time you work with Microsoft Excel, you can do one of the following:

- Store your functions in the Personal macro workbook.
- Save the workbook with your custom VBA function in the XLStart folder.
- Set up a reference to the workbook containing your custom functions.

A Quick Test of a Function

After you write your custom function, you can quickly try it out in the Immediate window. To display the value of a function, open the Immediate window and type a question mark (?) followed by the function name. Remember to enclose the function's arguments in parentheses.

For example, type:

```
? SumItUp(54, 367.24)
```

and press Enter. Your function procedure runs, using the values you passed for the m and n arguments. The result of the function appears on a line below:

```
421.24
```

PASSING ARGUMENTS TO FUNCTION PROCEDURES

Procedures (both subroutines and functions) often take arguments. *Arguments* are one or more values needed for a procedure to do something. Arguments are entered within parentheses. Multiple arguments are separated with commas.

Having used Excel for a while, you already know that Excel's built-in functions can produce different results based on the values you supply to them. For example, if cells A4 and A5 contain the numbers 5 and 10, respectively, the Sum function =SUM(A4:A5) will return 15, unless you change the values entered in the specified cells. Just like you can pass any values to Excel's built-in functions, you can pass values to custom VBA procedures.

Let's see how you can pass some values from a subroutine procedure to the SumItUp function. We will write a procedure that collects the user's first and last name. Next, we will call the SumItUp function to get the sum of characters in a person's first and last name.

⦿ **Hands-On 4.4   Passing Arguments to Functions (Example 1)**

1. Type the following NumOfCharacters subroutine in the same module (Sample1) where you entered the SumItUp function:

```
Sub NumOfCharacters()
  Dim f As Integer
  Dim l As Integer

  f = Len(InputBox("Enter first name:"))
  l = Len(InputBox("Enter last name:"))
  MsgBox SumItUp(f,l)
End Sub
```

2. Place the mouse pointer within the code of the NumOfCharacters procedure and press **F5**. Visual Basic displays the input box asking for the first name. This box is generated by the following function: `InputBox("Enter first name:")`. For more information on the use of this function, see the section titled "Using the InputBox Function" later in this chapter.

3. Enter any name, and press **Enter** or click **OK**. Visual Basic takes the text you entered and supplies it as an argument to the `Len` function. The `Len` function calculates the number of characters in the supplied text string. Visual Basic places the result of the `Len` function in the `f` variable for further reference. After that, Visual Basic displays the next input box, this time asking for the last name.

4. Enter any last name, and press **Enter** or click **OK**.
Visual Basic passes the last name to the `Len` function to get the number of characters. Then that number is stored in the `l` variable. What happens next? Visual Basic encounters the `MsgBox` function. This function tells Visual Basic to display the result of the `SumItUp` function. However, because the result is not yet ready, Visual Basic jumps quickly to the `SumItUp` function to perform the calculation using the values saved earlier in the `f` and `l` variables. Inside the function procedure, Visual Basic substitutes the `m` argument with the value of the `f` variable and the `n` argument with the value of the `l` variable. Once the substitution is done, Visual Basic adds up the two numbers and returns the result to the `SumItUp` function.

There are no more tasks to perform inside the function procedure, so Visual Basic returns to the subroutine and provides the `SumItUp` function's result as an argument to the `MsgBox` function. Now a message appears on the screen displaying the total number of characters.

5. Click **OK** to exit the message box.
You can run the NumOfCharacters procedure as many times as you'd like, each time supplying different first and last names.

To pass a specific value from a function to a subroutine, assign the value to the name of the function. For example, the `NumOfDays` function shown here passes the value of 7 to the subroutine `DaysInAWeek`.

```
Function NumOfDays()
   NumOfDays = 7
End Function

Sub DaysInAWeek()
   MsgBox "There are " & NumOfDays & " days in a week."
End Sub
```

Specifying Argument Types

In the preceding section, you learned that functions perform some calculations based on data received through their arguments. When you declare a function procedure, you list the names of arguments inside a set of parentheses. Argument names are like variables. Each argument name refers to whatever value you provide at the time the function is called. When a subroutine calls a function procedure, it passes the required arguments as variables to it. Once the function does something, the result is assigned to the function name. Notice that the function procedure's name is used as if it were a variable.

Like variables, functions can have types. The result of your function procedure can be String, Integer, Long, and so on. To specify the data type for your function's result, add the keyword As and the name of the desired data type to the end of the function declaration line—for example:

```
Function MultiplyIt(num1, num2) As Integer
```

Let's look at an example of a function that returns an Integer number, although the arguments passed to it are declared as Single data types in a calling subroutine.

Hands-On 4.5   Passing Arguments to Functions (Example 2)

1. Add a new module to the **ProcAndFunctions (Chap04_ExcelPrimer. xlsm)** project and change the module's name to **Sample2**.
2. Activate the **Sample2** module and enter the HowMuch subroutine as shown here:

```
Sub HowMuch()
    Dim num1 As Single
    Dim num2 As Single
    Dim result As Single

    num1 = 45.33
    num2 = 19.24

    result = MultiplyIt(num1, num2)
    MsgBox result
End Sub
```

3. Enter the **MultiplyIt** function procedure below the HowMuch subroutine:

```
Function MultiplyIt(num1, num2) As Integer
    MultiplyIt = num1 * num2
End Function
```

Because the values stored in the variables num1 and num2 are not whole numbers, you may want to assign the Integer data type to the result of the function to ensure that the result is a whole number. If you don't assign the data type to the MultiplyIt function's result, the HowMuch procedure will display the result in the data type specified in the declaration line of the result variable. Instead of 872, the result of the multiplication will be 872.1492.

4. Run the HowMuch procedure.

How about passing different values each time you run the procedure? Instead of hardcoding the values to be used in the multiplication, you can use the `InputBox` function to ask the user for the values at runtime—for example:

```
num1 = InputBox("Enter a number:")
```

The InputBox function is discussed in detail in a later section of this chapter.

Passing Arguments by Reference and by Value

In some procedures, when you pass arguments as variables, Visual Basic can suddenly change the value of the variables. To ensure that the called function procedure does not alter the value of the passed-in arguments, you should precede the name of the argument in the function's declaration line with the keyword `ByVal`. Let's look at the following example.

(⊙) Hands-On 4.6   Passing Arguments to Functions (Example 3)

1. Add a new module to the **ProcAndFunctions (Chap04_ExcelPrimer. xlsm)** project and change the module's name to **Sample3**.
2. Activate the **Sample3** module and type the procedures shown here:

```
Sub ThreeNumbers()
  Dim num1 As Integer, num2 As Integer, num3 As Integer
  num1 = 10
  num2 = 20
  num3 = 30

  MsgBox MyAverage(num1, num2, num3)
  MsgBox num1
  MsgBox num2
  MsgBox num3
End Sub

Function MyAverage(ByVal num1, ByVal num2, ByVal num3)
  num1 = num1 + 1

  MyAverage = (num1 + num2 + num3) / 3
End Function
```

To prevent the function from altering values of arguments, use the keyword `ByVal` before the arguments' names (see the "Know Your Keywords: ByRef and ByVal" sidebar).

3. Run the ThreeNumbers procedure.

The ThreeNumbers procedure assigns values to three variables and then calls the `MyAverage` function to calculate and return the average of the numbers stored in these variables. The function's arguments are the variables `num1`, `num2`, and `num3`. Notice that all of the function arguments are preceded with the keyword `ByVal`. Also, notice that prior to the calculation of the average, the `MyAverage` function changes the value of the `num1` variable. Inside the function procedure, the `num1` variable equals 11 (10 + 1). Therefore, when the function passes the calculated average to the ThreeNumbers procedure, the `MsgBox` function displays the result as 20.3333333333333 and not 20, as expected. The next three `MsgBox` functions show the contents of each of the variables. The values stored in these variables are the same as the original values assigned to them—10, 20, and 30.

What will happen if you omit the keyword `ByVal` in front of the `num1` argument in the `MyAverage` function's declaration line? The function's result will still be the same, but the contents of the `num1` variable displayed by `MsgBox num1` is now 11. The `MyAverage` function has not only returned an unexpected result (20.3333333333333 instead of 20) but also modified the original data stored in the `num1` variable. To prevent Visual Basic from permanently changing the values supplied to the function, use the `ByVal` keyword.

SIDEBAR *Know Your Keywords: ByRef and ByVal*

Because any of the variables passed to a function procedure (or a subroutine) can be changed by the receiving procedure, it is important to know how to protect the original value of a variable. Visual Basic has two keywords that give or deny permission to change the contents of a variable—`ByRef` and `ByVal`. By default, Visual Basic passes information into a function procedure (or a subroutine) by reference (`ByRef` keyword), referring to the original data specified in the function's argument at the time the function is called. So, if the function alters the value of the argument, the original value is changed. You will get this result if you omit the `ByVal` keyword in front of the `num1` argument in the `MyAverage` function's declaration line. If you want the function procedure to change the original value, you don't need to explicitly insert the `ByRef` keyword, because passed variables default to `ByRef`. When you use the `ByVal` keyword in front of an argument name, Visual Basic passes the argument by value. This means that Visual Basic makes a copy of the original data and passes that copy to a function. If the function changes the value of an argument passed by value, the original data does not change—only the copy changes. That's why when the `MyAverage` function changed the value of the `num1` argument, the original value of the `num1` variable remained the same.

Using Optional Arguments

At times you may want to supply an additional value to a function. Let's say you have a function that calculates the price of a meal per person. Sometimes, however, you'd like the function to perform the same calculation for a group of two or more people. To indicate that a procedure argument is not always required, precede the name of the argument with the Optional keyword. Arguments that are optional come at the end of the argument list, following the names of all the required arguments.

Optional arguments must always be the Variant data type. This means that you can't specify the optional argument's type by using the As keyword. In the preceding section, you created a function to calculate the average of three numbers. Suppose that sometimes you'd like to use this function to calculate the average of two numbers. You could define the third argument of the MyAverage function as optional.

To preserve the original MyAverage function, let's create the Avg function to calculate the average for two or three numbers.

(⦿) **Hands-On 4.7   Writing Functions with Optional Arguments**

1. Add a new module to the **ProcAndFunctions (Chap04_ExcelPrimer. xlsm)** project and change the module's name to **Sample4**.
2. Activate the **Sample4** module and enter the function procedure Avg shown here:

```
Function Avg(num1, num2, Optional num3)
    Dim totalNums As Integer

    totalNums = 3

    If IsMissing(num3) Then
      num3 = 0
      totalNums = totalNums - 1
    End If

    Avg = (num1+num2+num3)/totalNums
End Function
```

Let's take a few minutes to analyze the Avg function. This function can take up to three arguments. The arguments num1 and num2 are required. The argument num3 is optional. Notice that the name of the optional argument is preceded with the Optional keyword. The optional argument is listed at the end of the argument list. Because the type of the num1, num2, and num3 arguments is not declared, Visual Basic treats all these arguments as Variants. Inside the function procedure, the totalNums variable is declared as an Integer and then assigned a beginning value of 3. Because the function has to be capable of calculating an average of two or three numbers, the handy built-in function `IsMissing` checks for the number of supplied arguments. If the third (optional) argument is not supplied, the `IsMissing` function puts in its place the value of zero (0), and at the same time it deducts the value of 1 from the value stored in the `totalNums` variable. Hence, if the optional argument is missing, `totalNums` is 2. The next statement calculates the average based on the supplied data, and the result is assigned to the name of the function.

The `IsMissing` function allows you to determine whether the optional argument was supplied. This function returns the logical value true if the third argument is not supplied, and it returns false when the third argument is given. The `IsMissing` function is used here with the decision-making statement `If…Then`. (See Chapter 5 for a detailed description of decision-making statements used in VBA.) If the `num3` argument is missing (`IsMissing`), then (`Then`) Visual Basic supplies a zero for the value of the third argument (`num3 = 0`) and reduces the value stored in the argument `totalNums` by one (`totalNums = totalNums - 1`).

3. Now call this function from the Immediate window like this:

```
?Avg(2,3)
```

As soon as you press **Enter,** Visual Basic displays the result: 2.5. If you enter the following:

```
?Avg(2,3,5)
```

this time the result is 3.3333333333333.

As you've seen, the `Avg` function allows you to calculate the average of two or three numbers. You decide which values and how many values (two or three) you want to average. When you start typing the values for the function's arguments in the Immediate window, Visual Basic displays the name of the optional argument enclosed in square brackets.

How else can you run the `Avg` function? On your own, run this function from a worksheet. Make sure you run it with two and then with three arguments.

TESTING A FUNCTION PROCEDURE

To test whether a custom function does what it was designed to do, write a simple subroutine that will call the function and display its result. In addition, the subroutine should show the original values of arguments. This way, you'll be able to quickly determine when the values of arguments were altered. If the function procedure uses optional arguments, you'll also need to check those situations in which the optional arguments may be missing.

LOCATING BUILT-IN FUNCTIONS

VBA comes with numerous built-in functions. These functions can be looked up in the Visual Basic online help:

https://docs.microsoft.com/en-us/office/vba/Language/Reference/functions-visual-basic-for-applications

Take, for example, the `MsgBox` or `InputBox` function. One of the features of a good program is its interaction with the user. When you work with Microsoft Excel, you interact with the application by using various dialog boxes. When you make a mistake, a dialog box comes up and displays a message informing you of the error. When you write your own procedures, you can also inform the users about an unexpected error or the result of a specific calculation. You do this with the help of the `MsgBox` function. So far you have seen a simple implementation of this function. In the next section, you will find out how to control the way your message looks. You will also learn how to get information from the user with the `InputBox` function.

GETTING TO KNOW THE MSGBOX FUNCTION

The `MsgBox` function that you have used thus far was limited to displaying a message to the user in a simple one-button dialog box. You closed the message box by clicking the OK button or pressing the Enter key. You create a simple message box by following the `MsgBox` function name with the text enclosed in quotation marks. In other words, to display the message "The procedure is complete." you write the following statement:

```
MsgBox "The procedure is complete."
```

You can quickly try out the foregoing instruction by entering it in the Immediate window. When you type this instruction and press Enter, Visual Basic displays the message box shown in Figure 4.4.

FIGURE 4.4 To display a message to the user, place the text as the argument of the `MsgBox` function.

The MsgBox function allows you to use other arguments that make it possible to set the number of buttons that should be available in the message box or change the title of the message box from the default, "Microsoft Excel." You can also assign your own help topic.

The syntax of the MsgBox function is as follows:

```
MsgBox (prompt [, buttons] [, title], [, helpfile, context])
```

Notice that while the MsgBox function has five arguments, only the first one, prompt, is required. The arguments listed in square brackets are optional. When you enter a long text string for the prompt argument, Visual Basic decides how to break the text so it fits the message box. Let's do some exercises in the Immediate window to learn various text formatting techniques.

Hands-On 4.8 Formatting Text for Display in the MsgBox Function

1. Enter the following instruction in the Immediate window. Be sure to enter the entire text string on one line, and then press **Enter**.

```
MsgBox "All processes completed successfully. Now connect an
    external storage device to your computer. The following
    procedure will copy the workbook file to the attached
    device."
```

As soon as you press **Enter**, Visual Basic shows the resulting dialog box (Figure 4.5).

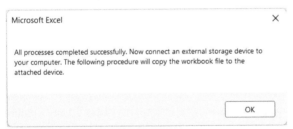

FIGURE 4.5 This long message will look more appealing when you take the text formatting into your own hands.

When you write a VBA procedure that requires long messages, you can break your message text into several lines using the VBA Chr function. The Chr function takes one argument (a number from 0 to 255), and it returns a character represented by this number. For example, Chr(13) returns a carriage return character (this is the same as pressing the Enter key), and Chr(10) returns a linefeed character (useful for adding spacing between the text lines).

```
Sub LongTextMessage()
    MsgBox "All processes completed successfully. " & Chr(13) _
        & "Now connect an external storage device to " & Chr(13) _
```

```
    & "your computer. The following procedure " & Chr(13) _
    & "will copy the workbook file to the attached device."
End Sub
```

Figure 4.6 depicts the message box after running the LongTextMessage procedure.

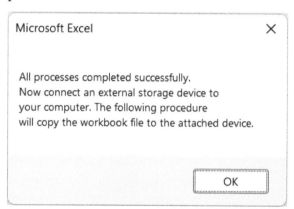

Microsoft Excel   ✕

All processes completed successfully.
Now connect an external storage device to
your computer. The following procedure
will copy the workbook file to the attached device.

OK

FIGURE 4.6 You can break a long text string into several lines by using the `Chr(13)` function.

You must surround each text fragment with quotation marks. The `Chr(13)` function indicates a place where you'd like to start a new line. The string concatenation character (&) is used to add a carriage return character to a concatenated string.

Quoted text embedded in a text string requires an additional set of quotation marks, as shown in the revised statement here:

```
Sub LongTextMessageRev()
    MsgBox "All processes completed successfully. " & _
        Chr(13) _
    & "Now connect an external storage device to " & _
        Chr(13) & "your computer. " & _
    "The following procedure ""TestProc()""" & _
        Chr(13) & "will copy the workbook file " & _
    "to the attached device."
End Sub
```

When you enter exceptionally long text messages on one line, it's easy to make a mistake. As you recall, Visual Basic has a special line continuation character (an underscore _) that allows you to break a long VBA statement into several lines. Unfortunately, the line continuation character cannot be used in the Immediate window.

2. Add a new module to the **ProcAndFunctions (Chap04_ExcelPrimer. xlsm)** project and change the module's name to **Sample5**.
3. Activate the **Sample5** module and enter the **LongTextMessage** and **LongTextMessageRev** subroutines as shown earlier. Be sure to precede each line continuation character (_) with a space.

4. Execute each procedure.
Notice that the text entered on several lines is more readable, and the code is easier to maintain.

To improve the readability of your message, you may want to add more spacing between the text lines by including blank lines. To do this, use two Chr(13) or two Chr(10) functions, as shown in the following step.

5. Enter the following LongTextMessage2 procedure and run it:

```
Sub LongTextMessage2()
    MsgBox "All processes completed successfully. " & _
        Chr(10) & Chr(10) _
    & "Now connect an external storage device " & _
        Chr(13) & Chr(13) _
    & "to your computer. The following procedure " & _
        Chr(10) & Chr(10) _
    & "will copy the workbook file to the attached device."
End Sub
```

Figure 4.7 displays the message box generated by the LongTextMessage2 procedure.

FIGURE 4.7 You can increase the readability of your message by increasing spacing between the selected text lines.

Now that you've mastered the text formatting techniques, let's take a closer look at the next argument of the MsgBox function. Although the buttons argument is optional, it is frequently used. The buttons argument specifies how many and what types of buttons you want to appear in the message box. This argument can be a constant or a number, as shown in Table 4.1. If you omit this argument, the resulting message box includes only the OK button, as you've seen in the preceding examples.

TABLE 4.1 Settings for the MsgBox buttons argument.

Constant	Value	Description
Button settings		
vbOKOnly	0	Displays only an OK button. This is the default.
vbOKCancel	1	OK and Cancel buttons.
vbAbortRetryIgnore	2	Abort, Retry, and Ignore buttons.
vbYesNoCancel	3	Yes, No, and Cancel buttons.
vbYesNo	4	Yes and No buttons.
vbRetryCancel	5	Retry and Cancel buttons.
Icon settings		
vbCritical	16	Displays the Critical Message icon.
vbQuestion	32	Displays the Question Message icon.
vbExclamation	48	Displays the Warning Message icon.
vbInformation	64	Displays the Information Message icon.
Default button settings		
vbDefaultButton1	0	The first button is the default.
vbDefaultButton2	256	The second button is the default.
vbDefaultButton3	512	The third button is the default.
vbDefaultButton4	768	The fourth button is the default.
Message box modality		
vbApplicationModal	0	The user must respond to the message before continuing to work in the current application.
vbSystemModal	4096	All applications are suspended until the user responds to the message box.
Other MsgBox display settings		
vbMsgBoxHelpButton	16384	Adds Help button to the message box.
vbMsgBoxSetForeground	65536	Specifies the message box window as the foreground window.
vbMsgBoxRight	524288	Text is right aligned.
vbMsgBoxRtlReading	1048576	Text appears as right-to-left reading on Hebrew and Arabic systems.

When should you use the buttons argument? Suppose you want the user of your procedure to respond to a question with Yes or No. Your message box may then require two buttons. If a message box includes more than one button, one of them is considered a default button. When the user presses Enter, the default button is selected automatically. Because you can display various types of messages (critical, warning, information), you can visually indicate the importance of the message by including in the buttons argument the graphical representation (icon) for the chosen message type.

In addition to the type of message, the `buttons` argument can include a setting to determine whether the message box must be closed before a user switches to another application. It's quite possible that the user may want to switch to another program or perform another task before responding to the question posed in your message box. If the message box is application modal (`vbApplication Modal`), the user must close the message box before continuing to use your application. On the other hand, if you want to suspend all the applications until the user responds to the message box, you must include the `vbSystemModal` setting in the `buttons` argument.

The `buttons` argument settings are divided into five groups: button settings, icon settings, default button settings, message box modality, and other `MsgBox` display settings. Only one setting from each group can be included in the `buttons` argument. To create a `buttons` argument, you can add up the values for each setting you want to include. For example, to display a message box with two buttons (Yes and No), the question mark icon, and the No button as the default button, look up the corresponding values in Table 4.1 and add them up. You should arrive at 292 (4 + 32 + 256).

Let's go back to the Immediate window for more testing of the capabilities of the `MsgBox` function.

⊚ Hands-On 4.9   Using the MsgBox Function with Arguments (Example 1)

1. To quickly see the message box using the calculated message box argument, enter the following statement in the Immediate window, and press Enter:

```
MsgBox "Do you want to proceed?", 292
```

The resulting message box is shown in Figure 4.8.

FIGURE 4.8 You can specify the number of buttons to include in the message box by using the optional `buttons` argument.

When you derive the `buttons` argument by adding up the constant values, your procedure becomes less readable. There's no reference table where you can check the hidden meaning of 292. To improve the readability of your `MsgBox` function, it's better to use the constants instead of their values.

2. Now enter the following revised statement on one line in the Immediate window and press Enter.

```
MsgBox "Do you want to proceed?", vbYesNo + vbQuestion +
vbDefaultButton2
```

This statement (which must be entered on one line) produces the same result shown in Figure 4.8 and is more readable.

The following example shows how to use the `buttons` argument inside the Visual Basic procedure.

Hands-On 4.10   Using the MsgBox Function with Arguments (Example 2)

1. Add a new module to the **ProcAndFunctions (Chap04_ExcelPrimer. xlsm)** project and change the module's name to **Sample6**.
2. Activate the **Sample6** module and enter the MsgYesNo subroutine shown here, and then run it:

```
Sub MsgYesNo()
    Dim question As String
    Dim myButtons As Integer

    question = "Do you want to open a new workbook?"
    myButtons = vbYesNo + vbQuestion + vbDefaultButton2

    MsgBox question, myButtons
End Sub
```

In the foregoing subroutine, the `question` variable stores the text of your message. The settings for the `buttons` argument is placed in the `myButtons` variable. Instead of using the names of constants, you can use their values, as in the following:

```
myButtons = 4 + 32 + 256
```

However, by specifying the names of the `buttons` argument's constants, you make your procedure easier to understand for yourself and others who may work with this procedure in the future.

The `question` and `myButtons` variables are used as arguments for the `MsgBox` function. When you run the procedure, you see the result displayed, as shown in Figure 4.8. Notice that the No button is selected. It's the default button for this dialog box. If you press Enter, Excel removes the `MsgBox` from the screen. Nothing happens because your procedure does not have any more instructions following the `MsgBox` function.

To change the default button, use the `vbDefaultButton1` setting instead.

The third argument of the `MsgBox` function is `title`. While this is also an optional argument, it's very handy, as it allows you to create procedures that don't provide visual clues to the fact that you programmed them with Microsoft Excel. Using this argument, you can set the title bar of your message box to any text you want.

Suppose you want the MsgYesNo procedure to display in its title the text "New workbook." The following MsgYesNo2 procedure demonstrates the use of the `title` argument:

```
Sub MsgYesNo2()
    Dim question As String
    Dim myButtons As Integer
    Dim myTitle As String

    question = "Do you want to open a new workbook?"
    myButtons = vbYesNo + vbQuestion + vbDefaultButton2
    myTitle = "New workbook"

    MsgBox question, myButtons, myTitle
End Sub
```

The text for the `title` argument is stored in the variable `myTitle`. If you don't specify the value for the `title` argument, Visual Basic displays the default text, "Microsoft Excel."

Notice that the arguments are listed in the order determined by the `Msg-Box` function. If you would like to list the arguments in any order, you must precede the value of each argument with its name:

```
MsgBox title:=myTitle, prompt:=question, buttons:=myButtons
```

The last two optional arguments—`helpfile` and `context`—are used by programmers who are experienced with using help files in the Windows environment.

The `helpfile` argument indicates the name of a special help file that contains additional information you may want to display to your VBA procedure user. When you specify this argument, the Help button will be added to your message box.

Returning Values from the MsgBox Function

When you display a simple message box dialog with one button, clicking the OK button or pressing the Enter key removes the message box from the screen. However, when the message box has more than one button, your procedure should detect which button was pressed. To do this, you must save the result of the message box in a variable. Table 4.2 shows values that the `MsgBox` function returns.

TABLE 4.2 Values returned by the `MsgBox` function.

Button Selected	Constant	Value
OK	vbOK	1
Cancel	vbCancel	2
Abort	vbAbort	3
Retry	vbRetry	4
Ignore	vbIgnore	5
Yes	vbYes	6
No	vbNo	7

Let's revise the MsgYesNo2 procedure to show which button the user has chosen.

Hands-On 4.11   Using the MsgBox Function with Arguments (Example 3)

1. Activate the **Sample6** module and enter the MsgYesNo3 subroutine as shown here:

```
Sub MsgYesNo3()
    Dim question As String
    Dim myButtons As Integer
    Dim myTitle As String

    Dim myChoice As Integer

    question = "Do you want to open a new workbook?"
    myButtons = vbYesNo + vbQuestion + vbDefaultButton2
    myTitle = "New workbook"
    myChoice = MsgBox(question, myButtons, myTitle)

    MsgBox myChoice
End Sub
```

In the foregoing procedure, we assigned the result of the `MsgBox` function to the variable `myChoice`. Notice that the arguments of the `MsgBox` function are now listed in parentheses:

```
myChoice = MsgBox(question, myButtons, myTitle)
```

2. Run the **MsgYesNo3** procedure.

When you run the MsgYesNo3 procedure, a two-button message box is displayed. When you click on the Yes button, the statement `MsgBox myChoice` displays the number 6. When you click the No button, the number 7 is displayed.

GETTING TO KNOW THE INPUTBOX FUNCTION

The `InputBox` function displays a dialog box with a message that prompts the user to enter data. This dialog box has two buttons—OK and Cancel. When you click OK, the `InputBox` function returns the information entered in the text box. When you select Cancel, the function returns the empty string (""). The syntax of the `InputBox` function is as follows:

```
InputBox(prompt [, title] [, default] [, xpos] [, ypos]
    [, helpfile, context])
```

The first argument, `prompt`, is the text message that you want to display in the dialog box. Long text strings can be entered on several lines by using the `Chr(13)` or `Chr(10)` functions (see examples of using the `MsgBox` function earlier in this chapter). All the remaining `InputBox` arguments are optional.

The second argument, `title`, allows you to change the default title of the dialog box. The default value is "Microsoft Excel."

The third argument of the `InputBox` function, `default`, allows the display of a default value in the text box. If you omit this argument, the empty edit box is displayed.

The following two arguments, `xpos` and `ypos`, let you specify the exact position where the dialog box should appear on the screen. If you omit these arguments, the box appears in the middle of the current window. The `xpos` argument determines the horizontal position of the dialog box from the left edge of the screen. When omitted, the dialog box is centered horizontally. The `ypos` argument determines the vertical position from the top of the screen. If you omit this argument, the dialog box is positioned vertically approximately one-third of the way down the screen. Both `xpos` and `ypos` are measured in special units called *twips*. One twip is equivalent to approximately 0.0007 inches.

The last two arguments, `helpfile` and `context`, are used in the same way as the corresponding arguments of the `MsgBox` function discussed earlier in this chapter.

Now that you know the meaning of the `InputBox` function's arguments, let's look at some examples of using this function.

(•) **Hands-On 4.12   Using the InputBox Function (Example 1)**

1. Add a new module to the **ProcAndFunctions (Chap04_ExcelPrimer. xlsm)** project and change the module's name to **Sample7**.
2. Activate the **Sample7** module and enter the Informant subroutine shown here:

```
Sub Informant()
    InputBox prompt:="Enter your place of birth:" & Chr(13) _
        & " (e.g., Boston, Great Falls, etc.) "
End Sub
```

This procedure displays a dialog box with two buttons, as shown in Figure 4.9. The input prompt is displayed on two lines.

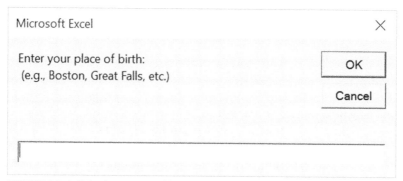

FIGURE 4.9 A dialog box generated by the Informant subroutine.

As with the `MsgBox` function, if you plan on using the data entered by the user in the dialog box, you should store the result of the `InputBox` function in a variable.

3. Type the Informant2 procedure shown here to assign the result of the `InputBox` function to the variable `town`:

```
Sub Informant2()
    Dim myPrompt As String
    Dim town As String

    Const myTitle = "Enter data"

    myPrompt = "Enter your place of birth:" & Chr(13) _
        & "(e.g., Boston, Great Falls, etc.)"
    town = InputBox(myPrompt, myTitle)

    MsgBox "You were born in " & town & ".", , "Your response"
End Sub
```

Notice that this time the arguments of the `InputBox` function are listed within parentheses. Parentheses are required if you want to use the result of the `InputBox` function later in your procedure. The Informant2 subroutine uses a constant to specify the text to appear in the title bar of the dialog box. Because the constant value remains the same throughout the execution of your procedure, you can declare the input box title as a constant. However, if you'd rather use a variable, you still can. When you run a procedure using the `InputBox` function, the dialog box generated by this function always appears in the same area of the screen. To change the location of the dialog box, you must supply the `xpos` and `ypos` arguments, as explained earlier.

4. Run the Informant2 procedure.
5. To display the dialog box in the top left-hand corner of the screen, modify the `InputBox` function in the Informant2 procedure as follows and then run it:

```
town = InputBox(myPrompt, myTitle, , 1, 200)
```

Notice that the argument `myTitle` is followed by two commas. The second comma marks the position of the omitted `default` argument. The next two arguments determine the horizontal and vertical position of the dialog box. If you omit the second comma after the `myTitle` argument, Visual Basic will use the number 1 as the value of the `default` argument. If you precede the values of arguments by their names (for example, `prompt:=myPrompt`, `title:=myTitle, xpos:=1, ypos:=200`), you won't have to remember to place a comma in the place of each omitted argument.

What will happen if you enter a number instead of the name of a town? Because users often supply incorrect data in an input dialog box, your procedure must verify that the supplied data can be used in further data manipulations. The `InputBox` function itself does not provide a facility for data validation. To validate user input, you must learn additional VBA instructions that are presented in the next chapter.

Determining and Converting Data Types

The result of the `InputBox` function is always a string. If the user enters a number, the string value the user entered should be converted to a numeric value before your procedure can use this number in mathematical computations. Visual Basic can convert values from one data type to another.

NOTE	*Refer to Chapter 3 for more information about using the `Var-Type` function to determine the data type of a variable and common data type conversion functions.*

Let's try out a procedure that suggests what type of data the user should enter by supplying a default value in the InputBox dialog.

⊚ Hands-On 4.13   Using the InputBox Function (Example 2)

1. Activate the **Sample7** module in the **ProcAndFunctions (Chap04_ExcelPrimer.xlsm)** project and enter the following AddTwoNums procedure:

```
Sub AddTwoNums()
    Dim myPrompt As String
    Dim value1 As String
    Dim value2 As Integer
    Dim mySum As Single

    Const myTitle = "Enter data"

    myPrompt = "Enter a number:"
    value1 = InputBox(myPrompt, myTitle, 0)
    value2 = 2
    mySum = value1 + value2

    MsgBox "The result is " & mySum & _
        " (" & value1 & " + " & CStr(value2) + ")", _
        vbInformation, "Total"
End Sub
```

The AddTwoNums procedure displays the dialog box shown in Figure 4.10. Notice that this dialog box has two special features that are obtained by using the `InputBox` function's optional `title` and `default` arguments. Instead of the default title "Microsoft Excel," the dialog box displays a text string defined by the contents of the `myTitle` constant. The zero entered as the default value in the edit box suggests that the user enter a number instead of text. Once the user provides the data and clicks OK, the user's input is assigned to the variable `value1`.

```
value1 = InputBox(myPrompt, myTitle, 0)
```

2. Run the AddTwoNums procedure, supply any number when prompted, and then click **OK**.

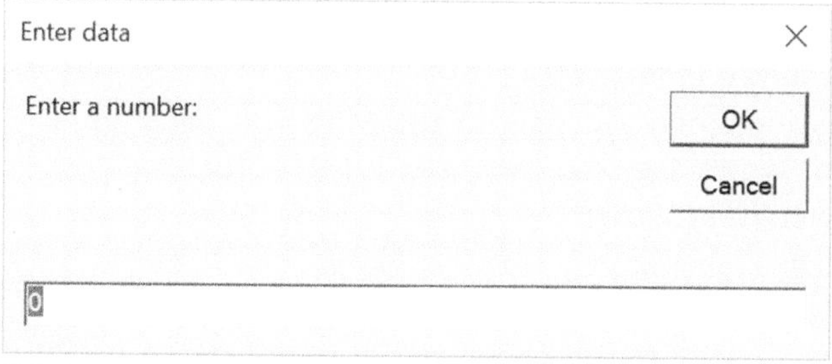

FIGURE 4.10 To suggest that the user enter a specific type of data, you may want to provide a default value in the edit box.

The data type of the variable `value1` is String.

3. You can check the data type easily if you follow the foregoing instruction in the procedure code with this statement:

```
MsgBox VarType(value1)
```

When Visual Basic runs the foregoing line, it will display a message box with the number 8. Recall from Chapter 3 (Table 3.3) that this number represents the String data type.

The statement `mySum = value1 + value2` adds the value stored in the `value2` variable to the user's input and assigns the result of the calculation to the variable `mySum`. Because the `value1` variable's data type is String, prior to using this variable's data in the computation, Visual Basic goes to work behind the scenes to perform the data type conversion. Visual Basic understands the need for conversion. Without it, the two incompatible data types (String and Integer) would generate a Type mismatch error. The procedure ends with the `MsgBox` function displaying the result of the calculation and showing the user how the total was derived. Notice that the `value2` variable must be converted from Integer to String data type using the `CStr` function to display it in the message box:

```
MsgBox "The result is " & mySum & _
     " (" & value1 & " + " & CStr(value2) + ")", _
     vbInformation, "Total"
```

USING THE INPUTBOX METHOD

In addition to the built-in `InputBox` VBA function, there is also the Excel `InputBox` method. If you activate the Object Browser window and type "inputbox" in the search box and press Enter, Visual Basic will display two occurrences of `InputBox`—one in the Excel library and the other one in the VBA library, as shown in Figure 4.11.

The `InputBox` method available in the Microsoft Excel library has a slightly different syntax than the `InputBox` function that was covered earlier in this chapter. Its syntax is:

```
expression.InputBox(prompt, [title], [default], [left], [top], _
[helpfile], [helpcontextID], [type])
```

All bracketed arguments are optional. The `prompt` argument is the message to be displayed in the dialog box, `title` is the title for the dialog box, and `default` is a value that will appear in the text box when the dialog box is initially displayed.

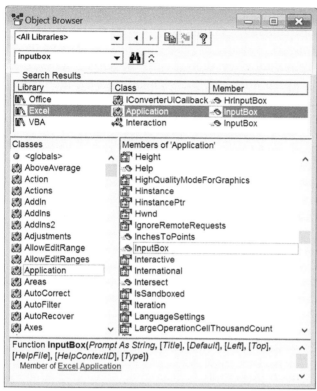

FIGURE 4.11 Don't forget to use the Object Browser when researching Visual Basic functions and methods.

The `left` and `top` arguments specify the position of the dialog box on the screen. The values for these arguments are entered in points. Note that one point equals 1/72 inch. The arguments `helpfile` and `helpcontextID` identify the name of the help file and the specific number of the help topic to be displayed when the user clicks the Help button.

The last argument of the `InputBox` method, `type`, specifies the return data type. If you omit this argument, the `InputBox` method will return text. The values of the `type` argument are shown in Table 4.3.

TABLE 4.3 Data types returned by the `InputBox` method.

Value	Type of Data Returned
0	A formula
1	A number
2	A string (text)
4	A logical value (True or False)
8	A cell reference, as a Range object
16	An error value (for example, #N/A)
64	An array of values

You can allow the user to enter a number or text in the edit box if you use 3 for the `type` argument. This value is obtained by adding up the values for a number (1) and a string (2), as shown in Table 4.3. The `InputBox` method is quite useful for VBA procedures that require a user to select a range of cells in a worksheet.

Let's look at an example procedure that uses the Excel `InputBox` method.

Hands-On 4.14   Using the Excel InputBox Method

1. Close the Object Browser window if you opened it before.
2. In the **Sample7** module, enter the following **WhatRange** procedure:

```
Sub WhatRange()
    Dim newRange As Range
    Dim tellMe As String

    tellMe = "Use the mouse to select a range:"
    Set newRange = Application.InputBox(prompt:=tellMe, _
        Title:="Range to format", _
        Type:=8)
    newRange.NumberFormat = "0.00"
    newRange.Select
End Sub
```

The WhatRange procedure begins with a declaration of an object variable—`newRange`. As you recall from Chapter 3, object variables point to the location of the data. The range of cells that the user selects is assigned to the object variable `newRange`. Notice the keyword `Set` before the name of the variable:

```
Set newRange = Application.InputBox(prompt:=tellMe, _
    Title:="Range to format", _
    Type:=8)
```

The `Type` argument (`Type:=8`) enables the user to select any range of cells. When the user highlights the cells, the next instruction:

```
newRange.NumberFormat = "0.00"
```

changes the format of the selected cells. The last instruction selects the range of cells that the user highlighted.

3. Press **Alt+F11** to activate the Microsoft Excel Application window, and then press **Alt+F8** and choose **WhatRange** procedure and run it.
   Visual Basic displays a dialog box prompting the user to select a range of cells in the worksheet.
4. Use the mouse to select any cells you want. Figure 4.12 shows how Visual Basic enters the selected range reference in the edit box as you drag the mouse to select the cells.

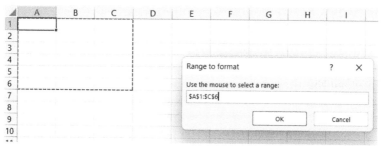

FIGURE 4.12 Using Excel's InputBox method, you can get the range address from the user.

5. When you're done selecting cells, click **OK** in the dialog box.
The selected range is now formatted. To check this out, enter a whole number in any of the selected cells. The number should appear formatted with two decimal places.

6. Rerun the procedure, and when the dialog box appears, click **Cancel**.
When you click the Cancel button or press Esc, Visual Basic displays an error message—"*Object Required.*" When you click the Debug button in the error dialog box, Visual Basic will highlight the line of code that caused the error. Because you don't want to select anything when you cancel the dialog box, you must find a way to ignore the error that Visual Basic displays. Using a special statement, On Error GoTo *labelname*, you can take a detour when an error occurs. This instruction has the following syntax:

```
On Error GoTo labelname
```

This instruction should be placed just below the variable declaration lines. Labelname can be any word you want, except for a Visual Basic keyword. If an error occurs, Visual Basic will jump to the specified label, as shown in Step 8 ahead.

7. Choose **Run | Reset** to cancel the procedure you were running.

8. Modify the **WhatRange** procedure so it looks like the **WhatRange2** procedure shown here:

```
Sub WhatRange2()
    Dim newRange As Range
    Dim tellMe As String

    On Error GoTo VeryEnd

    tellMe = "Use the mouse to select a range:"
    Set newRange = Application.InputBox(prompt:=tellMe, _
        Title:="Range to format", _
        Type:=8)
    newRange.NumberFormat = "0.00"
    newRange.Select
```

```
    VeryEnd:
    End Sub
```

9. Run the modified procedure and click **Cancel** as soon as the input box appears.

   Notice that this time the procedure does not generate the error when you cancel the dialog box. When Visual Basic encounters the error, it jumps to the `VeryEnd` label placed at the end of the procedure. The statements placed between `On Error Goto VeryEnd` and the `VeryEnd` labels are ignored. In Chapter 9 you will find other examples of trapping errors in your VBA procedures.

Subroutines and Functions: Which Should You Use?

Create a subroutine when...	Create a function when...
You want to perform some actions.	You want to perform a simple calculation more than once.
You want to get input from the user.	You must perform complex computations.
You want to display a message on the screen.	You must call the same block of instructions more than once.
	You want to check if a certain expression is True or False.

SUMMARY

In this chapter, you learned the difference between subroutine procedures that perform actions and function procedures that return values. While you can create subroutines by recording or typing code directly into the Visual Basic module, function procedures cannot be recorded because they can take arguments. You must write them manually. You learned how to pass arguments to functions and determine the data type of a function's result. You increased your repertoire of VBA keywords with the `ByVal`, `ByRef`, and `Optional` keywords. You also learned how, with the help of parameters, subprocedures can pass values back to the calling procedures. After working through this chapter, you should be able to create some custom functions of your own that are suited to your specific needs. You should also be able to interact easily with your procedure users by employing the `MsgBox` and `InputBox` functions as well as the Excel `InputBox` method.

The next chapter will introduce you to decision making. You will learn how to change the course of your VBA procedure based on the results of the conditions that you supply.

Chapter 5

ADDING DECISIONS TO EXCEL VBA PROGRAMS

A QUICK INTRODUCTION TO CONDITIONAL STATEMENTS

Visual Basic for Applications, like other programming languages, offers special statements that allow you to include decision points in your own procedures. But what is decision making? Suppose someone approaches you with the question, "Do you like the color red?" After giving this question some thought, you'll answer "yes" or "no." If you're undecided or simply don't care, you might answer "maybe" or "perhaps." In programming, you must be decisive. Only "yes" or "no" answers are allowed. In programming, all decisions are based on supplied answers. If the answer is positive, the procedure executes a specified block of instructions. If the answer is negative, the procedure executes another block of instructions or simply doesn't do anything. In this chapter, you will learn how to use VBA conditional statements to alter the flow of your program. Conditional statements are often referred to as "control structures," as they give you the ability to control the flow of your VBA procedure by skipping over certain statements and "branching" to another part of the procedure.

RELATIONAL AND LOGICAL OPERATORS

You make decisions in your VBA procedures by using conditional expressions inside the special control structures. A *conditional expression* is an expression that uses one of the relational operators listed in Table 5.1, one of the logical operators listed in Table 5.2, or a combination of both. When

Visual Basic encounters a conditional expression in your program, it evaluates the expression to determine whether it is true or false.

TABLE 5.1 Relational operators in VBA.

Operator	Description
=	Equal to
<>	Not equal to
>	Greater than
<	Less than
>=	Greater than or equal to
<=	Less than or equal to

TABLE 5.2 Logical operators in VBA.

Operator	Description
AND	All conditions must be true before an action can be taken.
OR	At least one of the conditions must be true before an action can be taken.
NOT	Used for negating a condition. If a condition is true, NOT makes it false. If a condition is false, NOT makes it true.

USING IF...THEN STATEMENT

The simplest way to get some decision making into your VBA procedure is to use the If...Then statement. Suppose you want to choose an action depending on a condition. You can use the following structure:

```
If condition Then statement
```

For example, to delete a blank row from a worksheet, first check if the active cell is blank. If the result of the test is true, go ahead and delete the entire row that contains that cell:

```
If ActiveCell = "" Then Selection.EntireRow.Delete
```

If the active cell is not blank, Visual Basic will ignore the statement following the Then keyword.

Sometimes you may want to perform several actions when the condition is true. Although you could add other statements on the same line by separating them with colons, your code will look clearer if you use the multiline version of the If...Then statement, as shown here:

```
If condition Then
    statement1
    statement2
    statementN
End If
```

For example, to perform some actions when the value of the active cell is greater than 50, you can write the following block of instructions:

```
If ActiveCell.Value > 50 Then
  MsgBox "The exact value is " & ActiveCell.Value
  Debug.Print ActiveCell.Address & ": " & ActiveCell.Value
End If
```

In this example, the statements between the `Then` and the `End If` keywords are not executed if the value of the active cell is less than or equal to 50. Notice that the block `If...Then` statement must end with the keywords `End If`.

How does Visual Basic make a decision? It evaluates the condition it finds between the `If...Then` keywords. Let's try to evaluate the following condition: `ActiveCell.Value > 50`.

NOTE	*Please note files for the "Hands-On" project may be found in the companion files.*

⊙ Hands-On 5.1   Evaluating Conditions in the Immediate Window

1. Open a new Microsoft Excel workbook.
2. Select any cell in a blank worksheet and enter **50**.
3. Switch to the Visual Basic Editor window.
4. Activate the Immediate window.
5. Type the following statement, and press **Enter** when you're done:

   ```
   ? ActiveCell.Value > 50
   ```

   When you press Enter, Visual Basic writes the result of this test—false. When the result of the test is false, Visual Basic will not bother to read the statement following the `Then` keyword in your code. It will simply go on to read the next line of your procedure, if there is one. If there are no more lines to read, the procedure will end.

6. Now change the operator to less than or equal to, and have Visual Basic evaluate the following condition:

   ```
   ? ActiveCell.Value <= 50
   ```

   This time, the test returns true, and Visual Basic will jump to whatever statement or statements it finds after the `Then` keyword.

7. Close the Immediate window.

Now that you know how Visual Basic evaluates conditions, let's try the `If... Then` statement in a VBA procedure.

Hands-On 5.2   Writing a VBA Procedure with a Simple If…Then Statement

1. Open a new workbook and save it as **C:\VBAPrimerExcel2021_ ByExample\Chap05_ExcelPrimer.xlsm**.
2. Switch to the Visual Basic Editor screen and rename the VBA project **Decisions**.
3. Insert a new module in the **Decisions (Chap05_ExcelPrimer.xlsm)** project and rename this module **IfThen**.
4. In the IfThen module, enter the following procedure:

```
Sub SimpleIfThen()
   Dim weeks As String
   weeks = InputBox("How many weeks are in a year?", "Quiz")
   If weeks <> 52 Then MsgBox "Try Again"
End Sub
```

The SimpleIfThen procedure stores the user's answer in the variable named weeks. The variable's value is then compared to the number 52. If the result of the comparison is true (that is, if the value stored in the variable weeks is not equal to 52), Visual Basic will display the message "Try Again."

5. Run the SimpleIfThen procedure and enter a number other than 52.
6. Rerun the SimpleIfThen procedure and enter the number **52**.
   When you enter the correct number of weeks, Visual Basic does nothing. The procedure simply ends. It would be nice to display a message when the user guesses right.
7. Enter the following instruction on a separate line before the End   Sub keywords:

```
If weeks = 52 Then MsgBox "Congratulations!"
```

8. Run the SimpleIfThen procedure again and enter **52**.
   When you enter the correct answer, Visual Basic does not execute the statement MsgBox "Try Again." When the procedure is executed, the statement to the right of the Then keyword is ignored if the result from evaluating the supplied condition is false. As you recall, a VBA procedure can call another procedure. Let's see whether it can also call itself.
9. Modify the first If statement in the SimpleIfThen procedure as follows:

```
If weeks <> 52 Then MsgBox "Try Again": SimpleIfThen
```

We added a colon and the name of the SimpleIfThen procedure to the end of the existing If…Then statement. If the user enters the incorrect answer, he will see a message, and as soon as he clicks the OK button in the message box, the input box will appear again, and he will get another chance to supply the correct answer. The user will be able to keep on guessing for a long time. In fact, he won't be able to exit the procedure gracefully until he supplies the correct answer. If he clicks Cancel, he will have to deal with the unfriendly error message *"Type mismatch."* You saw in the previous chapter how to use the `On Error GoTo labelname` statement to go around the error, at least temporarily until you learn more about error handling in Chapter 9. For now, you may want to revise your SimpleIfThen procedure as follows:

```
Sub SimpleIfThen()
    Dim weeks As String
    On Error GoTo VeryEnd
    weeks = InputBox("How many weeks are in a year:", "Quiz")
    If weeks <> 52 Then MsgBox "Try Again": SimpleIfThen
    If weeks = 52 Then MsgBox "Congratulations!"
    VeryEnd:
End Sub
```

10. Run the SimpleIfThen procedure a few times by supplying incorrect answers. The error trap that you added to your procedure allows the user to quit guessing without having to deal with the ugly error message.

SIDEBAR *Two Formats for the* If...Then *Statement*

The `If...Then` statement has two formats—single line and multiline. The single-line format is good for short or simple statements like:

```
If secretCode <> 01W01 Then MsgBox "Access denied"
```

Or

```
If secretCode = 01W01 Then alpha = True : beta = False
```

Here, `secretCode`, `alpha`, and `beta` are the names of variables. In the first example, Visual Basic displays the message "Access denied" if the value of `secretCode` is not equal to 01W01. In the second example, Visual Basic sets the value of `alpha` to true and `beta` to false when the `secretCode` variable is equal to 01W01. Notice that the second statement to be executed is separated from the first by a colon. The multiline `If...Then` statement is clearer when there are more statements to be executed when the condition is true or when the statement to be executed is extremely long, as in the following example:

```
If ActiveSheet.Name = "Sheet1" Then
    ActiveSheet.Move after:= Sheets(Worksheets.Count)
End If
```

Here, Visual Basic examines the active sheet name. If it is Sheet1, the condition `ActiveSheet.Name = "Sheet1"` is true, and Visual Basic proceeds to execute the line following the `Then` keyword. As a result, the active sheet is moved to the last position in the workbook.

<table>
<tr><td rowspan="3">NOTE</td><td colspan="2">If Block Instructions and Indenting
To make the If blocks easier to read and understand, use indentation. Compare the following:</td></tr>
<tr><td>

```
If condition Then
      action
End If
```

</td><td>

```
If condition Then
      action
End If
```

</td></tr>
<tr><td colspan="2">In the If...Then block statement on the right, you can easily see where the block begins and where it ends.</td></tr>
</table>

USING IF...THEN...ELSE STATEMENT

Now you know how to display a message or take an action when one or more conditions are true or false. What should you do, however, if your procedure needs to take one action when the condition is true and another action when the condition is false? By adding the Else clause to the simple If...Then statement, you can direct your procedure to the appropriate statement depending on the result of the test.

The If...Then...Else statement has two formats—single line and multiline. The single-line format is as follows:

```
If condition Then statement1 Else statement2
```

The statement following the Then keyword is executed if the condition is true, and the statement following the Else clause is executed if the condition is false—for example:

```
If Sales > 5000 Then Bonus = Sales * 0.05 Else MsgBox "No
Bonus"
```

If the value stored in the variable Sales is greater than 5000, Visual Basic will calculate the bonus using the following formula: Sales * 0.05. However, if the variable Sales is not greater than 5000, Visual Basic will display the message "No Bonus."

The If...Then...Else statement should be used to decide which of the two actions to perform. When you need to execute more statements when the condition is true or false, it's better to use the multiline format of the If...Then...Else statement:

```
If condition Then
   statements to be executed if condition is True
Else
   statements to be executed if condition is False
End If
```

Notice that the multiline (block) If...Then...Else statement ends with the End If keywords. Use the indentation shown in the previous section to make this block structure easier to read. Here's a code example that uses the foregoing syntax:

```
If ActiveSheet.Name = "Sheet1" Then
    ActiveSheet.Name = "My Sheet"
    MsgBox "This sheet has been renamed."
Else
    MsgBox "This sheet name is not default."
End If
```

If the condition (`ActiveSheet.Name = "Sheet1"`) is true, Visual Basic will execute the statements between `Then` and `Else` and ignore the statement between `Else` and `End If`. If the condition is false, Visual Basic will omit the statements between `Then` and `Else` and execute the statement between `Else` and `End If`. Let's look at the complete procedure example.

Hands-On 5.3   Writing a VBA Procedure with an If…Then…Else Statement

1. Insert a new module into the **Decisions (Chap05_ExcelPrimer.xlsm)** project.
2. Change the module name to **IfThenElse**.
3. Enter the following WhatTypeOfDay procedure and then run it:

```
Sub WhatTypeOfDay()
    Dim response As String
    Dim question As String
    Dim strmsg1 As String, strmsg2 As String
    Dim myDate As Date

    question = "Enter any date in the format mm/dd/yyyy:" _
        & Chr(13) & " (e.g., 11/22/2021)"
    strmsg1 = "weekday"
    strmsg2 = "weekend"
    response = InputBox(question)
    myDate = Weekday(CDate(response))
    If myDate >= 2 And myDate <= 6 Then
        MsgBox strmsg1
    Else
        MsgBox strmsg2
    End If
End Sub
```

The foregoing procedure asks the user to enter any date. The user-supplied string is then converted to the Date data type with the built-in `CDate` function. Finally, the `Weekday` function converts the date into an integer that indicates the day of the week. The day of the week constants are listed in Table 5.3. The integer is stored in the variable `myDate`. The conditional test is performed to check whether the value of the variable `myDate` is greater than or equal to 2 (`>=2`) and less than or equal to 6 (`<=6`). If the result of the test is true, the user is told that the supplied date is a weekday; otherwise, the program announces that it's a weekend.

4. Run the procedure from the Visual Basic window. Run it a few times, each time supplying a different date. Check the Visual Basic answers against your desktop or wall calendar.

TABLE 5.3   Values returned by the built-in Weekday function.

Constant	Value
vbSunday	1
vbMonday	2
vbTuesday	3
vbWednesday	4
vbThursday	5
vbFriday	6
vbSaturday	7

USING IF...THEN...ELSEIF STATEMENT

Quite often you will need to check the results of several different conditions. To join a set of If conditions together, you can use the ElseIf clause. Using the If...Then...ElseIf statement, you can supply more conditions to evaluate than is possible with the If...Then...Else statement discussed earlier.

Here's the syntax of the If...Then...Else statement:

```
If condition1 Then
    statements to be executed if condition1 is True
ElseIf condition2 Then
    statements to be executed if condition2 is True
ElseIf condition3 Then
    statements to be executed if condition3 is True
ElseIf conditionN Then
statements to be executed if conditionN is True
Else
    statements to be executed if all conditions are False
End If
```

The Else clause is optional; you can omit it if there are no actions to be executed when all conditions are false. Your procedure can include any number of ElseIf statements and conditions. The ElseIf clause always comes before the Else clause. The statements in the ElseIf clause are executed only if the condition in this clause is true.

Let's look at the following code example:

```
If ActiveCell.Value = 0 Then
    ActiveCell.Offset(0, 1).Value = "zero"
```

```
ElseIf ActiveCell.Value > 0 Then
   ActiveCell.Offset(0, 1).Value = "positive"
ElseIf ActiveCell.Value < 0 Then
   ActiveCell.Offset(0, 1).Value = "negative"
End if
```

This example checks the value of the active cell and enters the appropriate label (zero, positive, negative) in the adjoining column. Notice that the `Else` clause is not used. If the result of the first condition (`ActiveCell.Value = 0`) is false, Visual Basic jumps to the next `ElseIf` statement and evaluates its condition (`ActiveCell.Value > 0`). If the value is not greater than zero, Visual Basic skips to the next `ElseIf` and the condition `ActiveCell.Value < 0` is evaluated.

Let's see how the `If…Then…ElseIf` statement works in a complete procedure.

Hands-On 5.4   Writing a VBA Procedure with an If…Then…ElseIf Statement

1. Insert a new module into the current VBA project.
2. Rename the module **IfThenElseIf**.
3. Enter the following WhatValue procedure:

```
Sub WhatValue()
   Range("A1").Select
   If ActiveCell.Value = 0 Then
      ActiveCell.Offset(0, 1).Value = "zero"
   ElseIf ActiveCell.Value > 0 Then
      ActiveCell.Offset(0, 1).Value = "positive"
   ElseIf ActiveCell.Value < 0 Then
      ActiveCell.Offset(0, 1).Value = "negative"
   End If
End Sub
```

Because you need to run the WhatValue procedure several times to test each condition, let's have Visual Basic assign a temporary keyboard shortcut to this procedure.

4. Open the Immediate window and type the following statement:

```
Application.OnKey "^+y", "WhatValue"
```

When you press **Enter**, Visual Basic runs the `OnKey` method that assigns the WhatValue procedure to the key sequence Ctrl+Shift+Y. This keyboard shortcut is only temporary—it will not work when you restart Microsoft Excel. To assign the shortcut key to a procedure, use the Options button in the Macro dialog box accessed from Developer | Macros in the Microsoft Excel window.

5. Now switch to the Microsoft Excel window and activate **Sheet2**.
6. Type **0** (zero) in cell A1 and press **Enter**. Then press **Ctrl+Shift+Y**.

7. Visual Basic calls the WhatValue procedure and enters "zero" in cell B1.

8. Enter any number greater than zero in cell A1 and press **Ctrl+Shift+Y**.
   Visual Basic again calls the WhatValue procedure. Visual Basic evaluates the first condition, and because the result of this test is false, it jumps to the `ElseIf` statement. The second condition is true, so Visual Basic executes the statement following `Then` and skips over the next statements to the `End If`. Because there are no more statements following the `End If`, the procedure ends. Cell B1 now displays the word "positive."

9. Enter any number less than zero in cell A1 and press **Ctrl+Shift+Y**.
   This time, the first two conditions return false, so Visual Basic goes to examine the third condition. Because this test returns true, Visual Basic enters the word "negative" in cell B1.

10. Enter any text in cell A1 and press **Ctrl+Shift+Y**.
    Visual Basic's response is "positive." However, this is not a satisfactory answer. You may want to differentiate between positive numbers and text by displaying the word "text." To make the WhatValue procedure smarter, you need to learn how to make more complex decisions by using nested `If...Then` statements.

NESTED IF...THEN STATEMENTS

You can make more complex decisions in your VBA procedures by placing an `If...Then` or `If...Then...Else` statement inside another `If...Then` or `If...Then...Else` statement.

Structures in which an `If` statement is contained inside another `If` block are referred to as nested `If` statements. The following TestConditions procedure is a revised version of the WhatValue procedure created in the previous section. The WhatValue procedure has been modified to illustrate how nested `If...Then` statements work.

```
Sub TestConditions()
    Range("A1").Select
    If IsEmpty(ActiveCell) Then
        MsgBox "The cell is empty."
    Else
        If IsNumeric(ActiveCell.Value) Then
            If ActiveCell.Value = 0 Then
                ActiveCell.Offset(0, 1).Value = "zero"
            ElseIf ActiveCell.Value > 0 Then
                ActiveCell.Offset(0, 1).Value = "positive"
            ElseIf ActiveCell.Value < 0 Then
                ActiveCell.Offset(0, 1).Value = "negative"
            End If
        Else
```

```
            ActiveCell.Offset(0, 1).Value = "text"
        End If
    End If
End Sub
```

To make the TestConditions procedure easier to understand, each If...Then statement is shown with different formatting. You can now clearly see that the procedure uses three If...Then blocks. The first If block (in bold) checks whether the active cell is empty. If this is true, the message is displayed, and Visual Basic skips over the Else part until it finds the matching End If. This statement is located just before the End Sub keywords. If the active cell is not empty, the IsEmpty(ActiveCell) condition returns false, and Visual Basic runs the single underlined If block following the Else format- ted in bold. This (underlined) If...Then...Else statement is said to be nested inside the first If block (in bold). This statement checks if the value of the active cell is a number. Notice that this is done with the help of another built-in function—IsNumeric. If the value of the active cell is not a number, the condition is false, so Visual Basic jumps to the statement following the underlined Else and enters "text" in cell B1. However, if the active cell con- tains a number, Visual Basic runs the double-underlined If block, evaluat- ing each condition and making the appropriate decision. The first If block (in bold) is called the outer If statement. This outer statement contains two inner If statements (single and double underlined).

USING THE SELECT CASE STATEMENT

To avoid complex nested If statements that are difficult to follow, you can use the Select Case statement instead. The syntax of this statement is as follows:

```
Select Case testexpression
    Case expressionlist1
        statements if expressionlist1 matches testexpression
    Case expressionlist2
        statements if expressionlist2 matches testexpression
    Case expressionlistN
        statements if expressionlistN matches testexpression
    Case Else
        statements to be executed if no values match
testexpression
    End Select
```

You can place any number of Case clauses to test between the keywords Select Case and End Select. The Case Else clause is optional. Use it when you expect that there may be conditional expressions that return false. In the Select Case statement, Visual Basic compares each expression- list with the value of testexpression.

Here's the logic behind the `Select Case` statement. When Visual Basic encounters the `Select Case` clause, it makes note of the value of `testexpression`. Then it proceeds to test the expression following the first `Case` clause. If the value of this expression (`expressionlist1`) matches the value stored in `testexpression`, Visual Basic executes the statements until another `Case` clause is encountered and then jumps to the `End Select` statement. If, however, the expression tested in the first `Case` clause does not match `testexpression`, Visual Basic checks the value of each `Case` clause until it finds a match. If none of the `Case` clauses contain the expression that matches the value stored in `testexpression`, Visual Basic jumps to the `Case Else` clause and executes the statements until it encounters the `End Select` keywords. Notice that the `Case Else` clause is optional. If your procedure does not use `Case Else` and none of the `Case` clauses contain a value matching the value of `testexpression`, Visual Basic jumps to the statements following `End Select` and continues executing your procedure.

Let's look at an example of a procedure that uses the `Select Case` statement. In Chapter 4, you learned quite a few details about the `MsgBox` function, which allows you to display a message with one or more buttons. You also learned that the result of the `MsgBox` function can be assigned to a variable. Using the `Select Case` statement, you can now decide which action to take based on the button the user pressed in the message box.

**⊚ Hands-On 5.5   Writing a VBA Procedure with a
              Select Case Statement**

1. Insert a new module into the current VBA project.
2. Rename the new module **SelectCase**.
3. Enter the following TestButtons procedure:

```
Sub TestButtons()
  Dim question As String
  Dim bts As Integer
  Dim myTitle As String
  Dim myButton As Integer

  question = "Do you want to open a new workbook?"
  bts = vbYesNoCancel + vbQuestion + vbDefaultButton1
  myTitle = "New Workbook"
  myButton = MsgBox(prompt:=question, _
      buttons:=bts, _
      title:=myTitle)
  Select Case myButton
    Case 6
        Workbooks.Add
    Case 7
        MsgBox "You can open a new book manually later."
    Case Else
```

```
      MsgBox "You pressed Cancel."
   End Select
End Sub
```

The first part of the TestButtons procedure displays a message with three buttons: Yes, No, and Cancel. The value of the button selected by the user is assigned to the variable myButton. If the user clicks Yes, the variable myButton is assigned the vbYes constant or its corresponding value—6. If the user selects No, the variable myButton is assigned the constant vbNo or its corresponding value—7. Lastly, if Cancel is pressed, the contents of the variable myButton will equal vbCancel, or 2. The Select Case statement checks the values supplied after the Case clause against the value stored in the variable myButton. When there is a match, the appropriate Case statement is executed.

The TestButtons procedure will work the same if you use the constants instead of button values:

```
Select Case myButton
   Case vbYes
      Workbooks.Add
   Case vbNo
      MsgBox "You can open a new book manually later."
   Case Else
      MsgBox "You pressed Cancel."
End Select
```

You can omit the Else clause. Simply revise the Select Case statement as follows:

```
Select Case myButton
   Case vbYes
      Workbooks.Add
   Case vbNo
      MsgBox "You can open a new book manually later."
   Case vbCancel
      MsgBox "You pressed Cancel."
End Select
```

4. Run the TestButtons procedure three times, each time selecting a different button.

Using Is with the Case Clause

Sometimes a decision is made based on a relational operator, listed in Table 5.1, such as whether the test expression is greater than, less than, or equal to. The Is keyword lets you use a conditional expression in a Case clause. The syntax for the Select Case clause using the Is keyword is shown here:

```
Select Case testexpression
   Case Is condition1
```

```
   statements if condition1 is True
 Case Is condition2
   statements if condition2 is True
 Case Is conditionN
   statements if conditionN is True
End Select
```

Although using Case Else in the Select Case statement isn't required, it's always a good idea to include one, just in case the variable you are testing has an unexpected value. The Case Else statement is a good place to put an error message. For example, let's compare some numbers:

```
Select Case myNumber
 Case Is <=10
   MsgBox "The number is less than or equal to 10."
 Case 11
   MsgBox "You entered eleven."
 Case Is >=100
   MsgBox "The number is greater than or equal to 100."
 Case Else
   MsgBox "The number is between 12 and 99."
End Select
```

Assuming that the variable myNumber holds 120, the third Case clause is true, and the only statement executed is the one between the Case Is >=100 and the Case Else clause.

Specifying a Range of Values in a Case Clause

In the preceding example you saw a simple Select Case statement that uses one expression in each Case clause. Many times, however, you may want to specify a range of values in a Case clause. Do this by using the To keyword between the values of expressions, as in the following example:

```
Select Case unitsSold
 Case 1 To 100
   Discount = 0.05
 Case Is <= 500
   Discount = 0.1
 Case 501 To 1000
   Discount = 0.15
 Case Is > 1000
   Discount = 0.2
End Select
```

Let's analyze the foregoing Select Case block with the assumption that the variable unitsSold currently holds the value 99. Visual Basic compares the value of the variable unitsSold with the conditional expression in the Case clauses. The first and third Case clauses illustrate how to use a range of values in a conditional expression by using the To keyword. Because units-Sold equals 99, the condition in the first Case clause is true; thus, Visual

Basic assigns the value 0.05 to the variable `Discount`. How about the second `Case` clause, which is also true? Although it's obvious that 99 is less than or equal to 500, Visual Basic does not execute the associated statement `Discount = 0.1`. The reason for this is that once Visual Basic locates a `Case` clause with a true condition, it doesn't bother to look at the remaining `Case` clauses. It jumps over them and continues to execute the procedure with the instructions that may be following the `End Select` statement.

Specifying Multiple Expressions in a Case Clause

You may specify multiple conditions within a single `Case` clause by separating each condition with a comma, as shown in the following code example:

```
Select Case myMonth
  Case "January", "February", "March"
    Debug.Print myMonth & ": 1st Qtr."
  Case "April", "May", "June"
    Debug.Print myMonth & ": 2nd Qtr."
  Case "July", "August", "September"
    Debug.Print myMonth & ": 3rd Qtr."
  Case "October", "November", "December"
    Debug.Print myMonth & ": 4th Qtr."
End Select
```

SIDEBAR *Multiple Conditions with the* `Case` *Clause*

The commas used to separate conditions within a `Case` clause have the same meaning as the OR operator used in the `If` statement. The `Case` clause is true if at least one of the conditions is true.

Nesting means placing one type of control structure inside another control structure. You will see more nesting examples with the looping structures discussed in Chapter 7.

WRITING A VBA PROCEDURE WITH MULTIPLE CONDITIONS

The SimpleIfThen procedure that you worked with earlier evaluated only a single condition in the `If...Then` statement. This statement, however, can take more than one condition. To specify multiple conditions in an `If...Then` statement, use the logical operators AND and OR (listed in Table 5.2 at the beginning of this chapter). Here's the syntax with the AND operator:

```
If condition1 AND condition2 Then statement
```

In the foregoing syntax, both `condition1` and `condition2` must be true for Visual Basic to execute the statement to the right of the `Then` keyword—for example:

```
If sales = 10000 AND salary < 45000 Then SlsCom = Sales
    * 0.07
```

In this example:

```
Condition1 sales = 10000
Condition2 salary < 45000
```

When AND is used in the conditional expression, both conditions must be true before Visual Basic can calculate the sales commission (`SlsCom`). If either of these conditions is false, or both are false, Visual Basic ignores the statement after `Then`.

When it's good enough to meet only one of the conditions, you should use the OR operator. Here's the syntax:

```
If condition1 OR condition2 Then statement
```

The OR operator is more flexible. Only one of the conditions has to be true before Visual Basic can execute the statement following the `Then` keyword.

Let's look at this example:

```
If dept = "S" OR dept = "M" Then bonus = 500
```

In this example, if at least one condition is true, Visual Basic assigns 500 to the `bonus` variable. If both conditions are false, Visual Basic ignores the rest of the line.

Now let's look at a complete procedure example. Suppose you can get a 10% discount if you purchase 50 units of a product, each priced at $7.00. The IfThenAnd procedure demonstrates the use of the AND operator.

⦿ Hands-On 5.6   Writing a VBA Procedure with Multiple Conditions

1. Enter the following procedure in the IfThen module of the **Decisions (Chap05_ExcelPrimer.xlsm)** project:

```
Sub IfThenAnd()
    Dim price As Single
    Dim units As Integer
    Dim rebate As Single

    Const strmsg1 = "To get a rebate you must buy an additional "
    Const strmsg2 = "Price must equal $7.00"

    units = Range("B1").Value
    price = Range("B2").Value
```

```
   If price = 7 AND units >= 50 Then
      rebate = (price * units) * 0.1
      Range("A4").Value = "The rebate is: $" & rebate
   End If

   If price = 7 AND units < 50 Then
      Range("A4").Value = strmsg1 & 50 - units & " unit(s)."
   End If

   If price <> 7 AND units >= 50 Then
      Range("A4").Value = strmsg2
   End If

   If price <> 7 AND units < 50 Then
      Range("A4").Value = "You didn't meet the criteria."
   End If
End Sub
```

The IfThenAnd procedure just shown has four `If...Then` statements that are used to evaluate the contents of two variables: `price` and `units`. The AND operator between the keywords `If...Then` allows more than one condition to be tested. With the AND operator, all conditions must be true for Visual Basic to run the statements between the `Then...End If` keywords. Because the IfThenAnd procedure is based on the data entered in worksheet cells, it's more convenient to run it from the Microsoft Excel window.

2. Switch to the Microsoft Excel application window and choose **Developer | Macros**.
3. In the Macro dialog box, select the **IfThenAnd** macro and click the **Options** button.
4. While the cursor is blinking in the Shortcut key box, press **Shift+I** to assign the shortcut key Ctrl+Shift+I to your macro, and then click **OK** to exit the Macro Options dialog box.
5. Click **Cancel** to close the Macro dialog box.
6. Enter the sample data in a worksheet as shown in Figure 5.1.

	A	B	C
1	units	200	
2	price	7	
3			
4			

FIGURE 5.1 Sample test data in a worksheet.

7. Press **Ctrl+Shift+I** to run the IfThenAnd procedure.
8. Change the values of cells B1 and B2 so that every time you run the procedure, a different `If...Then` statement is true.

USING CONDITIONAL LOGIC IN FUNCTION PROCEDURES

To get more practice with the `Select Case` statement, let's use it in a function procedure. As you recall from Chapter 4, function procedures allow you to return a result to a subroutine. Suppose a subroutine must display a discount based on the number of units sold. You can get the number of units from the user and then run a function to determine which discount applies.

⊙ Hands-On 5.7 Writing a Function Procedure with a Select Case Statement

1. Enter the following subroutine in the **SelectCase** module:

```
Sub DisplayDiscount()
  Dim unitsSold As Integer
  Dim myDiscount As Single
  unitsSold = InputBox("Enter the number of units sold:")
  myDiscount = GetDiscount(unitsSold)
  MsgBox myDiscount
End Sub
```

2. Enter the following function procedure:

```
Function GetDiscount(unitsSold As Integer)
  Select Case unitsSold
    Case 1 To 200
      GetDiscount = 0.05
    Case Is <= 500
      GetDiscount = 0.1
    Case 501 To 1000
      GetDiscount = 0.15
    Case Is > 1000
      GetDiscount = 0.2
  End Select
End Function
```

3. Place the cursor anywhere within the code of the DisplayDiscount procedure and press **F5** to run it. Run the procedure several times, entering values to test each `Case` statement.
   The DisplayDiscount procedure passes the value stored in the variable `unitsSold` to the `GetDiscount` function. When Visual Basic encounters the `Select Case` statement, it checks whether the value of the first `Case` clause expression matches the value stored in the `unitsSold` parameter. If there is a match, Visual Basic assigns a 5% discount (0.05) to the function name, and then jumps to the `End Select` keywords. Because there are no more statements to execute inside the function procedure, Visual Basic returns to the calling procedure—DisplayDiscount. Here it assigns the

function's result to the variable `myDiscount`. The last statement displays the value of the retrieved discount in a message box.

SUMMARY

Conditional statements, which were introduced in this chapter, let you control the flow of your procedure. By testing the truth of a condition, you can decide which statements should be run and which should be skipped over. In other words, instead of running your procedure from top to bottom, line by line, you can execute only certain lines. If you are wondering what kind of conditional statement you should use in your VBA procedure, here are a few guidelines:

- If you want to supply only one condition, the simple `If...Then` statement is the best choice.
- If you need to decide which of two actions to perform, use the `If... Then...Else` statement.
- If your procedure requires two or more conditions, use the `If...Then... ElseIf` or `Select Case` statements.
- If your procedure has a great number of conditions, use the `Select Case` statement. This statement is more flexible and easier to comprehend than the `If...Then...ElseIf` statement.

Some decisions must be repeated. For example, you may want to repeat the same actions for each cell in a worksheet or each sheet in a workbook. The next chapter teaches you how to perform the same steps repeatedly.

Chapter 6

ADDING REPEATING ACTIONS TO EXCEL VBA PROGRAMS

A QUICK INTRODUCTION TO LOOPING STATEMENTS

N ow that you've learned how conditional statements can give your VBA procedures decision-making capabilities, it's time to go a step further. Not all decisions are easy. Sometimes you will need to perform several statements multiple times to arrive at a certain condition. On other occasions, however, after you've reached the decision, you may need to run the specified statements as long as a condition is true or until a condition becomes true. In programming, performing repetitive tasks is called *looping*. VBA has various looping structures that allow you to repeat a sequence of statements several times. In this chapter, you will learn how to loop through your code.

INTRODUCING LOOPING STATEMENTS

A loop is a programming structure that causes a section of program code to execute repeatedly. VBA provides several structures to implement loops in your procedures: Do...While, Do...Until, For...Next, For...Each, and While... Wend.

UNDERSTANDING DO...WHILE AND DO...UNTIL LOOPS

Visual Basic has two types of Do loop statements that repeat a sequence of statements either as long as or until a certain condition is true. The Do... While loop lets you repeat an action as long as a condition is true. This loop has the following syntax:

```
Do While condition
   statement1
   statement2
   statementN
Loop
```

When Visual Basic encounters this loop, it first checks the truth value of the condition. If the condition is false, the statements inside the loop are not executed. Visual Basic will continue to execute the program with the first statement after the Loop keyword. If the condition is true, the statements inside the loop are run one by one until the Loop statement is encountered. The Loop statement tells Visual Basic to repeat the entire process again, as long as the testing of the condition in the Do...While statement is true. Let's now see how you can put the Do...While loop to good use in Microsoft Excel.

In Chapter 5, you learned how to make a decision based on the contents of a cell. Let's take it a step further and see how you can repeat the same decision for a number of cells. Our task is to apply bold formatting to any cell in a column, as long as it's not empty.

NOTE	*Please note files for the "Hands-On" project may be found in the companion files.*

⊙ **Hands-On 6.1   Writing a VBA Procedure with a Do... While Statement**

1. Open a new workbook and save it as **C:\VBAPrimerExcel_ByExample\ Chap06_ExcelPrimer.xlsm**.
2. Switch to the Visual Basic Editor screen and change the name of the new project to **Repetition**.
3. Insert a new module into the Repetition project and change its name to **DoLoops**.
4. Enter the following procedure in the DoLoops module:

```
Sub ApplyBold()
   Do While ActiveCell.Value <> ""
      ActiveCell.Font.Bold = True
      ActiveCell.Offset(1, 0).Select
   Loop
End Sub
```

5. Press **Alt+F11** to switch to the Microsoft Excel application window, activate Sheet1, and then enter any data (text or numbers) in cells **A1:A7**.
6. When finished with the data entry, select cell **A1**.
7. Choose **Developer | Macros**. In the Macro dialog box, double-click the **ApplyBold** procedure (or highlight the procedure name and click **Run**). When you run the ApplyBold procedure, Visual Basic first evaluates the condition in the `Do While` statement—`ActiveCell.Value <>""`. The condition says: Perform the following statements as long as the value of the active cell is not an empty string (""). Because you have entered data in cell A1 and made this cell active (see Steps 5 to 6), the first test returns true. So Visual Basic executes the statement `ActiveCell.Font.Bold = True`, which applies the bold formatting to the active cell. Next, Visual Basic selects the cell in the next row (the Offset property is discussed in Chapter 3). Because the statement that follows is the `Loop` keyword, Visual Basic returns to the `Do While` statement and again checks the condition. If the newly selected active cell is not empty, Visual Basic repeats the statements inside the loop. This process continues until the contents of cell A8 are examined. Because this cell is empty, the condition is false, so Visual Basic skips the statements inside the loop. Because there are no more statements to execute after the `Loop` keyword, the procedure ends. Let's look at another `Do...While` loop example.

The `Do...While` loop has an alternative syntax that lets you test the condition at the bottom of the loop in the following way:

```
Do
    statement1
    statement2
    statementN
Loop While condition
```

When you test the condition at the bottom of the loop, the statements inside the loop are executed at least once. Let's take a look at an example:

```
Sub SignIn()
    Dim secretCode As String
    Do
        secretCode = InputBox("Enter your secret code:")
        If secretCode = "sp1045" Then Exit Do
    Loop While secretCode <> "sp1045"
End Sub
```

Notice that by the time the condition is evaluated, Visual Basic has already executed the statements one time. In addition to placing the condition at the end of the loop, the SignIn procedure shows how to exit the loop when a condition is reached. When the `Exit Do` statement is encountered, the loop ends immediately.

Another handy loop, Do...Until, allows you to repeat one or more statements until a condition becomes true. In other words, Do...Until repeats a block of code as long as something is false. Here's the syntax:

```
Do Until condition
   statement1
   statement2
   statementN
Loop
```

Using the foregoing syntax, you can now rewrite the previous ApplyBold procedure in the following way:

```
Sub ApplyBold2()
   Do Until IsEmpty(ActiveCell)
     ActiveCell.Font.Bold = True
     ActiveCell.Offset(1, 0).Select
   Loop
End Sub
```

The first line of this procedure says to perform the following statements until the first empty cell is reached. As a result, if the active cell is not empty, Visual Basic executes the two statements inside the loop. This process continues as long as the condition IsEmpty(ActiveCell) evaluates to false. Because the ApplyBold2 procedure tests the condition at the beginning of the loop, the statements inside the loop will not run if the first cell is empty. You will get the chance to try out this procedure in the next section.

Like the Do...While loop, the Do...Until loop has a second syntax that lets you test the condition at the bottom of the loop:

```
Do
   statement1
   statement2
   statementN
Loop Until condition
```

If you want the statements to execute at least once, place the condition on the line with the Loop statement no matter what the value of the condition.

Let's try out an example procedure that deletes empty sheets from a workbook.

**Hands-On 6.2   Writing a VBA Procedure with a
Do...Until Statement**

1. Enter the DeleteBlankSheets procedure, as shown here, in the DoLoops module that you created earlier.

```
Sub DeleteBlankSheets()
   Dim myRange As Range
   Dim shcount As Integer
```

```
   shcount = Worksheets.Count
   Do
     Worksheets(shcount).Select
     Set myRange = ActiveSheet.UsedRange
     If myRange.Address = "$A$1" And _
        Range("A1").Value = "" Then
        Application.DisplayAlerts = False
        Worksheets(shcount).Delete
        Application.DisplayAlerts = True
     End If
     shcount = shcount - 1
   Loop Until shcount = 1
End Sub
```

2. Press **Alt+F11** to switch to the Microsoft Excel window and manually insert three new worksheets into the current workbook. In one of the sheets, enter text or number in cell **A1**. On another sheet, enter some data in cells **B2** and **C10**. Do not enter any data on the third inserted sheet.

3. Run the **DeleteBlankSheets** procedure.

When you run this procedure, Visual Basic deletes the selected sheet whenever two conditions are true—the UsedRange property address returns cell A1 and cell A1 is empty. The UsedRange property applies to the Worksheet object and contains every nonempty cell on the worksheet, as well as all the empty cells that are among them. For example, if you enter something in cells B2 and C10, the used range is $B$2:$C$10. If you later enter data in cell A1, the UsedRange will be $A$1:$C$10. The used range is bounded by the farthest upper-left and farthest lower-right nonempty cell on a worksheet.

Because the workbook must contain at least one worksheet, the code is executed until the variable shcount equals one. The statement shcount = shcount - 1 makes sure that the shcount variable is reduced by one each time the statements in the loop are executed. The value of shcount is initialized at the beginning of the procedure with the following statement:

```
Worksheets.Count
```

Notice also that when deleting sheets, Excel normally displays the confirmation dialog box. If you'd rather not be prompted to confirm the deletion, use the following statement:

```
Application.DisplayAlerts = False
```

When you are finished, turn the system messages back on with the following statement:

```
Application.DisplayAlerts = True
```

SIDEBAR *Counters*

A *counter* is a numeric variable that keeps track of the number of items that have been processed. The DeleteBlankSheets procedure just shown declares the variable `shcount` to keep track of sheets that have been processed. A counter variable should be initialized (assigned a value) at the beginning of the program. This ensures that you always know the exact value of the counter before you begin using it. A counter can be incremented or decremented by a specified value. See other examples of using counters with the `For…Next` loop later in this chapter.

AVOIDING INFINITE LOOPS

If you don't design your loop correctly, you get an infinite loop—a loop that never ends. You will not be able to stop the procedure by using the Esc key. The following procedure causes the loop to execute endlessly because the programmer forgot to include the test condition:

```
Sub SayHello()
  Do
     MsgBox "Hello."
  Loop
End Sub
```

To stop the execution of the infinite loop, you must press Ctrl+Break. When Visual Basic displays the message box that says, "Code execution has been interrupted," click End to end the procedure.

EXECUTING A PROCEDURE LINE BY LINE

When you run procedures that use looping structures, it's sometimes hard to see whether the procedure works as expected. Occasionally, you'd like to watch the procedure execute in slow motion so that you can check the logic of the program. Let's examine how Visual Basic allows you to execute a procedure line by line.

(⊙) **Hands-On 6.3   Executing a Procedure Line by Line**

1. Insert a new sheet into the current workbook and enter any data in cells **A1:A5**.
2. Select cell **A1** and choose **Developer | Macros**.
3. In the Macro dialog box, select the **ApplyBold** procedure and click the **Step Into** button.

The VBE screen will appear with the name of the procedure highlighted in yellow, as shown in Figure 6.1. Notice the yellow arrow in the margin indicator bar of the Code window.

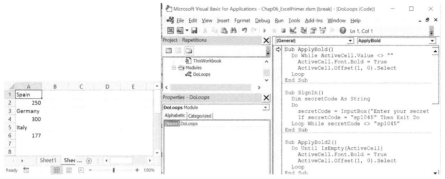

FIGURE 6.1 Watching the procedure code execute line by line.

4. Arrange the screens side by side as shown in Figure 6.1.
5. Make sure cell **A1** is selected and that it contains data.
6. Click the title bar in the Visual Basic window to move the focus to this window, and then press **F8**. The yellow highlight in the Code window jumps to this line:

```
Do While ActiveCell.Value <> ""
```

7. Continue pressing **F8** while watching both the Code window and the worksheet window.

NOTE	*You will find more information related to stepping through VBA procedures in Chapter 9.*

UNDERSTANDING WHILE...WEND LOOP

The `While...Wend` loop is functionally equivalent to the `Do...While` loop. This statement is a carryover from earlier versions of Microsoft Basic and is included in VBA for backward compatibility. The loop begins with the keyword `While` and ends with the keyword `Wend`. Here's the syntax:

```
While condition
    statement1
    statement2
    statementN
Wend
```

The condition is tested at the top of the loop. The statements are executed as long as the given condition is true. Once the condition is false, Visual Basic exits the loop.

Let's look at an example of a procedure that uses the `While...Wend` looping structure. We will change the row height of all nonempty cells in a worksheet.

Hands-On 6.4   Writing a VBA Procedure with a While...Wend Statement

1. Insert a new module into the current VBA project. Rename the module **WhileLoop**.
2. Enter the following procedure in the WhileLoop module.

```
Sub ChangeRHeight()
    While ActiveCell <> ""
        ActiveCell.RowHeight = 28
        ActiveCell.Offset(1, 0).Select
    Wend
End Sub
```

3. Switch to the Microsoft Excel window and enter some data in cells **B1:B4** of any worksheet.
4. Select cell **B1** and choose **Developer | Macros**.
5. In the Macro dialog, select the **ChangeRHeight** procedure and click **Run**.

The ChangeRHeight procedure sets the row height to 28 when the active cell is not empty. The next cell is selected by using the Offset property of the Range object. The statement `ActiveCell.Offset(1, 0).Select` tells Visual Basic to select the cell that is located one row below (1) the active cell and in the same column (0).

UNDERSTANDING FOR...NEXT LOOP

The `For...Next` loop is used when you know how many times you want to repeat a group of statements. The syntax of a `For...Next` loop looks like this:

```
For counter = start To end [Step increment]
    statement1
    statement2
    statementN
Next [counter]
```

The code in the brackets is optional. `Counter` is a numeric variable that stores the number of iterations. `Start` is the number at which you want to begin counting, and `end` indicates how many times the loop should be executed.

For example, if you want to repeat the statements inside the loop five times, use the following `For` statement syntax:

```
For counter = 1 To 5
```

```
    Your statements go here
  Next
```

When Visual Basic encounters the `Next` keyword, it will go back to the beginning of the loop and execute the statements inside the loop again, as long as `counter` hasn't reached the value in `end`. As soon as the value of `counter` is greater than the number entered after the `To` keyword, Visual Basic exits the loop. Because the variable `counter` automatically changes after each execution of the loop, sooner or later the value stored in `counter` exceeds the value specified. By default, every time Visual Basic executes the statements inside the loop, the value of the variable `counter` is increased by one. You can change this default setting by using the `Step` clause. For example, to increase the variable `counter` by three, use the following statement:

```
  For counter = 1 To 5 Step 3
    Your statements go here
  Next counter
```

When Visual Basic encounters the foregoing instruction, it executes the statements inside the loop twice. The first time in the loop, `counter` equals 1. The second time in the loop, `counter` equals 4 (3 + 1). After the second time inside the loop, `counter` equals 7 (4 + 3). This causes Visual Basic to exit the loop. Note that the `Step` increment is optional and isn't specified unless it's a value other than 1. You can also place a negative number after `Step`. Visual Basic will then decrement this value from `counter` each time it encounters the `Next` keyword. The name of the variable (`counter`) after the `Next` keyword is also optional. However, it's good programming practice to make your `Next` keywords explicit by including `counter`.

How can you use the `For...Next` loop in a Microsoft Excel worksheet? Suppose in your sales report you'd like to include only products that were sold in a particular month. When you imported data from a Microsoft Access table, you also got rows with the sold amount equal to zero. How can you quickly eliminate those "zero" rows? Although there are many ways to solve this problem, let's see how you can handle it with a `For...Next` loop.

Hands-On 6.5   Writing a VBA Procedure with a For...Next Statement

1. In the Visual Basic window, insert a new module into the current project and rename it **ForNextLoop**.
2. Enter the following procedure in the ForNextLoop module:

```
Sub DeleteZeroRows()
  Dim totalR As Integer
  Dim r As Integer

  Range("A1").CurrentRegion.Select
  totalR = Selection.Rows.Count
```

```
    Range("B2").Select

    For r = 1 To totalR - 1
       If ActiveCell = 0 Then
              Selection.EntireRow.Delete
              totalR = totalR - 1
       Else
              ActiveCell.Offset(1, 0).Select
       End If
    Next r
End Sub
```

Let's examine the DeleteZeroRows procedure line by line. The first two statements calculate the total number of rows in the current range and store this number in the variable totalR. Next, Visual Basic selects cell B2 and encounters the For keyword. Because the first row of the worksheet contains the column headings, decrease the total number of rows by one (totalR - 1). Visual Basic will need to execute the instructions inside the loop six times. The conditional statement (If...Then...Else) nested inside the loop tells Visual Basic to make a decision based on the value of the active cell. If the value is equal to zero, Visual Basic deletes the current row and reduces the value of totalR by one. Otherwise, the condition is false, so Visual Basic selects the next cell. Each time Visual Basic completes the loop, it jumps to the For keyword to compare the value of r with the value of totalR - 1.

3. Switch to the Microsoft Excel window and insert a new worksheet. Enter the data shown here:

	A	B
1	Product Name	Sales (in Pounds)
2	Apples	120
3	Pears	0
4	Bananas	100
5	Cherries	0
6	Blueberries	0
7	Strawberries	160

4. Choose **Developer | Macros.**
5. In the Macro dialog, select the **DeleteZeroRows** procedure and click **Run.** When the procedure ends, the sales worksheet does not include products that were not sold.

SIDEBAR *Paired Statements*

For and Next must be paired. If one is missing, Visual Basic generates the following error message: "For without Next."

UNDERSTANDING FOR...EACH...NEXT LOOP

When your procedure needs to loop through all of the objects of a collection or all of the elements in an array (arrays are covered in Chapter 7), the For Each...Next loop should be used. This loop does not require a counter variable. Visual Basic can figure out on its own how many times the loop should execute.

Let's take, for example, a collection of worksheets. To remove a worksheet from a workbook, you must first select it and then choose Home | Cells | Delete | Delete Sheet. To leave only one worksheet in a workbook, you need to use the same command several times, depending on the total number of worksheets. Because each worksheet is an object in a collection of worksheets, you can speed up the process of deleting worksheets by using the For Each...Next loop. This loop looks like the following:

```
For Each element In Group
   statement1
   statement2
   statementN
Next [element]
```

In the foregoing syntax, element is a variable to which all the elements of an array or collection will be assigned. This variable must be of the Variant data type for an array and an Object data type for a collection. Group is the name of a collection or an array.

Let's now see how to use the For Each...Next loop to remove some worksheets.

Hands-On 6.6   Writing a VBA Procedure with a For Each... Next Statement

1. Insert a new module into the current project and rename it **ForEachNextLoop**.
2. Type the following procedure in the **ForEachNextLoop** module:

```
Sub RemoveSheets()
  Dim mySheet As Worksheet

  Application.DisplayAlerts = False

  Workbooks.Add
  Sheets.Add After:=ActiveSheet, Count:=3

  For Each mySheet In Worksheets
    If mySheet.Name <> "Sheet1" Then
       ActiveWindow.SelectedSheets.Delete
    End If
  Next mySheet
```

```
    Application.DisplayAlerts = True
End Sub
```

Visual Basic will open a new workbook, add three new sheets after the default Sheet1 (ActiveSheet), and proceed to delete all the sheets except for Sheet1. Notice that the variable `mySheet` represents an object in a collection of worksheets. Therefore, this variable has been declared of the specific object data type Worksheet. The first instruction, `Application.DisplayAlerts = False`, makes sure that Microsoft Excel does not display alerts and messages while the procedure is running. The `For Each...Next` loop steps through each worksheet and deletes it as long as it is not Sheet1. When the procedure ends, the workbook has only one sheet—Sheet1.

3. Position the insertion point anywhere within the RemoveSheets procedure code and press **F5** to run it.

EXITING LOOPS EARLY

Sometimes you may not want to wait until the loop ends on its own. It's possible that a user has entered the wrong data, a procedure has encountered an error, or perhaps the task has been completed and there's no need to do additional looping. You can leave the loop early without reaching the condition that normally terminates it. Visual Basic has two types of `Exit` statements:

- The `Exit For` statement is used to end either a `For...Next` or a `For Each...Next` loop early.
- The `Exit Do` statement immediately exits any of the VBA `Do` loops.

The following procedure demonstrates how to use the `Exit For` statement to leave the `For Each...Next` loop early.

Hands-On 6.7   Writing a VBA Procedure with an Early Exit from a For Each...Next Statement

1. Enter the following procedure in the **ForEachNextLoop** module:

```
Sub EarlyExit()
    Dim myCell As Variant
    Dim myRange As Range

    Set myRange = Range("A1:H10")
    For Each myCell In myRange
        If myCell.Value = "" Then
            myCell.Value = "empty"
        Else
            Exit For
        End If
```

```
   Next myCell
End Sub
```

The EarlyExit procedure examines the contents of each cell in the specified range—A1:H10. If the active cell is empty, Visual Basic enters the text "empty" in the active cell. When Visual Basic encounters the first nonempty cell, it exits the loop.

2. Open a new workbook and enter a value in any cell within the specified range—**A1:H10**.
3. Choose **Developer | Macros**.
4. In the Macro dialog, select the **EarlyExit** procedure and click **Run**.

USING A DO...WHILE STATEMENT

The next example procedure demonstrates how to display today's date and time in Microsoft Excel's status bar for 10 seconds.

Hands-On 6.8   Writing a VBA Procedure with a Do... While Statement

1. Enter the following procedure in the **DoLoops** module:

```
Sub TenSeconds()
   Dim stopme

   stopme = Now + TimeValue("00:00:10")

   Do While Now < stopme
     Application.DisplayStatusBar = True
     Application.StatusBar = Now
   Loop

   Application.StatusBar = False
End Sub
```

In the TenSeconds procedure, the statements inside the Do...While loop will be executed as long as the time returned by the Now function is less than the value of the variable called stopme. The variable stopme holds the current time plus 10 seconds. (See the online help for other examples of using the built-in TimeValue function.)

The statement Application.DisplayStatusBar tells Visual Basic to turn on the status bar display. The next statement places the current date and time in the status bar. While the time is displayed for 10 seconds, the user cannot work with the system (the mouse pointer turns into the hourglass). After the 10 seconds are over (that is, when the condition Now < stopme evaluates to true), Visual Basic leaves the loop and executes the statement after the `Loop` keyword. This statement returns the default status bar message "Ready."

2. Press **Alt+F11** to switch to the Microsoft Excel application window.
3. Choose **Developer | Macros**. In the Macro dialog box, double-click the **TenSeconds** macro name (or highlight the macro name and click **Run**). Observe the date and time display in the status bar. The status bar should return to "Ready" after 10 seconds.

USING LOOPS AND CONDITIONALS

Let's combine the looping statements and some conditional logic to write a procedure that checks whether a certain sheet is part of a workbook.

(◉) **Hands-On 6.9   Writing a VBA Procedure with Loops and Conditionals**

1. Enter the following procedures in a new module:

```
Sub IsSuchSheet(strSheetName As String)
    Dim mySheet As Worksheet
    Dim counter As Integer

    counter = 0

Workbooks.Add
Sheets.Add After:=ActiveSheet, Count:=3
    For Each mySheet In Worksheets
        If mySheet.Name = strSheetName Then
            counter = counter + 1
            Exit For
        End If
    Next mySheet

    If counter = 1 Then
        MsgBox strSheetName & " exists."
    Else
        MsgBox strSheetName & " was not found."
    End If
End Sub

Sub FindSheet()
    Call IsSuchSheet("Sheet4")
End Sub
```

The IsSuchSheet procedure uses the `Exit For` statement to ensure that we exit the loop as soon as the sheet name passed in the procedure argument is found in the workbook. The FindSheet procedure is used to show you how to call one procedure from another.

2. To execute the IsSuchSheet procedure, run the FindSheet procedure.

SUMMARY

In this chapter, you learned how to repeat certain groups of statements using procedure loops. While working with several types of looping statements, you saw how each loop performs repetitions in a slightly different way. As you gain programming experience, you'll find it easier to choose the appropriate flow control structure for your task.

The next chapter will show you how arrays are used to work with larger sets of data.

Chapter 7

STORING MULTIPLE VALUES IN EXCEL VBA PROGRAMS

A QUICK INTRODUCTION TO WORKING WITH ARRAYS

I n previous chapters, you worked with many VBA procedures that used variables to hold specific information about an object, property, or value. For each single value that you wanted your procedure to manipulate, you declared a variable. But what if you have a series of values? If you had to write a VBA procedure to deal with larger amounts of data, you would have to create enough variables to handle all the data. Can you imagine the nightmare of storing in your program currency exchange rates for all the countries in the world? To create a table to hold the necessary data, you'd need at least three variables for each country: country name, currency name, and exchange rate. Fortunately, Visual Basic has a way to get around this problem. By clustering the related variables together, your VBA procedures can manage a large amount of data with ease. In this chapter, you'll learn how to manipulate lists and tables of data with arrays.

UNDERSTANDING ARRAYS

An *array* is a special type of variable that represents a group of similar values that are of the same data type (String, Integer, Currency, Date, etc.). The two most common types of arrays are one-dimensional arrays (lists) and two-dimensional arrays (tables). A one-dimensional array is sometimes referred to as a *list*. A shopping list, a list of the days of the week, and an employee list are examples of one-dimensional arrays or, simply, numbered lists. Each element in the list has an index value that allows accessing that element. For example, in the following illustration we have a one-dimensional array of six elements indexed from 0 to 5:

(0)	(1)	(2)	(3)	(4)	(5)

You can access the third element of this array by specifying index (2). By default, the first element of an array is indexed zero. You can change this behavior by using the `Option Base 1` statement or by explicitly coding the lower bound of your array as explained further in this chapter.

All elements of the array must be of the same data type. In other words, one array cannot store both strings and integers. Following are two examples of one-dimensional arrays: a one-dimensional array called cities that is populated with text (String data type—$) and a one-dimensional array called lotto that contains six lottery numbers stored as integers (Integer data type—%).

<table>
<tr><td colspan="2">A one-dimensional array: cities$</td><td colspan="2">A one-dimensional array: lotto%</td></tr>
<tr><td>cities(0)</td><td>Baltimore</td><td>lotto(0)</td><td>25</td></tr>
<tr><td>cities(1)</td><td>Atlanta</td><td>lotto(1)</td><td>4</td></tr>
<tr><td>cities(2)</td><td>Boston</td><td>lotto(2)</td><td>31</td></tr>
<tr><td>cities(3)</td><td>Washington</td><td>lotto(3)</td><td>22</td></tr>
<tr><td>cities(4)</td><td>New York</td><td>lotto(4)</td><td>11</td></tr>
<tr><td>cities(5)</td><td>Trenton</td><td>lotto(5)</td><td>5</td></tr>
</table>

As you can see, the contents assigned to each array element match the Array type. If you want to store values of different data types in the same array, you must declare the array as Variant. You will learn how to declare arrays in the next section.

A two-dimensional array may be thought of as a table or matrix. The position of each element in a table is determined by its row and column numbers. For example, an array that holds the yearly sales for each product your company sells has two dimensions (the product name and the year). The following is a diagram of an empty two-dimensional array.

(0,0)	(0,1)	(0,2)	(0,3)	(0,4)	(0,5)
(1,0)	(1,1)	(1,2)	(1,3)	(1,4)	(1,5)
(2,0)	(2,1)	(2,2)	(2,3)	(2,4)	(2,5)
(3,0)	(3,1)	(3,2)	(3,3)	(3,4)	(3,5)
(4,0)	(4,1)	(4,2)	(4,3)	(4,4)	(4,5)
(5,0)	(5,1)	(5,2)	(5,3)	(5,4)	(5,5)

You can access the first element in the second row of this two-dimensional array by specifying indexes (1, 0). Following are two examples of a two-dimensional array: an array named yearlyProductSales@ that stores yearly product sales using the Currency data type (@) and an array named exchange (of Variant data type) that stores the name of the country, its currency, and the U.S. dollar exchange rate.

A two-dimensional array: yearlyProductSales@

Walking Cane (0,0)	$25,023 (0,1)
Pill Crusher (1,0)	$64,085 (1,1)
Electric Wheelchair (2,0)	$345,016 (2,1)
Folding Walker (3,0)	$85,244 (3,1)

A two-dimensional array: exchange

Japan (0,0)	Japanese Yen (0,1)	108.83 (0,2)
Australia (1,0)	Australian Dollar (1,1)	1.28601 (1,2)
Canada (2,0)	Canadian Dollar (2,1)	1.235 (2,2)
Norway (3,0)	Norwegian Krone (3,1)	6.4471 (3,2)
Europe (4,0)	Euro (4,1)	0.816993 (4,2)

In these examples, the yearlyProductSales@ array can hold a maximum of 8 elements (4 rows * 2 columns = 8) and the exchange array will allow a maximum of 15 elements (5 rows * 3 columns = 15).

Although VBA arrays can have up to 60 dimensions, most people find it difficult to picture dimensions beyond 3-D. A three-dimensional array is an array of two-dimensional arrays (tables) where each table has the same number of rows and columns. A three-dimensional array is identified by three indexes: table, row, and column. The first element of a three-dimensional array is indexed (0, 0, 0).

Declaring Arrays

Because an array is a variable, you must declare it in a similar way that you declare other variables (by using the keywords `Dim`, `Private`, or `Public`). For fixed-length arrays, the array bounds are listed in parentheses following the variable name. If a variable-length, or dynamic, array is being declared, the variable name is followed by an empty pair of parentheses.

The last part of the array declaration is the definition of the data type that the array will hold. An array can hold any of the following data types: Integer, Long, Single, Double, Variant, Currency, String, Boolean, Byte, or Date. Let's look at some examples:

Array Declaration (one-dimensional)	Description
`Dim cities(5) as String`	Declares a 6-element array, indexed 0 to 5
`Dim lotto(1 to 6) as String`	Declares a 6-element array, indexed 1 to 6
`Dim supplies(2 to 11)`	Declares a 10-element array, indexed 2 to 11
`Dim myIntegers(-3 to 6)`	Declares a 10-element array, indexed −3 to 6 (the lower bound of an array can be 0, 1, or negative)
`Dim dynArray() as Integer`	Declares a variable-length array whose bounds will be determined at runtime (see examples later in this chapter)

Array Declaration (two-dimensional)	Description
`Dim exchange(4,2) as Variant`	Declares a two-dimensional array (five rows by three columns)
`Dim yearlyProductSales(3, 1) as Currency`	Declares a two-dimensional array (four rows by two columns)
`Dim my2Darray(1 to 3, 1 to7) as Single`	Declares a two-dimensional array (three rows indexed 1 to 3 by seven columns indexed 1 to 7)

Array Declaration (three-dimensional)	Description
`Dim exchange(2, 1 to 6, 4) as Variant`	Declares a three-dimensional array (the first dimension has three elements, the second dimension has six elements indexed 1 to 6, and the third dimension has five elements)

When you declare an array, Visual Basic automatically reserves enough memory space. The amount of the memory allocated depends on the array's size and data type. When you declare a one-dimensional array named lotto with six elements, Visual Basic sets aside 12 bytes—2 bytes for each element of the array (recall that the size of the Integer data type is 2 bytes, and hence $2 * 6 = 12$). The larger the array, the more memory space is required to store the data. Because arrays can eat up a lot of memory and impact your computer's performance, it's recommended that you declare arrays with only as many elements as you think you'll use.

SIDEBAR *What Is an Array Variable?*

An array is a group of variables that have a common name. While a typical variable can hold only one value, an array variable can store many individual values. You refer to a specific value in the array by using the array name and an index number.

SideBar *Subscripted Variables*

The numbers inside the parentheses of the array variables are called *subscripts*, and each individual variable is called a subscripted variable or element. For example, cities(5) is the sixth subscripted variable (element) of the array cities().

Array Upper and Lower Bounds

By default, VBA assigns zero (0) to the first element of the array. Therefore, number 1 represents the second element of the array, number 2 represents the third, and so on. With numeric indexing starting at 0, the one-dimensional array cities(5) contains six elements numbered from 0 to 5. If you'd rather start counting your array's elements at 1, you can explicitly specify a lower bound of the array by using an Option Base 1 statement. This instruction must be placed in the declaration section at the top of a VBA module before any Sub statements. If you don't specify Option Base 1 in a procedure that uses arrays, VBA assumes that the statement Option Base 0 is to be used and begins indexing your array's elements at 0. If you'd rather not use the Option Base 1 statement and still have the array indexing start at a number other than 0, you must specify the bounds of an array when declaring the array variable. The bounds of an array are its lowest and highest indices. Let's look at the following example:

```
Dim cities(3 To 6) As Integer
```

The foregoing statement declares a one-dimensional array with four elements. The numbers enclosed in parentheses after the array name specify the lower (3) and upper (6) bounds of the array. The first element of this array is indexed 3, the second 4, the third 5, and the fourth 6. Notice the keyword To between the lower and the upper indexes.

Initializing and Filling an Array

After you declare an array, you must assign values to its elements. This is often referred to as "initializing an array," "filling an array," or "populating an array." The three methods you can use to load data into an array are discussed in this section.

Filling an Array Using Individual Assignment Statements

Assume you want to store the names of your six favorite cities in a one-dimensional array named cities. After declaring the array with the Dim statement:

```
Dim cities(5) as String
```

or

```
Dim cities$(5)
```

you can assign values to the array variable like this:

```
cities(0) = "Baltimore"
cities(1) = "Atlanta"
cities(2) = "Boston"
cities(3) = "San Diego"
cities(4) = "New York"
cities(5) = "Denver"
```

Filling an Array Using the Array Function

VBA's built-in function `Array` returns an array of Variants. Because Variant is the default data type, the `As Variant` clause is optional in the array variable declaration:

```
Dim cities() as Variant
```

or

```
Dim cities()
```

Notice that you don't specify the number of elements between the parentheses.

Next, use the `Array` function as shown here to assign values to your cities array:

```
cities = Array("Baltimore", "Atlanta", "Boston", "San Diego",
"New York", "Denver")
```

When using the `Array` function for array population, the lower bound of an array is 0 or 1 and the upper bound is 5 or 6, depending on the setting of `Option Base` (see the previous section titled "Array Upper and Lower Bounds").

Filling an Array Using For...Next Loop

The easiest way to learn how to use loops to populate an array is by writing a procedure that fills an array with a specific number of integer values. Let's look at the example procedure here:

```
Sub LoadArrayWithIntegers()
  Dim myIntArray(1 To 10) As Integer
  Dim i As Integer

  'Initialize random number generator
  Randomize

  'Fill the array with 10 random numbers between 1 and 100
  For i = 1 To 10
    myIntArray(i) = Int((100 * Rnd) + 1)
  Next

  'Print array values to the Immediate window
```

```
    For i = 1 To 10
      Debug.Print myIntArray(i)
    Next
  End Sub
```

The foregoing procedure uses a For...Next loop to fill myIntArray with 10 random numbers between 1 and 100. The second loop is used to print out the values from the array. Notice that the procedure uses the Rnd function to generate a random number. This function returns a value less than 1 but greater than or equal to 0. You can try it out in the Immediate window by entering:

```
    x=rnd
    ?x
```

Before calling the Rnd function, the LoadArrayWithIntegers procedure uses the Randomize statement to initialize the random-number generator. To become more familiar with the Randomize statement and Rnd function, be sure to follow up with the Excel online help.

USING A ONE-DIMENSIONAL ARRAY

Having learned the basics of array variables, let's write a couple of VBA procedures to make arrays a part of your new skill set. The procedure in Hands-On 7.1 uses a one-dimensional array to programmatically display a list of six North American cities.

NOTE	*Please note files for the "Hands-On" project may be found in the companion files.*

(⊙) **Hands-On 7.1   Using a One-Dimensional Array**

1. Open a new workbook and save it as **C:\VBAPrimerExcel2021_ ByExample\Chap07_ExcelPrimer.xlsm**.
2. Switch to the Microsoft Visual Basic Editor window and rename the VBA project **Arrays**.
3. Insert a new module into the Arrays (Chap07_ExcelPrimer.xlsm) project and rename this module **StaticArrays**.
4. In the StaticArrays module, enter the following FavoriteCities procedure:

```
' start indexing array elements at 1
Option Base 1

Sub FavoriteCities()
  'now declare the array
  Dim cities(6) As String
```

```
     'assign the values to array elements
     cities(1) = "Baltimore"
     cities(2) = "Atlanta"
     cities(3) = "Boston"
     cities(4) = "San Diego"
     cities(5) = "New York"
     cities(6) = "Denver"

     'display the list of cities
     MsgBox cities(1) & Chr(13) & cities(2) & Chr(13) _
          & cities(3) & Chr(13) & cities(4) & Chr(13) _
          & cities(5) & Chr(13) & cities(6)
End Sub
```

Before the FavoriteCities procedure begins, the default indexing for an array is changed. Notice that the position of the `Option Base 1` statement is at the top of the module window before the `Sub` statement. This statement tells Visual Basic to assign the number 1 instead of the default 0 to the first element of the array. The array `cities()` of String data type is declared with six elements. Each element of the array is then assigned a value. The last statement uses the `MsgBox` function to display the list of cities. When you run this procedure in Step 5, the city names will appear on separate lines in the message box, as shown in Figure 7.1. You can change the order of the displayed data by switching the index values.

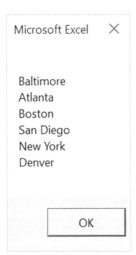

FIGURE 7.1 You can display the elements of a one-dimensional array with the `MsgBox` function.

5. Position the insertion point anywhere within the procedure code and press **F5** to run the FavoriteCities procedure.

6. On your own, modify the FavoriteCities procedure so that it displays the names of the cities in the reverse order (from 6 to 1).

USING A TWO-DIMENSIONAL ARRAY

Now that you know how to programmatically produce a list (a one-dimensional array), it's time to take a closer look at how you can work with tables of data. The following procedure creates a two-dimensional array that will hold the country name, currency name, and exchange rate for three countries.

⊙ **Hands-On 7.2   Storing Data in a Two-Dimensional Array**

1. In the **StaticArrays** module, enter the following procedure:

```
Sub Exchange()
    Dim t As String
    Dim r As String
    Dim Ex(3, 3) As Variant

    t = Chr(9)          ' tab
    r = Chr(13)         ' Enter

    Ex(1, 1) = "Japan"
    Ex(1, 2) = "Yen"
    Ex(1, 3) = 104.57
    Ex(2, 1) = "Mexico"
    Ex(2, 2) = "Peso"
    Ex(2, 3) = 11.2085
    Ex(3, 1) = "Canada"
    Ex(3, 2) = "Dollar"
    Ex(3, 3) = 1.2028
    MsgBox "Country " & t & t & "Currency" & t & "per US$" _
        & r & r _
        & Ex(1, 1) & t & t & Ex(1, 2) & t & Ex(1, 3) & r _
        & Ex(2, 1) & t & t & Ex(2, 2) & t & Ex(2, 3) & r _
        & Ex(3, 1) & t & t & Ex(3, 2) & t & Ex(3, 3) & r & r _
        & "* Sample Exchange Rates for Demonstration Only", , _
        "Exchange"
End Sub
```

2. Run the Exchange procedure.
3. When you run the Exchange procedure, you will see a message box with the exchange information presented in three columns, as shown in Figure 7.2.

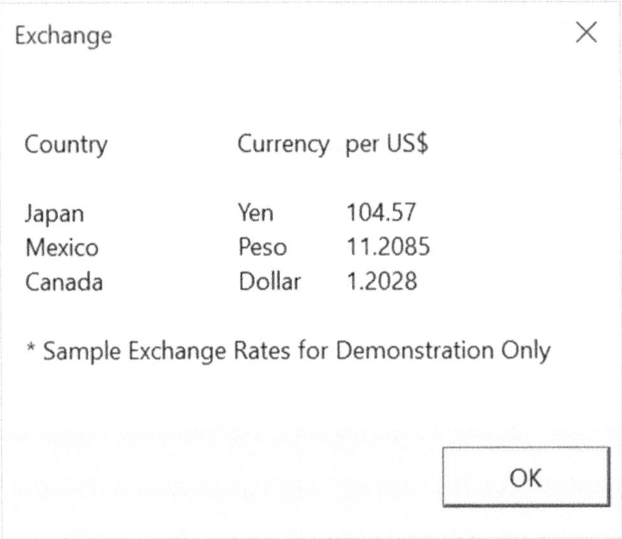

```
Exchange                              ✕


Country          Currency per US$

Japan            Yen      104.57
Mexico           Peso     11.2085
Canada           Dollar   1.2028

* Sample Exchange Rates for Demonstration Only



                              ┌─────────────┐
                              │     OK      │
                              └─────────────┘
```

FIGURE 7.2 The text displayed in a message box can be custom formatted.

USING A DYNAMIC ARRAY

The arrays introduced thus far in this chapter were static. A *static array* is an array of a specific size. Use a static array when you know in advance how big the array should be. The size of the static array is specified in the array's declaration statement. For example, the statement `Dim Fruits(9) As String` declares a static array called Fruits that is made up of 10 elements (assuming you have not changed the default indexing to 1). But what if you're not sure how many elements your array will contain? If your procedure depends on user input, the number of user-supplied elements might vary every time the procedure is executed. How can you ensure that the array you declare is not wasting memory? After you declare an array, VBA sets aside enough memory to accommodate the array. If you declare an array to hold more elements than what you need, you'll end up wasting valuable computer resources. The solution to this problem is making your arrays dynamic.

A *dynamic array* is an array whose size can change. You use a dynamic array when the array size is determined each time the procedure is run. A dynamic array is declared by placing empty parentheses after the array name:

```
Dim Fruits() As String
```

Before you use a dynamic array in your procedure, you must use the `ReDim` statement to dynamically set the lower and upper bounds of the array. For example, initially you may want to hold five fruits in the array:

```
Redim Fruits(1 To 5)
```

The ReDim statement redimensions arrays as the code of your procedure executes and informs Visual Basic about the new size of the array. This statement can be used several times in the same procedure.

The example procedure in Hands-On 7.3 will dynamically load data entered in a worksheet into a one-dimensional array.

⊚ Hands-On 7.3   Loading Worksheet Data into an Array

1. Insert a new module into the Arrays project and rename it **DynamicArrays**.
2. In the **DynamicArrays** module, enter the following procedure:

```vba
Sub LoadArrayFromWorksheet()
    Dim myDataRng As Range
    Dim myArray() As Variant
    Dim cnt As Integer
    Dim i As Integer
    Dim cell As Variant
    Dim r As Integer
    Dim last As Integer

    Set myDataRng = ActiveSheet.UsedRange

    'get the count of nonempty cells (text and numbers only)
    last = myDataRng.SpecialCells(xlCellTypeConstants, 3).Count

    If IsEmpty(myDataRng) Then
        MsgBox "Sheet is empty."
        Exit Sub
    End If

    ReDim myArray(1 To last)

    i = 1

    'fill the array from worksheet data
    'reformat all numeric values
    For Each cell In myDataRng
        If cell.Value <> "" Then
            If IsNumeric(cell.Value) Then
                myArray(i) = Format(cell.Value, "$#,#00.00")
            Else
                myArray(i) = cell.Value
            End If
            i = i + 1
        End If
    Next

    'print array values to the Immediate window
    For i = 1 To last
        Debug.Print myArray(i)
```

```
   Next
   Debug.Print "Items in the array: " & UBound(myArray)
End Sub
```

3. Switch to the Microsoft Excel application window of the Chap07_
   ExcelPrimer.xlsm workbook and enter some data in **Sheet2**. For example,
   enter your favorite fruits in cells A1:B6 and numbers in cells D1:D9.
4. Choose **Developer | Macros**. In the Macro dialog box, choose
   LoadArrayFromWorksheet, and click **Run**.
   When the procedure completes, check the data in the Immediate window.
   You should see the entries you typed in the worksheet. The numeric data
   should appear formatted with the currency format.

USING ARRAY FUNCTIONS

You can manipulate arrays with five built-in VBA functions: `Array`, `IsAr-`
`ray`, `Erase`, `LBound`, and `UBound`. The following sections demonstrate the
use of each of these functions in VBA procedures.

The Array Function

The `Array` function allows you to create an array during code execution
without having to dimension it first. This function always returns an array
of Variants. Using the `Array` function, you can quickly place a series of values in a list.

The CarInfo procedure shown here creates a fixed-size, one-dimensional, three-element array called auto.

(●) **Hands-On 7.4   Using the Array Function**

1. Insert a new module into the current project and rename it **Array_**
   Function.
2. Enter the following **CarInfo** procedure:

```
Option Base 1

Sub CarInfo()
   Dim auto As Variant
   auto = Array("Ford", "Black", "1999")
   MsgBox auto(2) & " " & auto(1) & ", " & auto(3)
   auto(2) = "4-door"
   MsgBox auto(2) & " " & auto(1) & ", " & auto(3)
End Sub
```

3. Run the CarInfo procedure.

The IsArray Function

Using the `IsArray` function, you can test whether a variable is an array. The `IsArray` function returns either true, if the variable is an array, or false, if it's not an array. Here's an example.

⊙ Hands-On 7.5 Using the IsArray Function

1. Insert a new module into the current project and rename it **IsArray_ Function**.
2. Enter the code of the **IsThisArray** procedure, as shown here:

```
Sub IsThisArray()
  ' declare a dynamic array
  Dim sheetNames() As String
      Dim totalSheets As Integer
  Dim counter As Integer

  ' count the sheets in the current workbook
  totalSheets = ActiveWorkbook.Sheets.Count

  ' specify the size of the array
  ReDim sheetNames(1 To totalSheets)

  ' enter and show the names of sheets
  For counter = 1 To totalSheets
    sheetNames(counter) = _
        ActiveWorkbook.Sheets(counter).Name
    MsgBox sheetNames(counter)
  Next counter

  ' check if this is indeed an array
  If IsArray(sheetNames) Then
    MsgBox "The sheetNames variable is an array."
  End If
End Sub
```

3. Run the IsThisArray procedure.

The Erase Function

When you want to remove the data from an array, you should use the `Erase` function. This function deletes all the data held by static or dynamic arrays. In addition, the `Erase` function reallocates all the memory assigned to a dynamic array. If a procedure has to use the dynamic array again, you must use the `ReDim` statement to specify the size of the array.

The following example shows how to erase the data from the array cities.

Hands-On 7.6   Using the Erase Function

1. Insert a new module into the current project and rename it **Erase_ Function**.

2. Enter the code of the FunCities procedure shown here:

```
' start indexing array elements at 1
Option Base 1

Sub FunCities()
' declare the array
Dim cities(1 To 5) As String

' assign the values to array elements
cities(1) = "Las Vegas"
cities(2) = "Orlando"
cities(3) = "Atlantic City"
cities(4) = "New York"
cities(5) = "San Francisco"

' display the list of cities
  MsgBox cities(1) & Chr(13) & cities(2) & Chr(13) _
    & cities(3) & Chr(13) & cities(4) & Chr(13) _
    & cities (5)
Erase cities

' show all that were erased
MsgBox cities(1) & Chr(13) & cities(2) & Chr(13) _
  & cities(3) & Chr(13) & cities(4) & Chr(13) _
  & cities (5)
End Sub
```

After the `Erase` function deletes the values from the array, the `MsgBox` function displays an empty message box.

3. Run the FunCities procedure.

The LBound and UBound Functions

The `LBound` and `UBound` functions return whole numbers that indicate the lower bound and upper bound of an array.

Hands-On 7.7   Using the LBound and UBound Functions

1. Insert a new module into the current project and rename it **L_and_ UBound_Function**.

2. Enter the code of the **FunCities2** procedure shown here:

```
Sub FunCities2()
  ' declare the array
  Dim cities(1 To 5) As String
```

```
' assign the values to array elements
cities(1) = "Las Vegas"
cities(2) = "Orlando"
cities(3) = "Atlantic City"
cities(4) = "New York"
cities(5) = "San Francisco"

    ' display the list of cities
MsgBox cities(1) & Chr(13) & cities(2) & Chr(13) _
    & cities(3) & Chr(13) & cities(4) & Chr(13) _
    & cities (5)
' display the array bounds
MsgBox "The lower bound: " & LBound(cities) & Chr(13) _
    & "The upper bound: " & UBound(cities)
End Sub
```

3. Run the FunCities2 procedure.

TROUBLESHOOTING ERRORS IN ARRAYS

When working with arrays, it's easy to make a mistake. If you try to assign more values than there are elements in the declared array, VBA will display the error message "Subscript out of range," as shown in Figure 7.3.

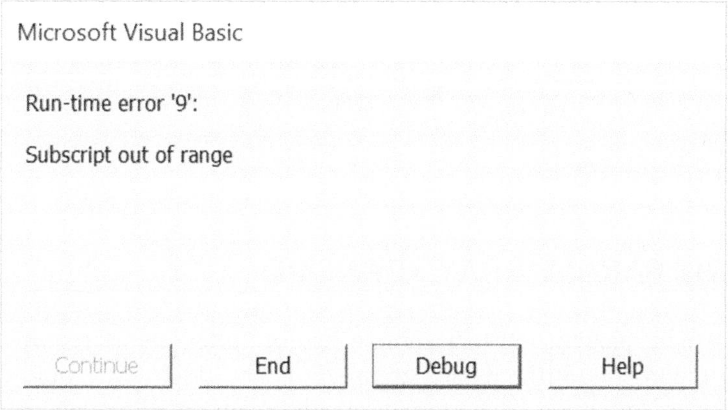

Microsoft Visual Basic

Run-time error '9':

Subscript out of range

| Continue | End | Debug | Help |

FIGURE 7.3 This error was caused by an attempt to access a nonexistent array element.

Suppose you declare a one-dimensional array that consists of six elements, and you are trying to assign a value to the seventh element. When you run the procedure, Visual Basic can't find the seventh element, so it displays the error message. When you click the Debug button, Visual Basic will highlight the line of code that caused the error.

To fix this type of error, you should begin by looking at the array's declaration statement. Once you know how many elements the array should hold, it's easy to figure out that the culprit is the index number that appears in the parentheses in the highlighted line of code. In the example shown in Figure 7.4, once we replace the line of code `cities(7) = "Denver"` with `cities(6) = "Trenton"` and press F5 to resume the procedure, the procedure will run as intended.

Another frequent error you may encounter while working with arrays is *Type mismatch*. To avoid this error, keep in mind that each element of an array must be of the same data type. If you attempt to assign to an element of an array a value that conflicts with the data type of the array declared in the `Dim` statement, you'll obtain the Type mismatch error during code execution. To hold values of different data types in an array, declare the array as Variant.

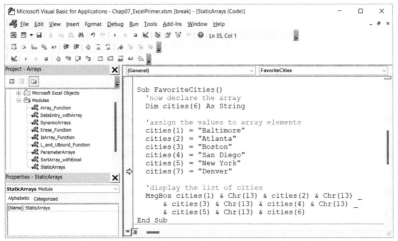

FIGURE 7.4 When you click the Debug button in the error message, Visual Basic highlights the statement that triggered the error.

USING THE PARAMARRAY KEYWORD

Values can be passed between subroutines or functions as required or optional arguments. If the passed argument is not absolutely required for the procedure to execute, the argument's name is preceded by the keyword `Optional`. Sometimes, however, you don't know in advance how many arguments you want to pass. A classic example is addition. You may want to add together two numbers. Later, you may use 3, 10, or 15 numbers.

Using the keyword `ParamArray`, you can pass an array consisting of any number of elements to your subroutines and function procedures.

The following AddMultipleArgs function will add up as many numbers as you require. This function begins with the declaration of an array, `myNumbers`. Notice the use of the `ParamArray` keyword. The array must be declared as an array of type Variant, and it must be the last argument in the procedure definition.

⊚ **Hands-On 7.8   Passing an Array to Procedures Using the**
               ParamArray Keyword

1. Insert a new module into the current project and rename it **ParameterArrays**.

2. In the ParameterArrays module, enter the following **AddMultipleArgs** function procedure:

```
Function AddMultipleArgs(ParamArray myNumbers() As Variant)
   Dim mySum As Single
   Dim myValue As Variant
   For Each myValue in myNumbers
     mySum=mySum+myValue
   Next
   AddMultipleArgs = mySum
End Function
```

3. To try out the AddMultipleArgs function, activate the Immediate window and type the following instruction:

```
?AddMultipleArgs(1, 23.24, 3, 24, 8, 34)
```

When you press **Enter**, Visual Basic returns the total of all the numbers in the parentheses: 93.24. You can supply an unlimited number of arguments. To add more values, enter additional values inside the parentheses and press Enter. Notice that each function argument must be separated by a comma.

DATA ENTRY WITH AN ARRAY

Earlier in this chapter you learned how to use various Array functions. The following procedure demonstrates how the simple `Array` function can speed up data entry.

⊚ **Hands-On 7.9   Using the Array Function to Enter Headings in a**
               Worksheet

1. Insert a new module into the current project and rename it **DataEntry_ withArray**.

2. In the EnterData_Array module, enter the following **ColumnHeads** procedure:

```
Sub ColumnHeads()
   Dim heading As Variant
   Dim cell As Range
   Dim i As Integer
   i = 0
   heading = Array("First Name", "Last Name", _
     "Position", "Salary")
   Workbooks.Add
```

```
For Each cell In Range("A1:D1")
  cell.Formula = heading(i)
i = i + 1
Next

Columns("A:D").Select
Selection.Columns.AutoFit
Range("A1").Select
End Sub
```

3. Switch to Microsoft Excel window and run the ColumnHeads procedure.

SORTING AN ARRAY WITH EXCEL

We all find it easier to work with sorted data. Some operations on arrays, like finding maximum and minimum values, require that the array is sorted. Once it is sorted, you can find the maximum value by assigning the upper bound index to the sorted array, as in the following:

```
y = myIntArray(UBound(myIntArray))
```

The minimum value can be obtained by reading the first value of the sorted array:

```
x = myIntArray(1)
```

So, how can you sort an array? This section demonstrates how you can use Excel to get your array data into the sorted order. An easy way to sort an array is copying your array values to a new worksheet, and then using the Excel built-in `Sort` function. After completing the sort, you can load your sorted values back into a VBA array. This technique is the simplest since you can use a macro recorder to get your sort statement started for you. And, with a large array, it is also faster than the classic bubble sort routine that is commonly used with arrays.

⊙ Hands-On 7.10   Using Excel to Sort a VBA Array

1. Insert a new module into the current project and rename it **SortArray_ withExcel**.

2. In the SortArray_withExcel module, enter the following **SortArrayWithExcel** procedure:

```
Sub SortArrayWithExcel()
  Dim myIntArray() As Integer
  Dim i As Integer
  Dim x As Integer
  Dim y As Integer
  Dim r As Integer
  Dim myDataRng As Range
```

```vba
'initialize random number generator
Randomize

ReDim myIntArray(1 To 10)

' Fill the array with 10 random numbers between 1 and 100
For i = 1 To 10
    myIntArray(i) = Int((100 * Rnd) + 1)
    Debug.Print "aValue" & i & ":" & vbTab & myIntArray(i)
Next

'write array to a worksheet
Worksheets.Add

r = 1    'row counter
With ActiveSheet
  For i = 1 To 10
      Cells(r, 1).Value = myIntArray(i)
      r = r + 1
  Next i
End With

'Use Excel Sort to order values in the worksheet
Set myDataRng = ActiveSheet.UsedRange

With ActiveSheet.Sort
  .SortFields.Clear
  .SortFields.Add Key:=Range("A1"), _
    SortOn:=xlSortOnValues, Order:=xlAscending, _
    DataOption:=xlSortNormal
  .SetRange myDataRng
  .Header = xlNo
  .MatchCase = False
  .Apply
End With

'free the memory used by array by using Erase statement
Erase myIntArray

ReDim myIntArray(1 To 10)

'load sorted values back into an array

For i = 1 To 10
  myIntArray(i) = ActiveSheet.Cells(i, 1).Value
Next

'write out sorted array to the Immediate Window

i = 1
For i = 1 To 10
```

```
    Debug.Print "aValueSorted: " & myIntArray(i)
    Next

    'find minimum and maximum values stored in the array
    x = myIntArray(1)
    y = myIntArray(UBound(myIntArray))
    Debug.Print "Min value=" & x & vbTab; "Max value=" & y
    End Sub
```

The SortArrayWithExcel procedure populates a dynamic array with 10 random Integer values and prints out this array to an Immediate window and a new worksheet. Next, the values entered in the worksheet are sorted in ascending order using the Excel Sort object. The sort statements have been generated by the macro recorder and then modified for this procedure's needs. Once sorted, the `Erase` statement is used to free the memory used by the dynamic array. Before reloading the array with the sorted values, the procedure redeclares the array variable using the `ReDim` statement. The last statements in the procedure demonstrate how to retrieve the minimum and maximum values from the array variable.

3. Switch to Microsoft Excel window and run the SortArrayWithExcel procedure.

SUMMARY

In this chapter, you learned how you can use arrays in complex VBA procedures that require many variables. You worked with examples of procedures that demonstrated how to declare and use a one-dimensional array (list) and a two-dimensional array (table). You saw the difference between static and dynamic arrays and practiced using five built-in VBA functions that are frequently used with arrays: `Array`, `IsArray`, `Erase`, `LBound`, and `UBound`. You also learned how to use a new keyword—`ParamArray`—and perform sorting of an array with Excel.

In the next chapter you will learn how to use collections instead of arrays to manipulate large amounts of data.

Chapter 8

KEEPING TRACK OF MULTIPLE VALUES
IN EXCEL VBA PROGRAMS

A QUICK INTRODUCTION TO
CREATING AND USING COLLECTIONS

In the previous chapter, you learned how arrays are used to manipulate multiple items quickly and easily. Instead of creating several variables to keep track of your data, you only needed to declare one variable. Using arrays instead of defining individual variables saves you from writing many lines of repetitive code. As you have seen so far, in programming there are many ways of performing the same task. The method you use depends on your needs. So it is with storing multiple values. In addition to arrays, you can maintain your items of data while your program is running by using a special type of object—the collection. Like arrays, collections are used for grouping variables.

Because collections have built-in properties and methods that allow you to add, remove, and count their elements, they make working with multiple data items much easier than arrays. Collections can also be used to hold objects. This is a more advanced feature of object-oriented programming that is beyond the scope of this primer book. In this chapter we will focus on learning the basic skills of using collections for tracking and maintaining data in your VBA procedures.

WORKING WITH BUILT-IN COLLECTIONS

A set of similar objects is known as a collection. In Microsoft Excel, for example, all open workbooks belong to the collection of Workbooks, and all the sheets in a workbook are members of the Worksheets collection. Collections are objects that contain other objects. No matter what collection you want to work with, you can do the following:

- Refer to a specific object in a collection by using an index value. For example, to refer to the second object in the collection of Worksheets, use either of the following statements:

```
Worksheets(2).Select
```

Or

```
Worksheets("Sheet2").Select
```

- Determine the number of items in the collection by using the Count property. For example, when you enter in the Immediate window the statement:

```
?Worksheets.Count
```

- VBA will return the total number of worksheets in the current workbook.

- Insert new items into the collection by using the Add method. For example, when you enter in the Immediate window the statement:

```
Worksheets.Add
```

- VBA will insert to the current workbook a new worksheet. The Worksheets collection now contains one more item.

- Cycle through every object in the collection by using the For Each... Next loop.

- Suppose that you opened a workbook containing five worksheets with the following names: "Daily wages," "Weekly wages," "Monthly wages," "Yearly salary," and "Bonuses." To delete the worksheets that contain the word "wages" in the name, you could write the following procedure:

```
Sub DeleteSheets()
  Dim ws As Worksheet
  Application.DisplayAlerts = False
  For Each ws In Worksheets
    If InStr(ws.Name, "wages") Then
      ws.Delete
    End If
  Next
  Application.DisplayAlerts = True
End Sub
```

- The statement Application.DisplayAlerts = False is used to suppress some prompts and messages that Excel displays while the code is running. In this case, we want to suppress the confirmation message that Excel displays when worksheets are deleted. The `In-Str` function is very useful for string comparisons as it allows you to find one string within another. The statement `InStr(ws.Name, "wages")` tells Excel to determine if the worksheet name (stored in ws object variable) contains the string of characters "wages."

Creating Your Own Collection

Collection is an object; it is a data type in VBA. To create a user-defined collection, begin by declaring an object variable of the Collection type:

```
Dim collection_name As Collection
Set collection_name = New Collection
```

Or

```
Dim collection_name As New Collection
```

Notice the `New` keyword. VBA uses this keyword to create a new instance of an object. The collection_name is the name of your collection. You can use any name if it is not one of the reserved words Excel uses for its own collections or other internal operations.

You can define more than one collection but each collection you define should have a distinct name so you can easily reference it in your code. Collections can be defined at the top of the standard module or within a procedure. They can also be defined in class modules which are often used in more advanced Excel VBA programming. Unlike arrays, collections do not require you to predefine their size. Once you define the object variable of the Collection type you are ready to begin adding items to the collection.

Adding Objects to a Custom Collection

After you've declared the Collection object, you can insert new items into the collection by using the `Add` method. The `Add` method looks like this:

```
object.Add item[, key, before, after]
```

You are required to specify only the object and the item. All arguments in the square brackets are optional. The object is the collection name. This is the same name that was used in the declaration of the Collection object. The item is the object that you want to add to the collection. For example, if the name of your collection is `colFruits`, the following statement adds several new items to it:

```
colFruits.Add "Apple"
colFruits.Add "Pear"
colFruits.Add "Strawberry"
colFruits.Add "Blueberry"
```

```
colFruits.Add "Orange"
colFruits.Add "Peach"
```

Although other arguments are optional, they are quite useful. It's important to understand that the items in a collection are automatically assigned numbers starting with 1. However, they can also be assigned a unique key value. Instead of accessing a specific item with an index (1, 2, 3, and so on), you can assign a key for that object at the time an object is added to a collection. For instance, if you are creating a collection of custom sheets, you could use a sheet name as a key. To identify an individual in a collection of students or employees, you could use their ID numbers as a key. For example, here's how you can add *James Allen* to `colPeople` collection, using his Employee ID as a key:

```
Dim colPeople As New Collection
colPeople.Add "James Allen", Key:="123456"
```

If you want to specify the position of the object in the collection, you should use either a `before` or `after` argument (do not use both). The `before` argument is the object before which the new object is added. The `after` argument is the object after which the new object is added.

For example, to add *Kiwi* to the `colFruits` collection so that it appears after the second item, use the following statement:

```
colFruits.Add "Kiwi", , , 2
```

or

```
colFruits.Add "Kiwi", After:=2
```

Notice that if you are not using the named argument `After`, you must place a comma for each of the preceding optional arguments that you are not specifying.

To enter *Cherry* in the first position, use the named `Before` argument:

```
colFruits.Add "Cherry", Before:=1
```

Using the optional `Before` or `After` arguments you can easily add elements in any position.

Each element of a collection can be a different data type. Please note that arrays can support different data types only if they are defined as Variants. To store a date item in your collection, use the following statement:

```
colFruits.Add #12/10/2021#, Key:="InvoiceDate"
```

To store a number in your collection, the following statement can be used:

```
colFruits.Add 100.99, Key:="InvoiceTotal"
```

Determining the Number of Items in Your Collection

Use the `Count` property to find out the number of items in your collection. To determine the current number of fruit items in the `colFruits`, write the following statement:

```
Debug.Print colFruits.Count
```

Accessing Items in a Collection

To refer to a specific item in your collection, use its index or key value.

For example, to find out the names of the first collection item, use this statement:

```
Debug.Print colFruits.Item(1)
```

Because the `Item` method is a default method of the collection, you may omit it from the statement, as shown here:

```
Debug.Print colFruits(1)
```

If you know the item key, then you can quickly retrieve it like this:

```
Debug.Print colPeople("123456")
```

By using the Key to access a collection item you can go to it directly without the need to iterate through all the items. Excel VBA does not provide a built-in method to check if the Key exists, but you can write your own function to return a Boolean value of True if the key exists. Here's how you would do it:

```
Function KeyExists(colName As Collection, _
        key As String) As Boolean
    On Error GoTo EndHere
    IsObject (colName.Item(key))
    KeyExists = True

EndHere:
End Function
```

The `IsObject` is a built-in VBA function that returns `True` if the passed to it expression (i.e., key name) represents an object variable. The statement `OnError GoTo EndHere` tells Excel to jump to the line `EndHere:` if the result of the `IsObject` function is `False`. The error handling statements introduced here are covered in detail in Chapter 9.

Removing Items from a Collection

Removing an item from your custom collection is as easy as adding an item. To remove an item, use the `Remove` method in the following format:

```
object.Remove index
```

`object` is the name of the custom collection that contains the object you want to remove. `index` is an expression specifying the position of the object in the collection. To remove the third fruit item from the `colFruits`, you simply write the following statement:

```
colFruits.Remove 3
```

Collections are reindexed automatically when an item is removed. Therefore, to remove all items from a custom collection you can use 1 for the `Index` argument, as in the following example:

```
Do While colFruits.Count > 0
  colFruits.Remove Index:=1
Loop
```

Another way to remove all objects from your collection is by using the `For Each...Next` loop. For example, to remove all objects from the `colFruits`, use the following looping structure:

```
Dim m As Variant

For Each m in colFruits
 colFruits.Remove 1
Next
```

Note that the control variable used in the `For Each...Next` loop must be declared as Variant or Object. Because collections are reindexed, the preceding statement will remove the first item of the collection on each iteration. After the loop completes, `colFruits` should have zero items. However, to be sure, use the `Count` property to find out.

```
Debug.Print colFruits.Count
```

You can also remove all items from a collection by setting the collection object variable to a new collection, like this:

```
Set colFruits = New Collection
```

Updating Items in a Collection

When you add an item to your collection that has a basic data type such as string, integer, long, currency, or date, your collection will be read-only. This means you will not be able to change the value of the item. Excel will display an error if you try to assign a value to an existing item in your collection:

```
' this statement will produce Run-time error 424 'Object required'
colFruits(4) = "Cranberry"
```

Therefore, if your procedure requires that the values are updated, you should group your items into an array. If you want to stick with the collection, to change an item, remove the item and add a new one. The only time that the collection is updatable is when it references objects, and this is a subject for the advanced VBA.

Let's proceed to the first Hands-On in this chapter where you put all your knowledge about collections into a VBA procedure.

> **NOTE** *Please note files for the "Hands-On" project may be found in the companion files.*

Hands-On 8.1   Creating and Manipulating a Custom Collection (Example 1)

1. Start Excel and create a new macro-enabled workbook named **Chap08_ExcelPrimer.xlsm** in your **C:\VBAPrimerExcel2021_ByExample** folder.
2. Press **Alt+F11** to switch to the Visual Basic Editor window.
3. Choose **Insert | Module** to add a new standard module.
4. In the Module1 Code window, enter the following **WorkWith_**Collection, **Display_Items** and **KeyExists** procedures.

```
Sub WorkWith_Collection()
    Dim colFruits As New Collection
    Dim itm As Variant
    Dim strColItems As String

    colFruits.Add "Apple"
    colFruits.Add "Pear"
    colFruits.Add "Strawberry"
    colFruits.Add "Blueberry"
    colFruits.Add "Orange"
    colFruits.Add "Peach"
    colFruits.Add "Kiwi", , , 2
    colFruits.Add "Mango", , 5
    colFruits.Add "Cherry", Before:=1
    colFruits.Add 100.99, Key:="InvoiceTotal"
    colFruits.Add #12/10/2021#, Key:="InvoiceDate"

    Debug.Print "Total Items in colFruits: " & colFruits.Count

    'call a procedure to display all items in the collection
    Display_Items colFruits, itm

    colFruits.Remove 3
     Debug.Print "New Total Items in colFruits: " & colFruits.Count

    For Each itm In colFruits
        strColItems = strColItems & ", " & itm
    Next

    ' remove a comma and a space from the beginning of
```

```
' the strColItems variable
strColItems = Mid(strColItems, 3, Len(strColItems))
Debug.Print strColItems


'Find if keys exist and if not display a message
'and go to the next line

If KeyExists(colFruits, "InvoiceDate") And _
    KeyExists(colFruits, "InvoiceTotal") Then
Debug.Print "Invoiced on: " & colFruits("InvoiceDate") & _
    vbCrLf & "Total: " & colFruits("InvoiceTotal")
Else
    MsgBox "Provided key(s) not found."
End If


' Remove all items from collection one by one
For Each itm In colFruits
    colFruits.Remove 1
Next
Debug.Print "Total Items in colFruits: " & colFruits.Count

End Sub


Sub Display_Items(col As Collection, myItm As Variant)

    For Each myItm In col
        Debug.Print myItm
    Next
End Sub


Function KeyExists(colName As Collection, _
        key As String) As Boolean

    On Error GoTo EndHere

    IsObject (colName.Item(key))
    KeyExists = True

EndHere:
End Function
```

5. Position the pointer anywhere within the WorkWith_Collection procedure and choose **Run | Run Sub/UserForm** to execute it.

6. Press **Ctrl+G** to open the Immediate Window and check the output of the procedure.

The WorkWith_Collection procedure performs various operations on the declared collection object variable `colFruits`. If you plan on using the same collection in other procedures in the same module, you will need to move its variable declaration statement to the top of the module.

Returning a Collection from a Function

Collections like arrays can be used as parameters or return values to functions or subroutine procedures. In Hands-On 8.2 you will collect entries from the user via the VBA InputBox function and store them into an array. Next, you will pass that array to a function and return a collection with the same items. Let's see how this is done.

Hands-On 8.2   Creating and Manipulating a Custom Collection (Example 2)

1. Choose **Insert | Module** to add a new standard module to the current VBA project.
2. In the Code window, enter the code shown as follows.
   Notice that the allItems variable is declared at the top of the module (above all the procedure code). This placement will make this variable available to all the procedures in this module.

```
Dim allItems As String

Sub ShowCollItems()
    Dim coll As Collection
    Dim myArray As Variant
    Dim itm As Variant

    ' get items from user input
    If AskForItems <> "" Then
        Debug.Print allItems
        ' extract items from the user input string (allItems)
        ' and place them in an array
        myArray = Split(allItems, ",")
        Debug.Print "Array has " & UBound(myArray) + 1 & " items."

        ' call function to create a collection from the array
        Set coll = CreateCollection(myArray)

        ' iterate through the collection to display each item
        For Each itm In coll
            Debug.Print itm
        Next
        Debug.Print "Total items in the collection: " & coll.Count
    End If
End Sub

Function AskForItems() As String
    allItems = InputBox("Enter your items separated by a comma", _
        "Demo - Get User Input", _
        "item1, item2")

    If allItems = "" Then
        AskForItems = ""
```

```
Else
   AskForItems = allItems
 End If
End Function

Function CreateCollection(arrMyItems As Variant) As Collection
     Dim coll As New Collection
     Dim i As Integer
     For i = 0 To UBound(arrMyItems)
         coll.Add arrMyItems(i)
     Next i
     'Return a collection
     Set CreateCollection = coll
End Function
```

3. Position the pointer anywhere within the ShowCollItems procedure and choose **Run | Run Sub/UserForm** to execute it.

4. Press **Ctrl+G** to open the Immediate Window and check the output of the procedure.

Let's review the previous code. The main procedure ShowCollItems declares three variables that we need for working with the array and collection. Notice that you don't need to use the New keyword to declare the collection because the collection is created inside the CreateCollection function. The declared object variable coll will be assigned a collection received from this function. In addition to the CreateCollection function, the ShowCollItem procedure relies on following functions: AskForItems and Split.

The custom function procedure AskForItems populates the allItems string variable (declared on the top of the module) with the values obtained from the user via the VBA InputBox function. The user is requested to input values as a comma-delimited string (each item must be separated by a comma). If the user does not enter any values and presses Cancel instead, the function will return an empty string to the calling procedure (ShowCollItems). If items are entered, then the entire string will be returned. If the string returned from the AskForItems function is not empty, we continue running the statements within the If block. If the string is empty, the procedure ends.

Within the If block, we print the contents of the allItems variable to the Immediate window. Next, we use the built-in VBA Split function to extract the values from the allItems string using a comma delimiter and return an array (myArray). We use the UBound function to find the number of items in the array. Because by default arrays are zero-based, we need to add 1 to the count to get the correct number of items. Refer to the previous chapter on arrays if you'd like to add code here to list the items in the myArray variable.

The next set of statements focuses on creating a collection. To do this we set the coll variable to the result obtained from the CreateCollection function. We call the CreateCollection function and pass it the myArray variable. Notice that myArray is a Variant and the CreateCollection function was defined to expect the parameter of the Variant type. Inside the CreateCollection function we start by declaring the coll variable of the Collection type. We also need a counter (i) to loop through the items of the array variable that we passed to this function. Note that the parameter name that the CreateCollection function expects can be any name you define.

Using the For…Next loop we loop through the items of the array starting from zero and add each array item to the collection. Once we are done looping, we pass the entire collection to the calling procedure— ShowCollItems. The coll is an object variable, so we need to use the `Set` keyword to return it from the function:

```
'Return a collection
Set CreateCollection = coll
```

Now we are back again in the ShowCollItems procedure, this time returning a collection. To view the collection items, we use the `For each Next` loop to print each item to the Immediate window. Note that the `itm` iterator must be defined as Variant. The procedure ends by printing the total number of collection items.

Using Custom and Built-in Collections Together

Let's apply our knowledge of custom collections to working with the Excel built-in collection of worksheets. As worksheets can contain various objects, you may need to collect different values stored within them. The GetNotes procedure in Hands-On 8.3 declares a custom collection object named col-Notes. We will use this collection to store notes that you insert in various worksheets of the active workbook.

Note: Currently in Excel for Microsoft 365 notes are used for making notes and annotations about the data in a worksheet. Notes look like yellow stickies and were formerly called comments. The comments are still in Excel, but they look different and are used when you want to discuss the data. Comments have a Reply box which allows you to discuss the data with other people. Comments are now threaded which means that when people reply to the comment, you can see several comments connected together, forming a conversation. In the following Hands-On you will work with notes.

⊙ Hands-On 8.3   Using a Custom Collection Object

1. Right-click any cell in Sheet1 of the Chap8_ExcelPrimer.xlsm workbook and choose **New Note** from the shortcut menu. You can also enter a note

by choosing Review | Notes | New Note. Type any text you want for your note. Click outside the note box to exit the edit mode. Add two new sheets to the workbook. Use the same technique to enter two notes in Sheet2. Enter different text for each note. Add a note in any cell on Sheet3. You should now have four notes in three worksheets.

2. Click the **File tab** and choose **Options**. In the Excel Options window's General section, in the area named "Personalize your copy of Microsoft Office," you should see a text box with your name. Delete your name and enter **Joan Smith**, and then click **OK**. Now, enter one note anywhere on Sheet2 and one note anywhere on Sheet3. These notes should be automatically stamped with Joan Smith's name. When you're done entering the note text, return to the Excel Options window and change the User name text box entry back to the way it was (your name).

3. Switch to the Visual Basic Editor and add a new module to the current project.

4. Use the Properties box to rename the module. Enter **MyCollection** next to the **Name** property.

5. In the MyCollection module, enter the **GetNotes** procedure, as shown here:

```
Sub GetNotes()
    Dim sht As Worksheet
    Dim colNotes As New Collection
    Dim myNote As Comment
    Dim i As Integer
    Dim t As Integer
    Dim strName As String

    strName = InputBox("Enter author's name:")
    For Each sht In ThisWorkbook.Worksheets
      sht.Select
      i = ActiveSheet.Comments.Count
      For Each myNote In ActiveSheet.Comments
          If myNote.Author = strName Then
            MsgBox myNote.Text
            If colNotes.Count = 0 Then
              colNotes.Add Item:=myNote, key:="first"
            Else
              colNotes.Add Item:=myNote, Before:=1
            End If
          End If
      Next
      t = t + i
    Next
    If colNotes.Count <> 0 Then MsgBox colNotes("first").Text
      MsgBox "Total notes in workbook: " & t & Chr(13) & _
      "Total notes in collection: " & colNotes.Count
      Debug.Print "Notes by " & strName
```

```
   For Each myNote In colNotes
      Debug.Print Mid(myNote.Text, Len(myNote.Author) + 2, _
         Len(myNote.Text))
   Next
End Sub
```

The foregoing procedure begins by declaring the custom collection object called colNotes. Next, the procedure prompts for an author's name and then loops through all the worksheets in the active workbook to locate this author's notes. Only notes entered by the specified author are added to the custom collection. It is important to note that we are working here with the note feature that is compatible with previous versions of Excel. To use the new comments feature using the Excel VBA you will need to declare myNote as CommentThreaded and make other changes in the procedure. Look for the example in the companion files.

The procedure assigns a key to the first note and then adds the remaining notes to the collection by placing them before the note that was added last (notice the use of the `before` argument). If the collection includes at least one note, the procedure displays a message box with the text of the note that was identified with the special `key` argument. Notice how the `key` argument is used in referencing an item in a collection. The procedure then prints the text of all the notes included in the collection to the Immediate window.

Text functions (`Mid` and `Len`) are used to get only the text of the note without the author's name. Next, the total number of notes in a workbook and the total number of notes in the custom collection are returned by the Count property.

6. Run the **GetNotes** procedure twice each time, supplying a different name of the author (your name and Joan Smith). Check the procedure results in the Immediate window.

Now let's modify the GetNotes procedure that you prepared in the previous Hands-On. At the end of the procedure, we'll display the contents of the items that are currently in the colNotes collection one by one and ask the user whether the item should be removed from the collection. If for any reason your name does not appear in the notes you entered after you've saved your workbook, enter Author for the name of the author. To resolve the issue of the author's name being sometimes removed from your notes, review the options available from File | Info. Choose Check for Issues next to the Inspect Workbook section and select Inspect Document to launch Document Inspector. Make sure that Comments are not selected.

Hands-On 8.4   Removing Items from the Custom ColNotes Collection

1. Add the following line to the declaration section of the GetNotes procedure:

```
Dim response As Integer
```

This statement declares the variable called `response`. You will use this variable to store the result of the `MsgBox` function.

2. Locate the following statement in the GetNotes procedure:

```
For Each myNote In colNotes
```

Precede the foregoing statement with the following line of code:

```
myID = 1
```

3. Locate the following statement in the GetNotes procedure:

```
Debug.Print Mid(myNote.Text, Len(myNote.Author) + 2, _
    Len(myNote.Text))
```

Enter the following block of instructions below that statement:

```
response = MsgBox("Remove this note?" & Chr(13) _
    & Chr(13) & myNote.Text, vbYesNo + vbQuestion)
        If response = 6 Then
                    colNotes.Remove Index:=myID
End If
```

4. Enter the following statements at the end of the procedure before the `End Sub` keywords:

```
Debug.Print "These notes remain in the collection:"
For Each myNote in colNotes
    Debug.Print Mid(myNote.Text, Len(myNote.Author) + 2, _
            Len(myNote.Text))
Next
```

The revised GetNotes procedure, named GetNotes2, is shown here. The procedure removes the specified notes from the custom collection. It does not delete the notes from the worksheets.

```
Sub GetNotes2()
    Dim sht As Worksheet
    Dim colNotes As New Collection
    Dim myNote As Comment
    Dim i As Integer
    Dim t As Integer
    Dim strName As String
    Dim response As Integer

    strName = InputBox("Enter author's name:")
    For Each sht In ThisWorkbook.Worksheets
      sht.Select
```

```
      i = ActiveSheet.Comments.Count
      For Each myNote In ActiveSheet.Comments
      If myNote.Author = strName Then
        MsgBox myNote.Text
        If colNotes.Count = 0 Then
          colNotes.Add Item:=myNote, key:="first"
        Else
          colNotes.Add Item:=myNote, Before:=1
        End If
      End If
        Next
      t = t + i
    Next
    If colNotes.Count <> 0 Then MsgBox colNotes("first").Text
      MsgBox "Total notes in workbook: " & t & Chr(13) & _
      "Total notes in collection:" & colNotes.Count
      Debug.Print "Notes by " & strName

      For Each myNote In colNotes
       Debug.Print Mid(myNote.Text, Len(myNote.Author) + 2, _
       Len(myNote.Text))
       response = MsgBox("Remove this note?" & Chr(13) _
        & Chr(13) & myNote.Text, vbYesNo + vbQuestion)
       If response = 6 Then
         colNotes.Remove index:=1
       End If
      Next

      MsgBox "Total notes in workbook: " & t & Chr(13) & _
      "Total notes in collection: " & colNotes.Count
      Debug.Print "These notes remain in the collection:"

      For Each myNote In colNotes
        Debug.Print Mid(myNote.Text, Len(myNote.Author) + 2, _
         Len(myNote.Text))
      Next
  End Sub
```

5. Run the GetNotes2 procedure and remove one of the notes displayed in the message box.
6. To delete all notes from the workbook, run the following code:

```
Sub DeleteWorkbookNotes()
  Dim myComment As Comment
  Dim sht As Worksheet

  For Each sht In ThisWorkbook.Worksheets
      For Each myComment In sht.Comments
          myComment.Delete
      Next
  Next
End Sub
```

COLLECTIONS VERSUS ARRAYS

As you have seen so far, both collections and arrays provide a very convenient way for storing and manipulating groups of similar items. Most people find collections easier to use and master than arrays. However, before you decide which grouping structure you should use for storing items in your program, examine your needs. Arrays are usually faster and more convenient to use if you know ahead of time the number of items you are going to store. If the number of elements varies and you often need to add and remove elements, collections may be more efficient to use.

Let's do some feature comparison: collections versus arrays.

- Custom collections you create use 1 by default as a first element. Arrays by default are zero-based. You need to use the `Option Base 1` statement to force the numbering of array items to start at position 1.
- You don't need to specify the size of your collection up front as collections are dynamically allocated. Arrays, on the other hand, require that you define their size and if you need to change the array size further in your procedure you must use the `ReDim` keyword. Each time you re-dimension the array, Excel takes up more resources.
- It's very easy to add or remove items from the collection with the `Add` and `Remove` methods. With arrays, before you can add or remove items, you need to find the size of the array by using its upper and lower bounds.
- You can add new items to a collection in any position. To perform the same task using arrays you must write more code.
- Collections can store items of different data types. Arrays can only store items of different data types when they are declared as a Variant.
- You can use the For and For Each loop to access items in a collection, while with arrays you must first set and verify the upper and lower bounds to iterate through the items.
- Collections allow you to use Keys to access a particular item directly, while arrays don't provide this feature.

WATCHING THE EXECUTION OF YOUR VBA PROCEDURES

To help you understand what's going on when your code runs and how one procedure passes information to a function and receives back a function result, let's walk through the ShowCollItems procedure you created in Hands-On 8.2. Treat this exercise as a brief introduction to the debugging techniques that are covered in detail in the next chapter.

(•) Hands-On 8.5   Code Walkthrough

1. In the VBE Editor screen locate the ShowCollItems procedure.
2. Set a breakpoint by clicking in the left margin next to the following line of
   code, as shown in Figure 8.1:

```
If AskForItems <> "" Then
```

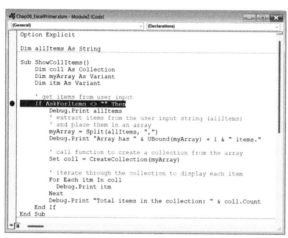

FIGURE 8.1 A red circle in the margin indicates a breakpoint. The statement with a breakpoint is displayed as white text on a red background.

3. Choose **View | Immediate window** and position the window next to the
   procedure as shown in Figure 8.2.
4. Click anywhere within the code of the ShowCollItems procedure and press
   F5 or choose **Run | Run Sub/User Form**.
   Visual Basic should now jump to the line where you set a breakpoint (see
   Figure 8.2).

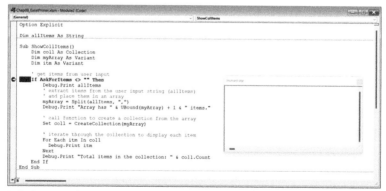

FIGURE 8.2 When Visual Basic encounters a breakpoint while running a procedure, it switches to the Code window and displays a yellow arrow in the margin to the left of the statement at which the procedure is suspended.

5. Step through the code one statement at a time by pressing **F8**.
   Visual Basic runs the current statement which in this case is a call to the
   AskForItems function procedure. The yellow highlight moves to the line
   with the name of this function as shown in Figure 8.3.

FIGURE 8.3 When you press the F8 key you activate a step mode when each press of the key jumps to the next line of code, allowing you to step through the procedure.

6. Press **F8** again and the highlight should move to the first line of the
   function procedure. Press **F8** again to execute this line.
   You should now be presented with the Input box where you need to enter
   the items you want to include in the array (see Figure 8.4).

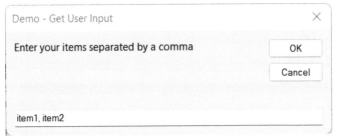

FIGURE 8.4 The Function procedure asks for items separated by a comma. These items will be used to fill an array variable.

7. Enter four names of your best friends or family members or any items you
   want separated by a comma and click **OK**. Clicking Cancel will terminate
   the procedure.
   When you click OK you should see the Immediate window filled with the
   data you entered (see Figure 8.5). All Debug statements in your procedures
   wrote results to the Immediate window while the code was executing.

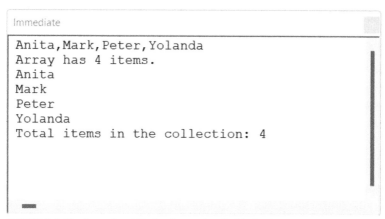

```
Immediate

Anita,Mark,Peter,Yolanda
Array has 4 items.
Anita
Mark
Peter
Yolanda
Total items in the collection: 4
```

FIGURE 8.5 The Immediate Window is populated with the data generated by the Debug Print statements.

This was a quick run through the VBA procedure. To go slower and gain more understanding of what's happening in the code, you need to put in more breakpoints next to the lines where you would like Visual Basic to temporarily stop the code execution.

8. Erase all data in the Immediate window by clicking anywhere within it, then press **Ctrl+A**, and then **Delete**.
   Let's add more breakpoints and execute the procedure again.

9. Add the breakpoints as shown in Figure 8.6.

FIGURE 8.6 Adding multiple breakpoints on important lines in VBA procedures allows you to better troubleshoot your own or someone else's code.

10. Position the cursor within the ShowCollItems procedure and press F5.
    Keep pressing F5 to quickly execute the code between the set breakpoints. At any time when you need to step line by line, press the F8 key. While your procedure execution is in the break mode with the yellow highlight on

some code statement, you can use the Immediate window to find out the contents of your variables or issue other commands that will allow you to check the returned values. For example, after you type entries in the dialog box, you can find the contents of the `allItems` variable by typing `?allI-tems` in the Immediate window and pressing Enter.

11. Keep pressing **F8** to execute the function procedure step by step. The yellow highlight should eventually move to the line that tells Visual Basic to return the `allItems` variable from this function:

```
AskForItems = allItems
```

12. Press **F8** until the execution moves to the ShowAllItems procedure. Press **F8** and you should see the output of the `Debug.Print   allItems` statement in the Immediate window.

13. Press **F8** again when the yellow highlight reaches the line that uses the `Split` function to extract items from the `allItems` string variable into the `myArray` varriable:

```
myArray = Split(allItems, ",")
```

14. Press **F8** to fill the `myArray` variable.

15. Find the first element of the `myArray` variable by typing the following in the Immediate window and pressing Enter:

```
?myArray(0)
```

You should see the first item you entered.

16. Continue pressing the **F8** key and examining each line of code until the execution moves to the CreateCollection function procedure.

17. Press **F8** again to move to the For Next loop within the CreateCollection procedure. Let's use the Immediate Window to find out what was passed to this function.

18. In the Immediate Window, type `?Ubound(arrMyItems)` and press **Enter**. You should see the count of the total items you entered. Recall that arrays are zero-based by default, so the actual count is `?Ubound(arrMyItems) + 1`.

19. Press **F8** until you are out of the loop that adds individual array items to the coll object variable.

20. When you reach the last statement of the CreateCollection procedure (`Set CreateCollection = coll`), type `?coll.count` to return the total number of items in your collection.

21. Press **F8** to pass the collection back to the calling procedure (**ShowAllItems**) and exit the function by pressing **F8** again.

Now you should be positioned on the next statement in the ShowAllItems procedure. This statement will loop through the collection as you continue pressing **F8**. All collection items and the total count will be written to the Immediate window.

22. Press F8 until you reach the end of the procedure. The code execution will stop. You can repeat this entire walkthrough again for more practice before we clear the breakpoints in the next step.
23. Select **Debug | Clear All Breakpoints**.
24. Choose **File | Save** to save the changes in the workbook.
25. Choose **File | Close and Return to Microsoft Excel**.
26. Close the **Chap08_ExcelPrimer.xlsm** workbook.

SIDEBAR *VBA Debugging Tools*

Visual Basic provides many debugging tools to help you analyze how your application operates, as well as to locate the source of errors in your procedures. See the next chapter for details on working with these tools.

SUMMARY

This chapter walked you through the process of building your own custom collection object that can be used to track and manipulate data in your VBA program. You also learned how to build an array and convert it into a collection. After making some comparisons between collections and arrays you learned how to analyze your VBA procedures by stepping through the programming code. As your procedures become more complex, you will need to start using special tools for tracing errors, which are covered in the next chapter.

Chapter 9

EXCEL TOOLS FOR
TESTING AND DEBUGGING

A QUICK INTRODUCTION
TO TESTING VBA PROGRAMS

I t does not take much for an error to creep into your VBA procedure. The truth is that no matter how careful you are, it is rare that all your VBA procedures will work correctly the first time. There are three types of errors in VBA: syntax errors, logic errors, and runtime errors. This chapter introduces you to the Visual Basic Editor tools that are available for you to use in the process of analyzing the code of your VBA procedures and locating the source of errors.

TESTING VBA PROCEDURES

Because most of the procedures we wrote earlier were quite short, finding errors wasn't very difficult. However, locating the source of errors in longer and more complex procedures is more tedious and time-consuming. Fortunately, Visual Basic Editor provides a set of handy tools that can make the process of tracking down your VBA problems easier, faster, and less frustrating. Bugs are errors in computer programs. Debugging is the process of locating and fixing those errors by stepping through the code of your procedure or checking the values of variables.

When testing your VBA procedure, use the following guidelines:

- To analyze your procedure, step through your code one line at a time by pressing F8 or choose Debug | Step Into.

- To locate an error in a specific place in your procedure, use a break-point.
- To monitor the value of a variable or expression used by your procedure, add a watch expression.
- To get to sections of code that interest you, set up a bookmark to jump quickly to the desired location.

Each of these guidelines is demonstrated in a hands-on scenario in this chapter.

STOPPING A PROCEDURE

While testing your VBA procedure you may want to halt its execution. This can be done simply by pressing the Esc key, which causes Visual Basic to stop your program and display the message shown in Figure 9.1. VBA also offers other methods of stopping your procedure. When you stop your procedure, you enter what is called a break mode.

To enter break mode, do one of the following:

- Press the Ctrl+Break key combination
- Set one or more breakpoints
- Insert the `Stop` statement into your procedure code
- Add a watch expression

A break occurs when the execution of your VBA procedure is suspended. Visual Basic remembers the values of all variables and the statement from which the execution of the procedure should resume when the user decides to continue by clicking Run Sub/UserForm on the toolbar (or the Run menu option with the same name), or by clicking the Continue button in the dialog box. The error dialog box shown in Figure 9.1 informs you that the procedure was halted. The buttons in this dialog are described in Table 9.1.

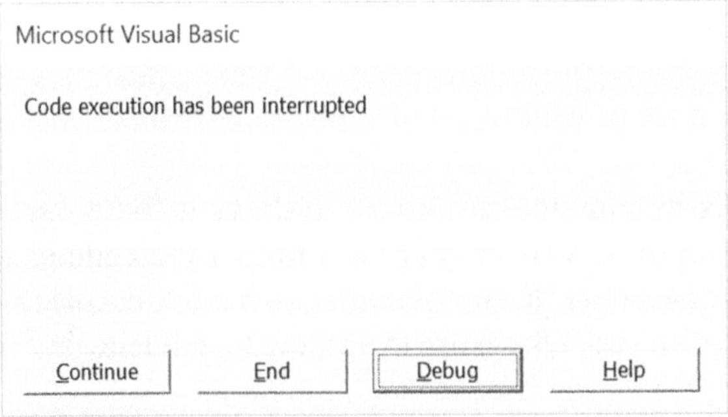

```
Microsoft Visual Basic

Code execution has been interrupted




         Continue          End           Debug          Help
```

FIGURE 9.1 This message appears when you press Esc or Ctrl+Break while your VBA procedure is running.

TABLE 9.1 Error dialog buttons.

`Continue`	Click this button to resume code execution. This button will be grayed out if an error was encountered.
`End`	Click this button if you do not want to troubleshoot the procedure at this time. VBA will stop code execution.
`Debug`	Click this button to enter break mode. The Code window will appear, and VBA will highlight the line at which the procedure execution was suspended. You can examine, debug, reset, or step through the code.
`Help`	Click this button to view the online help that explains the cause of this error message.

You can prevent application users from halting your procedure by including the following statement in the procedure code:

```
Application.EnableCancelKey = xlDisabled
```

When the user presses Esc or Ctrl+Break while the procedure is running, nothing happens. The Application object's EnableCancelKey property disables these keys.

USING BREAKPOINTS

If you know more or less where you can expect a problem in the code of your procedure, suspend code execution on a given line by pressing F9 to set a breakpoint on that line. When VBA gets to that line while running your procedure, it will immediately display the Code window. At this point, you can step through the procedure code line by line by pressing F8 or choosing Debug | Step Into. To see how this works, let's look at the following scenario. Assume that during the execution of the ChangeCode procedure in Hands-On 9.1, the following line of code could get you in trouble:

```
ActiveCell.FormulaR1C1 "=VLOOKUP(RC[1],Codes.xlsx!R1C1:R6C2,2)"
```

NOTE	*Please note files for the "Hands-On" project may be found in the companion files.*

⊙ Hands-On 9.1   Setting Breakpoints in a VBA Procedure

1. Copy the **Chap09_ExcelPrimer.xlsm** and **Codes.xlsx** workbooks from the companion files to your **C:\VBAPrimerExcel2021_ByExample** folder.
2. Start Microsoft Excel and open both these files (**Chap09_ExcelPrimer. xlsm, Codes.xlsx**) from the **C:\VBAPrimerExcel2021_ByExample** folder.
3. Examine the data in both workbooks. It should look like Figures 9.2 and 9.3.

⊿	A	B	C	D
1	Teacher	Position	Amount	Code
2	Ann Marie Smith	A	6500	227.163-23-220
3	Barbara Kaufman	A	6500	227.163-14-100
4	John Frederick	A	6500	211.163-23-330
5	Katherine Stein	B	6300	211.163-23-330
6	Christine Martin	B	6300	211.163-23-330
7	Mark O'Brian	B	6300	211.163-23-220
8	Jorge Rodriguez	B	6300	227.163-11-100
9				

FIGURE 9.2 The data entered in column D of this worksheet will be used to look up the equivalent code from column B in the Codes.xlsx workbook (see Figure 9.3).

4. Close the **Codes.xlsx** workbook. Leave the other file open.

5. With Chap09_ExcelPrimer.xlsm active, switch to the Visual Basic Editor window.

6. In Project Explorer, open the Modules folder in the **Debugging (Chap09_ ExcelPrimer.xlsm)** project and double-click the **Breaks** module.

The Breaks Module Code window lists the following ChangeCode procedure:

⊿	A	B	C
1	211.163-23-220	65	
2	211.163-23-330	73	
3	211.163-28-330	78	
4	227.163-11-100	67	
5	227.163-14-100	62	
6	227.163-23-220	66	
7			
8			
9			

Sheet1   ⊕

FIGURE 9.3 The ChangeCode procedure uses this code table for lookup purposes.

```
Sub ChangeCode()
    Workbooks.Open Filename:="C:\VBAPrimerExcel2021_
ByExample\Codes.xlsx"
    Windows("Chap09_ExcelPrimer.xlsm").Activate
    Columns("D:D").Insert Shift:=xlToRight
    Range("D1").Formula = "Simple Code"
    Columns("D:D").SpecialCells(xlBlanks).Select
    ActiveCell.FormulaR1C1 = "=VLookup(RC[1],Codes.
xlsx!R1C1:R6C2,2)"
    Selection.FillDown
        With Columns("D:D")
            .EntireColumn.AutoFit
            .Select
        End With
```

```
    Selection.Copy
    Selection.PasteSpecial Paste:=xlValues
    Rows("1:1").Select
        With Selection
            .HorizontalAlignment = xlCenter
            .VerticalAlignment = xlBottom
            .Orientation = xlHorizontal
        End With
    Workbooks("Codes.xlsx").Close
End Sub
```

7. In the `ChangeCode` procedure, click anywhere on the line containing the following statement:

```
ActiveCell.FormulaR1C1 = "=VLookup(RC[1],Codes.
xlsx!R1C1:R6C2,2)"
```

8. Set a breakpoint by pressing **F9** (or choosing **Debug | Toggle Breakpoint** or clicking in the margin indicator to the left of the line).
   When you set the breakpoint, Visual Basic displays a red circle in the margin. At the same time, the line that has the breakpoint is indicated as white text on a red background as in Figure 9.4. The color of the breakpoint can be changed on the Editor Format tab in the Options dialog box (Tools menu).

9. Press **F5** to run the ChangeCode procedure.
   When you run the procedure, Visual Basic will execute all the statements until it encounters the breakpoint. Figure 9.5 shows the yellow arrow in the margin to the left of the statement at which the procedure was suspended, and the statement inside a box with a yellow background. The arrow and the box indicate the current statement or the statement that is about to be executed. If the current statement also contains a breakpoint, the margin displays both indicators overlapping one another (the circle and the arrow).

```
(General)                                              ChangeCode
  Option Explicit

  Sub ChangeCode()
      Workbooks.Open Filename:="C:\VBAPrimerExcel2021_ByExample\Codes.xlsx"
      Windows("Chap09_ExcelPrimer.xlsm").Activate
      Columns("D:D").Insert Shift:=xlToRight
      Range("D1").Formula = "Simple Code"
      Columns("D:D").SpecialCells(xlBlanks).Select
●     ActiveCell.FormulaR1C1 = "=VLookup(RC[1],Codes.xlsx!R1C1:R6C2,2)"
      Selection.FillDown
          With Columns("D:D")
              .EntireColumn.AutoFit
              .Select
          End With
      Selection.Copy
      Selection.PasteSpecial Paste:=xlValues
      Rows("1:1").Select
          With Selection
              .HorizontalAlignment = xlCenter
              .VerticalAlignment = xlBottom
              .Orientation = xlHorizontal
          End With
      Workbooks("Codes.xlsx").Close
  End Sub
```

FIGURE 9.4 The line of code where the breakpoint is set is displayed in the color specified on the Editor Format tab in the Options dialog box.

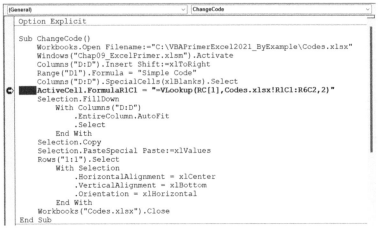

FIGURE 9.5 When Visual Basic encounters a breakpoint, it displays the Code window and indicates the current statement.

While in break mode, you can change code, add new statements, execute the procedure one line at a time, skip lines, set the next statement, use the Immediate window, and more. When Visual Basic is in break mode, all the options on the Debug menu are available. If you change certain code while you work in break mode, VBA will prompt you to reset the project by displaying the following error message: "*This action will reset your project, proceed anyway?*" You can click OK to stop the program's execution and proceed editing your code or click Cancel to delete the new changes and continue running the code from the point at which it was suspended.

10. Press **F5** (or choose **Run Sub/UserForm**) to continue running the procedure.
Visual Basic leaves break mode and continues to run the procedure statements until it reaches the end of the procedure. When the procedure finishes executing, Visual Basic does not automatically remove the breakpoint. Notice that the line of code with the VLookup function is still highlighted in red.

In this example you have set only one breakpoint. Visual Basic allows you to set any number of breakpoints in a procedure. This way, you can suspend and continue the execution of your procedure as you please. You can analyze the code of your procedure and check the values of variables while execution is suspended. You can also perform various tests by typing statements in the Immediate window.

11. Remove the breakpoint by choosing **Debug | Clear All Breakpoints** or by pressing **Ctrl+Shift+F9** or by clicking on the red circle in the margin area to remove the breakpoint.
All the breakpoints are removed. If you had set several breakpoints in a given procedure and would like to remove only one or some of them, click

on the line containing the breakpoint that you want to remove and press F9 (or choose Debug | Clear Breakpoint or simply click the red dot in the margin). You should clear the breakpoints when they are no longer needed. The breakpoints are automatically removed when you close the file.

12. Switch to the Microsoft Excel application window and notice that a new column with the looked-up codes, like the one in Figure 9.6, was added on Sheet1 of the Chap09_ExcelPrimer.xlsm workbook.

	A	B	C	D	E
1	Teacher	Position	Amount	Simple Code	Code
2	Ann Marie Smith	A	6500	66	227.163-23-220
3	Barbara Kaufman	A	6500	62	227.163-14-100
4	John Frederick	A	6500	73	211.163-23-330
5	Katherine Stein	B	6300	73	211.163-23-330
6	Christine Martin	B	6300	73	211.163-23-330
7	Mark O'Brian	B	6300	65	211.163-23-220
8	Jorge Rodriguez	B	6300	67	227.163-11-100
9					

FIGURE 9.6 This worksheet was modified by the ChangeCode procedure in Hands-On 9.1.

When to Use a Breakpoint

Consider setting a breakpoint if you suspect that your procedure never executes a certain block of code.

In break mode, you can quickly find out the contents of the variable at the cursor in the Code window by holding the mouse pointer over it. For example, in the VarValue procedure shown in Figure 9.7, the breakpoint has been set on the `Workbooks.Add` statement. When Visual Basic encounters this statement, the Code window (break mode) appears. Because Visual Basic has already executed the statement that stores the name of Active-Workbook in the variable `strName`, you can quickly find out the value of this variable by resting the mouse pointer over its name. The name of the variable and its current value appear in a tooltip frame.

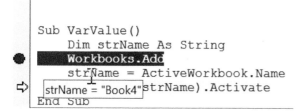

```
Sub VarValue()
    Dim strName As String
    Workbooks.Add
    strName = ActiveWorkbook.Name
    strName = "Book4" strName).Activate
End Sub
```

FIGURE 9.7 In break mode, you can find out the value of a variable by resting the mouse pointer on that variable.

NOTE	*To show the values of several variables used in a procedure at once, you should use the Locals window, which is discussed later in this chapter.*

USING THE IMMEDIATE WINDOW IN BREAK MODE

Once the procedure execution is suspended and the Code window appears, you can activate the Immediate window and type VBA instructions to find out, for instance, which cell is currently active or the name of the active sheet. You can also use the Immediate window to change the contents of variables in order to correct values that may be causing errors.

Figure 9.8 shows the suspended ChangeCode procedure and the Immediate window with the questions that were asked of Visual Basic while in break mode.

```
(General)                                      ChangeCode

Option Explicit

Sub ChangeCode()
    Workbooks.Open Filename:="C:\VBAPrimerExcel2021_ByExample\Codes.xlsx"
    Windows("Chap09_ExcelPrimer.xlsm").Activate
    Columns("D:D").Insert Shift:=xlToRight
    Range("D1").Formula = "Simple Code"
    Columns("D:D").SpecialCells(xlBlanks).Select
    ActiveCell.FormulaR1C1 = "=VLookup(RC[1],Codes.xlsx!R1C1:R6C2,2)"
    Selection.FillDown
        With Columns("D:D")
            .EntireColumn.AutoFit
            .Select
        End With
    Selection.Copy
    Selection.PasteSpecial Paste:=xlValues
    Rows("1:1").Select
        With Selection
            .HorizontalAlignment = xlCenter
            .VerticalAlignment = xlBottom
            .Orientation = xlHorizontal
        End With
    Workbooks("Codes.xlsx").Close
End Sub

Immediate

?ActiveCell.Address
$E$9
?ActiveSheet.Name
Sheet1
```

FIGURE 9.8 When the code execution is suspended, you can find the values of your variables and execute additional commands by entering appropriate statements in the Immediate window.

USING THE STOP AND ASSERT STATEMENTS

Sometimes you won't be able to test your procedure right away. If you set up your breakpoints and then close the file, Excel will remove your breakpoints, and the next time you are ready to test your procedure, you'll have to begin by setting up breakpoints again. To postpone the task of testing your procedure until you reopen the file, insert a Stop statement into your code wherever you want to halt a procedure. Figure 9.9 shows a Stop statement before the For Each...Next loop. Visual Basic will suspend the execution of the StopExample procedure when it encounters the Stop statement. The screen will display the Code window in break mode.

Although the Stop statement has the same effect as setting a breakpoint, it has one disadvantage—all Stop statements stay in the procedure until you

```
(General)                                              StopExample
    Sub StopExample()
        Dim curCell As Range
        Dim num As Integer

        ActiveWorkbook.Sheets(1).Select
        ActiveSheet.UsedRange.Select
        num = Selection.Columns.Count
        Selection.Resize(1, num).Select
        Stop
        For Each curCell In Selection
            Debug.Print curCell.Text
        Next
    End Sub
```

FIGURE 9.9 You can insert a Stop statement anywhere in the code of your VBA procedure. The procedure will halt when it gets to the Stop statement, and the Code window will appear with the line highlighted.

remove them. When you no longer need to stop your procedure, you must locate and remove all the Stop statements.

A very powerful and easy-to-apply debugging technique is utilizing Debug.Assert statements. Assertions allow you to write code that checks itself while running. By including assertions in your programming code, you can verify that a particular condition or assumption is true. Assertions give you immediate feedback when an error occurs. They are great for detecting logic errors early in the development phase instead of hearing about them later from your end users. The fact that your procedure ran on your system without generating an error does not mean that there are no bugs in that procedure. Don't assume anything—always test for validity of expressions and variables in your code. The Debug.Assert statement takes any expression that evaluates to True or False and activates the break mode when that expression evaluates to False. The syntax for Debug.Assert is shown here:

```
Debug.Assert condition
```

where condition is a VBA code or expression that returns True or False. If condition evaluates to False or 0 (zero), VBA will enter break mode. For example, when running the following looping structure, the code will stop executing when the variable i equals 50:

```
Sub TestDebugAssert()
    Dim i As Integer

    For i = 1 To 100
        Debug.Assert i <> 50
    Next
End Sub
```

Keep in mind that Debug.Assert does nothing if the condition is False or zero. The execution simply stops on that line of code and the VBE screen opens with the line containing the false statement highlighted so that you can start debugging your code. You may need to write an error handler to handle the identified error. Error-handling procedures are discussed later in this chapter.

While you can stop the code execution by using the `Stop` statement (see the previous section), `Debug.Assert` differs from the `Stop` statement in its conditional aspect; it will stop your code only under specific conditions. Conditional breakpoints can also be set by using the Watch window (see the next section).

After you have debugged and tested your code, comment out or remove the `Debug.Assert` statements from your final code. The easiest way to do this is to use Edit | Replace in the VBE editor screen. To comment out the statements, enter Debug.Assert in the Find What box. In the Replace With box, enter an apostrophe followed by Debug.Assert.

To remove the `Debug.Assert` statements from your code, enter `Debug.Assert` in the Find What box. Leave the Replace With box empty but be sure to mark the Use Pattern Matching check box.

USING THE WATCH WINDOW

Many errors in procedures are caused by variables that assume unexpected values. If a procedure uses a variable whose value changes in various locations, you may want to stop the procedure and check the current value of that variable. Visual Basic offers a special Watch window that allows you to keep an eye on variables or expressions while your procedure is running.

To add a watch expression to your procedure, perform the following:

- In the Code window, select the variable whose value you want to monitor.

- Choose **Debug | Add Watch**.

- The screen will display the Add Watch dialog box, as shown in Figure 9.10. The Add Watch dialog box contains three sections, which are described in Table 9.2.

FIGURE 9.10 The Add Watch dialog box allows you to define conditions that you want to monitor while a VBA procedure is running.

TABLE 9.2 Add Watch dialog options.

Expression	Displays the name of a variable that you have highlighted in your procedure. If you opened the Add Watch dialog box without selecting a variable name, type the name of the variable you want to monitor in the Expression text box.
Context	In this section you should indicate the name of the procedure that contains the variable and the name of the module where this procedure is located.
Watch Type	Specifies how to monitor the variable. If you choose the Watch Expression option button, you will be able to read the value of the variable in the Watch window while in break mode. If you choose Break When Value Is True, Visual Basic will automatically stop the procedure when the variable evaluates to true (nonzero). The last option button, Break When Value Changes, stops the procedure each time the value of the variable or expression changes.

You can add a watch expression before running a procedure or after execution of your procedure has been suspended. The difference between a breakpoint and a watch expression is the breakpoint always stops a procedure in a specified location and the watch stops the procedure only when the specified condition (Break When Value Is True or Break When Value Changes) is met. Watches are extremely useful when you are not sure where the variable is being changed. Instead of stepping through many lines of code to find the location where the variable assumes the specified value, you can simply put a watch expression on the variable and run your procedure as normal. Let's see how this works.

(◉) Hands-On 9.2   Watching the Values of VBA Expressions

1. The Breaks Module Code window lists the following WhatDate procedure:

```
Sub WhatDate()
   Dim curDate As Date
   Dim newDate As Date
   Dim x As Integer

   curDate = Date
   For x = 1 To 365
     newDate = Date + x
   Next
End Sub
```

The WhatDate procedure uses the For...Next loop to calculate the date that is x days in the future. If you run this procedure, you won't get any result unless you insert the following instruction in the code of the procedure:

```
MsgBox "In " & x & " days, it will be " & NewDate
```

In this example, however, you don't care to display the individual dates, day after day. What if all you want to do is to stop the program when the value of the variable x reaches 211? In other words, what date will be 211 days from now? To get the answer, you could insert the following statement into your procedure:

```
If x = 211 Then MsgBox "In " & x & " days it will be " &
NewDate
```

Introducing new statements into your procedure just to get an answer about the value of a certain variable when a specific condition occurs will not always be viable. Instead of adding MsgBox or other debug statements to your procedure code that you will later need to delete, you can use the Watch window and avoid extra code maintenance. If you add watch expressions to the procedure, Visual Basic will stop the For...Next loop when the specified condition is met, and you'll be able to check the values of the desired variables.

2. Choose **View | Watch Window**.
   An empty Watches window should appear. This window is divided into four areas: Expression, Value, Type and Context. The Expression column will list all the watch expressions that you'll set in this Hands-On. The Value column will list the value of the expression at the time of transition into break mode. The Type column will list the expression type and the Context column will list the context of the watch expression. Let's set a few watches for the WhatDate procedure.

3. Choose **Debug | Add Watch**.

4. In the Expression text box, enter the following expression: **x = 211**. In the Context section, choose **WhatDate** from the Procedure combo box and **Breaks** from the Module combo box. In the Watch Type section, select the **Break When Value Is True** option button.

5. Click **OK** to close the Add Watch dialog box. You have now added your first watch expression.
   Visual Basic places your expression x = 211 in the first line of the Watches window. Notice that the Value column will show <Out of context> entry. This entry will change as you run your procedure. Now let's add another expression to the Watch window for tracking the current date.

6. In the Code window, position the insertion point anywhere within the name of the curDate variable.

7. Choose **Debug | Add Watch** and click **OK** to set up the default watch type with Watch Expression.
   Notice that a new line is added to the Watches window with the curDate variable in the Expression column. Let's add another variable to the Watches window.

8. In the Code window, position the insertion point anywhere within the name of the newDate variable.

9. Choose **Debug | Add Watch** and click **OK** to set up the default watch type with Watch Expression.

   Notice that newDate now appears in the Expression column of the Watch window. After performing the foregoing steps, the WhatDate procedure contains the following three watches:

   x = 211—Break When Value is True
   curDate—Watch Expression
   newDate—Watch Expression

10. Position the insertion point anywhere inside the code of the WhatDate procedure, and press **F5**.

    Figure 9.11 shows the Watches window when Visual Basic stops the procedure when x equals 211.

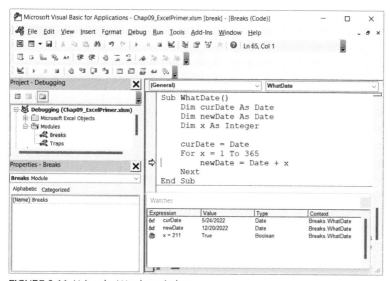

FIGURE 9.11 Using the Watches window.

Notice that the value of the variable x in the Watch window is the same as the value that you specified in the Add Watch dialog. In addition, the Watch window shows the value of both variables—curDate and newDate. The procedure is in break mode. You can press F5 to continue or you can ask another question, such as "What date will be in 277 days?" The next step shows how to do this.

11. Choose **Debug | Edit Watch** and enter the following expression: **x = 277**.

12. Click **OK** to close the Edit Watch dialog box.

    Notice that the Watch window now displays a new value for the expression. x is now False.

13. Press **F5** to continue running the procedure.

The procedure stops again when the value of `x` equals 277. The value of `curDate` is the same; however, the `newDate` variable now contains a new value—a date that is 277 days from now. You can change the value of the expression again or finish running the procedure.

14. Press **F5** to finish running the procedure.

When your procedure is running and a watch expression has a value, the Watch window displays the value of the watch expression. If you open the Watch window after the procedure has finished, you will see <out of context> instead of the variable values. In other words, when the watch expression is out of context, it does not have a value.

Removing Watch Expressions

To remove the watch expressions, click on the expression in the Watch window that you want to remove, and press Delete. You may now remove all the watch expressions you had defined in the preceding example.

USING QUICK WATCH

In break mode you can check the value of an expression for which you have not defined a watch expression by using the Quick Watch dialog box displayed in Figure 9.12.

FIGURE 9.12 The Quick Watch dialog box shows the value of the selected expression in a VBA procedure.

The Quick Watch dialog box can be accessed in the following ways:

- While in break mode, position the insertion point anywhere inside the name of a variable or expression you wish to watch.
- Choose Debug | Quick Watch.
- Press Shift+F9.

The Add button in the Quick Watch dialog box allows you to add the expression to the Watch window. Let's find out how to work with this dialog box.

(●) **Hands-On 9.3   Using the Quick Watch Dialog Box**

1. Make sure that the WhatDate procedure you entered in the previous Hands-On exercise does not contain any watch expressions. See the section called "Removing Watch Expressions" for instructions on how to remove a watch expression from the Watch window.
2. In the WhatDate procedure, position the insertion point on the name of the variable x.
3. Choose **Debug | Add Watch**.
4. Enter the following expression: **x = 50**.
5. Choose the **Break When Value Is True** option button and click **OK**.
6. Run the WhatDate procedure.
   Visual Basic will suspend procedure execution when x equals 50. Notice that the Watch window does not contain the newDate or the curDate variables. To check the values of these variables, you can position the mouse pointer over the appropriate variable name in the Code window, or you can invoke the Quick Watch dialog box.
7. In the Code window, position the mouse pointer inside the newDate variable and press **Shift+F9**.
   The Quick Watch dialog shows the name of the expression and its current value.
8. Click **Cancel** to return to the Code window.
9. In the Code window, position the mouse pointer inside the curDate variable and press **Shift+F9**.
   The Quick Watch dialog now shows the value of the variable curDate.
10. Click **Cancel** to return to the Code window.
11. Press **F5** to continue running the procedure.
12. In the Watch window, highlight the line containing the expression x = 50 and press **Delete** to remove it.
13. Close the Watch window.

USING THE LOCALS WINDOWS AND THE CALL STACK DIALOG BOX

During the execution of a VBA procedure, you can keep an eye on all the declared variables and their current values by choosing View | Locals Window before you run the procedure. Figure 9.13 shows a list of variables and their corresponding values in the Locals window, which is displayed while Visual Basic is in the break mode.

The Locals window contains three columns. The Expression column displays the names of variables that are declared in the current procedure. The first row displays the name of the module preceded by the plus sign. When you click the plus sign, you can check if any variables have been declared at the module level. For class modules, the system variable Me is defined. For standard modules, the first variable is the name of the current module. The global variables and variables in other projects are not accessible from the Locals window.

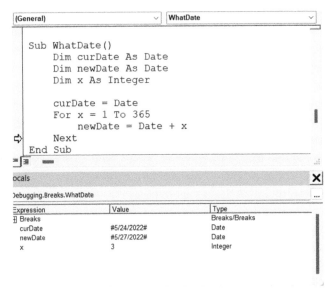

FIGURE 9.13 The Locals window displays the current values of all the declared variables in the current VBA procedure.

The second column shows the current values of variables. In this column, you can change the value of a variable by clicking it and typing the new value. After changing the value, press Enter to register the change. You can also press Tab, Shift+Tab, or the up or down arrows, or click anywhere within the Locals window after you've changed the variable value. The third column displays the type of each declared variable.

To observe the values of variables in the Locals window, perform the following Hands-On exercise.

Hands-On 9.4   Using the Locals and Call Stack Windows

1. Choose **View | Locals Window**.
2. Click anywhere inside the WhatDate procedure and press **F8**.
   By pressing F8, you place the procedure in break mode. The Locals window displays the name of the current module and the local variables and their beginning values.
3. Press **F8** a few more times while keeping an eye on the Locals window.
   The Locals window also contains a button with three dots. This button opens the Call Stack dialog box shown in Figure 9.14, which displays a list

of all active procedure calls. An active procedure call is a procedure that is started but not completed. You can also activate the Call Stack dialog box by choosing **View | Call Stack**. This option is available only in break mode.

FIGURE 9.14 The Call Stack dialog box displays a list of the procedures that are started but not completed.

The Call Stack dialog box is especially helpful for tracing nested procedures. Recall that a nested procedure is a procedure that is being called from within another procedure. If a procedure calls another, the name of the called procedure is automatically added to the Calls list in the Call Stack dialog box. When Visual Basic has finished executing the statements of the called procedure, the procedure name is automatically removed from the Call Stack dialog box. You can use the Show button in the Call Stack dialog box to display the statement that calls the next procedure listed in the dialog box.

4. Press **F5** to continue running the WhatDate procedure.
5. Close the Locals window.

NAVIGATING WITH BOOKMARKS

In the process of analyzing or reviewing your VBA procedures, you will often find yourself jumping to certain areas of code. Using the built-in bookmark feature, you can easily mark the spots in your code that you want to navigate between.

To set up a bookmark:

- Click anywhere in the statement that you want to define as a bookmark.
- Choose **Edit | Bookmarks | Toggle Bookmark** or click the **Toggle Bookmark** button on the Edit toolbar as illustrated in Figure 9.15.
- Visual Basic will place a rounded blue rectangle in the left margin beside the statement.

Once you've set up two or more bookmarks, you can jump between the marked locations of your code by choosing Edit | Bookmarks | Next Bookmark or simply by clicking the Next Bookmark button on the Edit toolbar. You can remove bookmarks at any time by choosing Edit | Bookmarks | Clear All Bookmarks or by clicking the Clear All Bookmarks button on the Edit toolbar. To remove a single bookmark, click anywhere in the bookmarked statement and choose Edit | Bookmarks | Toggle Bookmark or click the Toggle Bookmark button on the Edit toolbar.

```
(General)                                     ChangeCode

  Option Explicit
                        Edit
  Sub ChangeCode()
      Workbooks.Open Filename:="C:\                      el2021_ByExample\Codes.xlsx"
      Windows("Chap09_ExcelPrimer.xl     Toggle Bookmark  te
      Columns("D:D").Insert Shift:=xlToRight
      Range("D1").Formula = "Simple Code"
      Columns("D:D").SpecialCells(xlBlanks).Select
      ActiveCell.FormulaR1C1 = "=VLookup(RC[1],Codes.xlsx!R1C1:R6C2,2)"
      Selection.FillDown
          With Columns("D:D")
              .EntireColumn.AutoFit
              .Select
          End With
      Selection.Copy
      Selection.PasteSpecial Paste:=xlValues
      Rows("1:1").Select
          With Selection
              .HorizontalAlignment = xlCenter
              .VerticalAlignment = xlBottom
              .Orientation = xlHorizontal
          End With
          Workbooks("Codes.xlsx").Close
  End Sub
```

FIGURE 9.15 Using bookmarks you can quickly jump between often-used sections of your procedures.

TRAPPING ERRORS

No one writes bug-free programs the first time. When you create VBA procedures, you must determine how your program will respond to errors. Many unexpected errors happen during runtime. For example, your procedure may try to give a workbook the same name as an open workbook. Runtime errors are often discovered by users who attempt to do something that the programmer has not anticipated. If an error occurs when the procedure is running, Visual Basic displays an error message and the procedure is stopped. Most often, the error message that VBA displays is quite cryptic to the user. You can prevent users from seeing many runtime errors by including error-handling code in your VBA procedures. This way, when Visual Basic encounters an error, instead of displaying a default error message, it will show a much friendlier and more comprehensive error message.

In programming, mistakes and errors are not the same thing. A mistake, such as a misspelled or missing statement, a misplaced quote or comma, or assigning a value of one type to a variable of a different (and incompatible) type, can be removed from your program through proper testing and debugging. But even though your code may be free of mistakes, this does not mean that errors will not occur. An error is the result of an event or an operation that doesn't work as expected. For example, if your VBA procedure accesses a particular file on disk and someone has deleted this file or moved it to another location, you'll get an error no matter what. An error prevents the procedure from carrying out a specific task.

To implement error handling, place the `On Error` statement in your procedure. This statement tells VBA what to do if an error occurs while your program is running. VBA uses the `On Error` statement to activate an error-handling procedure that will trap runtime errors. Depending on the type of procedure, you can exit the error trap by using one of the following statements: `Exit Sub`, `Exit Function`, `Exit Property`, `End Sub`, `End Function`, or `End Property`. You should write an error-handling routine for each procedure. Table 9.3 shows how the `On Error` statement can be used.

TABLE 9.3 `On Error` statement options.

`On Error GoTo Label`	Specifies a label to jump to when an error occurs. This label marks the beginning of the error-handling routine. An error handler is a routine for trapping and responding to errors in your application. The label must appear in the same procedure as the `On Error` statement.
`On Error Resume Next`	When a runtime error occurs, Visual Basic ignores the line that caused the error, and does not display an error message but continues the procedure with the next line.
`On Error GoTo 0`	Turns off error trapping in a procedure. When VBA runs this statement, errors are detected but not trapped within the procedure.

Using the Err Object

Your error-handling code can utilize various properties and methods of the Err object. For example, to check which error occurred, check the value of Err.Number. The Number property of the Err object will tell you the value of the last error that occurred, and the Description property will return a description of the error. You can also find the name of the application that caused the error by using the Source property of the Err object (this is very helpful when your procedure launches other applications). After handling the error, use the `Err.Clear` statement to reset Err.Number back to zero.

To test your error-handling code you can use the `Raise` method of the Err object. For example, to raise the "Disk not ready" error, use the following statement:

```
Err.Raise 71
```

The OpenToRead procedure shown here demonstrates the use of the `Resume Next` and `Error` statements, as well as the `Err` object.

Hands-On 9.5 Writing a VBA Procedure with Error-Handling Code

1. Insert a new module into the Testing project and rename it **Traps.**
2. In the Traps module Code window, enter the Archive procedure as shown here:

```vba
Sub OpenToRead()
Dim myFile As String
Dim myChar As String
Dim myText As String
Dim FileExists As Boolean

FileExists = True

On Error GoTo ErrorHandler

myFile = InputBox("Enter the name of file to open:")
Open myFile For Input As #1
If FileExists Then
' loop until the end of file (EOF)
    Do While Not EOF(1)
        ' get one character
        myChar = Input(1, #1)
        ' store in the variable myText
        myText = myText + myChar
    Loop
    Debug.Print myText
    ' close the file
    Close #1
End If
Exit Sub

ErrorHandler:
  FileExists = False
  Select Case Err.Number
    Case 76
    MsgBox "The path you entered cannot be found."
    Case 53
    MsgBox "This file can't be found on the " & _
        "specified drive."
    Case 75
      Exit Sub
    Case Else
      MsgBox "Error " & Err.Number & " :" & _
        Error(Err.Number)
    Exit Sub
  End Select
  Resume Next
End Sub
```

The purpose of the OpenToRead procedure is to read the contents of the user-supplied text file character by character. When the user enters a filename, various errors can occur. For example, the filename or the path may be wrong, or the user may try to open a file that is already open. To trap these errors, the error-handling routine at the end of the OpenToRead procedure uses the Number property of the Err object.

There are several methods of reading a text file. In this example, to read data from a text file, the procedure uses the Windows Low-Level File I/O (Input / Output) method. Therefore, to open the file for reading, we need to use the Open statement, like this:

```
Open myFile For Input As #1
```

Here's the general syntax of the Open statement, followed by an explanation of each component:

```
Open pathname For mode[Access access][lock] As [#]filenumber
    [Len=reclength]
```

The Open statement has three required arguments: pathname, mode, and filenumber. Pathname is the name of the file you want to open. The filename may include the name of a drive and folder.

- Mode is a keyword that determines how the file was opened. Sequential files can be opened in one of the following modes: Input, Output, or Append. Use Input to read the file, Output to write to a file overwriting any existing file and Append to write to a file by adding to any existing information.
- The optional Access clause can be used to specify permissions for the file (Read, Write, or Read Write).
- The optional Lock argument determines which file operations are allowed for other processes. For example, if a file is open in a network environment, lock determines how other people can access it. The following lock keywords can be used: Shared, Lock Read, Lock Write, or Lock Read Write.
- Filenumber is a number from 1 to 511. This number is used to refer to the file in subsequent operations. You can obtain a unique file number using the Visual Basic built-in FreeFile function.
- The last element of the Open statement, reclength, specifies the buffer size (total number of characters) for sequential (text) files, or the record size for random-access files (text files where data is stored in records of equal length and fields separated by commas).

If the specified file exists, the procedure uses the Do...While loop to tell Visual Basic to execute the statements inside the loop until the end of the file has been reached. The end of the file is determined by the result of the

`EOF` function. The `Input` function is used to return the specified number of characters:

```
myChar = Input(1, #1)
```

`#1` is the file number that was used in the process of opening the file with the `Open` statement.

Each character being read is stored in the `myChar` variable. Next, the `myChar` variable is appended to the `myText` variable, like this:

```
myText = myText + myChar
```

The procedure then writes the contents of the myText variable to the Immediate window using the Debug.Print statement. When the file has been read, we must close it using the Close statement:

```
Close #1     ' close the file
```

The Err object contains information about runtime errors. If an error occurs while the procedure is running, the statement `Err.Number` will return the error number. If errors 76, 53, or 75 occur, Visual Basic will display user-friendly messages stored inside the `Select...Case` block and then proceed to the `Resume Next` statement, which will send it to the line of code following the one that caused the error. If another error occurs, Visual Basic will return its error code (Err.Number) and error description (Error (Err.Number)). At the beginning of the procedure, the variable `FileExists` is set to True. This way, if the program doesn't encounter an error, all the instructions inside the `If FileExists Then` block will be executed. However, if VBA encounters an error, the value of the `FileExists` variable will be set to False (see the first statement in the error-handling routine just below the `ErrorHandler` label). This way, Visual Basic will not cause another error while trying to read a file that caused the error on opening. Notice the `Exit Sub` statement before the `ErrorHandler` label. Put the `Exit Sub` statement just above the error-handling routine because you don't want Visual Basic to carry out the error handling if there are no errors.

To test the OpenToRead procedure and better understand error trapping, we will need a text file (see Step 3).

3. Use Windows Notepad to prepare a text file. Enter any text you want in this file. When done, save the file as **C:\VBAPrimerExcel2021_ByExample\ Vacation.txt**.

4. Run the OpenToRead procedure three times in step mode by using the F8 key, each time supplying one of the following:

   - Name of the C:\VBAPrimerExcel2021_ByExample\Vacation.txt file
   - Filename that does not exist on drive C
   - Path that does not exist on your computer (e.g., K:\Test)

Setting Error Trapping Options in a VBA Project

You can specify the error-handling settings for your current Visual Basic project by choosing Tools | Options and selecting the General tab (shown in Figure 9.16).

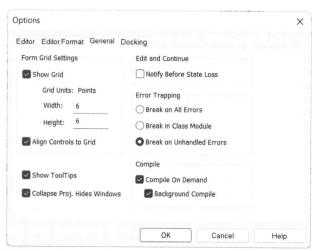

FIGURE 9.16 Setting the Error Trapping options in the Options dialog box will affect all instances of Visual Basic started after you change the setting.

The Error Trapping area located on the General tab determines how errors are handled in the Visual Basic environment. The following options are available:

- Break on All Errors

  This setting will cause Visual Basic to enter the break mode on any error, whether an error handler is active or whether the code is in a class module (class modules are not covered in this primer book).
- Break in Class Module

  This setting will trap any unhandled error in a class module. Visual Basic will activate a break mode when an error occurs and will highlight the line of code in the class module that produced this error.
- Break on Unhandled Errors

This setting will trap errors for which you have not written an error handler. The error will cause Visual Basic to activate a break mode. If the error occurs in a class module, the error will cause Visual Basic to enter break mode on the line of code that called the offending procedure of the class.

STEPPING THROUGH VBA PROCEDURES

Stepping through the code means running one statement at a time. This allows you to check every line in every procedure that is encountered. To start stepping through a procedure from the beginning, place the insertion point anywhere inside the code of your procedure and choose Debug | Step Into or press F8. Figure 9.17 shows the Debug menu, which contains several options that allow you to execute a procedure in step mode. When you run a procedure one statement at a time, Visual Basic executes each statement until it encounters the `End Sub` keywords. If you don't want Visual Basic to step through every statement, you can press F5 at any time to run the rest of the procedure without stepping through it.

File	Edit	View	Insert	Format	Debug
	Compile Debugging				
⛶	Step Into			F8	
⛶	Step Over			Shift+F8	
⛶	Step Out			Ctrl+Shift+F8	
⛶	Run To Cursor			Ctrl+F8	
	Add Watch...				
	Edit Watch...			Ctrl+W	
6J	Quick Watch...			Shift+F9	
⚓	Toggle Breakpoint			F9	
	Clear All Breakpoints			Ctrl+Shift+F9	
⇨	Set Next Statement			Ctrl+F9	
⟳	Show Next Statement				

FIGURE 9.17 The Debug menu offers many commands for stepping through VBA procedures.

Let's step through a procedure line by line.

⊙ Hands-On 9.6   Stepping through a VBA Procedure

1. Place the insertion point anywhere inside the code of the procedure whose execution you wish to trace. For example, try out the OpenToRead procedure you prepared in Hands-On 9.5.

2. Press **F8** or choose **Debug | Step Into**.
   Visual Basic executes the current statement and automatically advances to the next statement and suspends execution. While in break mode, you can activate the Immediate window, Watches window, or Locals window to see the effect of a particular statement on the values of variables and expressions. And if the procedure you are stepping through calls other pro-

cedures, you can activate the Call Stack window to see which procedures are currently active.

3. Press **F8** again to execute the selected statement.
   After executing this statement, Visual Basic will select the next statement, and the procedure execution will be halted again.

4. Continue stepping through the procedure by pressing **F8** or press **F5** to continue the code execution without stopping.
   You can also choose **Run | Reset** to stop the procedure at the current statement without executing the remaining statements.

Stepping Over a Procedure and Running to Cursor

When you step over procedures (Shift+F8), Visual Basic executes each procedure as if it were a single statement. This option is particularly useful if a procedure contains calls to other procedures and you don't want to step into these procedures because they have already been tested and debugged, or you want to concentrate only on the new code that has not yet been debugged.

Suppose that the current statement in MyProcedure (see Hands-On 9.7) calls the SpecialMsg procedure. If you choose Debug | Step Over (Shift+F8) instead of Debug | Step Into (F8), Visual Basic will quickly execute all the statements inside the SpecialMsg procedure and select the next statement in the calling procedure (MyProcedure). During the execution of the SpecialMsg procedure, Visual Basic continues to display the Code window with the current procedure.

(◉) Hands-On 9.7   Stepping over a Procedure

1. In the Breaks Module Code window, locate the following procedure:

```
Sub MyProcedure()
  Dim strName As String

  Workbooks.Add
  strName = ActiveWorkbook.Name
  ' choose Step Over to avoid stepping through the
  ' lines of code in the called procedure - SpecialMsg
  SpecialMsg strName
  Workbooks(strName).Close
End Sub

Sub SpecialMsg(n As String)
  If n = "Book2" Then
    MsgBox "You must change the name."
  End If
End Sub
```

2. Add a breakpoint at the following statement:

   ```
   SpecialMsg strName
   ```

3. Place the insertion point anywhere within the code of MyProcedure, and press **F5** to run it.
   Visual Basic halts execution when it reaches the breakpoint.

4. Press **Shift+F8** or choose **Debug | Step Over**.
   Visual Basic quickly runs the SpecialMsg procedure and advances to the statement immediately after the call to the SpecialMsg procedure.

5. Press **F5** to finish running the procedure without stepping through its code.

6. Remove the breakpoint you set in Step 2.
   Stepping over a procedure is particularly useful when you don't want to analyze individual statements inside the called procedure. Another command on the Debug menu, Step Out (Ctrl+Shift+F8), is used when you step into a procedure and then decide that you don't want to step all the way through it. When you choose this option, Visual Basic will execute the remaining statements in this procedure in one step and proceed to activate the next statement in the calling procedure. In the process of stepping through a procedure, you can switch between the Step Into, Step Over, and Step Out options. The option you select depends on which code fragment you wish to analyze at a given moment. The Debug menu's Run To Cursor (Ctrl+F8) command lets you run your procedure until the line you have selected is encountered. This command is useful if you want to stop the execution before a large loop or intend to step over a called procedure. Now, let's suppose you want to execute MyProcedure to the line that calls the SpecialMsg procedure.

7. Click inside the statement `SpecialMsg strName`.

8. Choose **Debug | Run To Cursor**. Visual Basic will stop the execution of the MyProcedure code when it reaches the specified line.

9. Press **Shift+F8** to step over the SpecialMsg procedure.

10. Press **F5** to execute the remaining statements in the procedure.

Setting the Next Statement

At times, you may want to rerun previous lines of code in the procedure or skip over a section of code that is causing trouble. In each of these situations, you can use the Set Next Statement option on the Debug menu. When you halt execution of a procedure, you can resume the procedure from any statement you want. Visual Basic will skip execution of the statements between the selected statement and the statement where execution was suspended. Suppose that in MyProcedure (see the code of this procedure in the preceding section) you have set a breakpoint on the statement calling the SpecialMsg procedure. To skip the execution of the SpecialMsg procedure, you can place the insertion point inside the statement `Work-books (strName).Close` and press Ctrl+F9 (or choose Debug | Set Next Statement).

Keep in mind that you can't use the Set Next Statement option unless you have suspended the execution of the procedure.

While skipping lines of code can be very useful in the process of debugging your VBA procedures, it should be done with care. When you use the Next Statement option, you tell Visual Basic that this is the line you want to execute next. All lines in between are ignored. This means that certain things that you may have expected to occur don't happen, which can lead to unexpected errors.

Showing the Next Statement

If you are not sure from which statement the execution of the procedure will resume, you can choose Debug | Show Next Statement and Visual Basic will place the cursor on the line that will run next. This is particularly useful when you have been looking at other procedures and are not sure where execution will resume. The Show Next Statement option is available only in break mode.

Stopping and Resetting VBA Procedures

At any time while stepping through the code of a procedure in the Code window, you can:

- Press F5 to execute the remaining instructions without stepping through.
- Choose Run | Reset to finish the procedure without executing the remaining statements.

When you reset your procedure, all the variables lose their current values. Numeric variables assume the initial value of zero, variable-length strings are initialized to a zero-length string (`""`), and fixed-length strings are filled with the character represented by the ASCII character code 0 or Chr(0). Variant variables are initialized to Empty, and the value of object variables is set to Nothing.

TERMINATING A PROCEDURE BASED ON A CONDITION

You may recall, in Chapter 1 (see Hands-On 1.20) we ran into an error while executing the Insert_NewSheet macro. We modified this macro to prompt the user for the sheet name using the Excel InputBox method. However, to make this macro error-proof, we need to ensure that the macro will not fail if the user clicks Cancel or enters a space or several blank spaces for the worksheet name. Let's address this problem now that you have more Excel VBA knowledge under your belt. Here is the Insert_NewSheet procedure as we modified it in Chapter 1.

```
Sub Insert_NewSheet()
'
' Insert_NewSheet Macro
' Insert and rename a worksheet
'

    Sheets.Add After:=ActiveSheet
    ActiveSheet.Name = Application.InputBox _
      ("Enter the name for your worksheet:", "Rename This Sheet")
End Sub
```

The `InputBox` method is a member of the Excel Application object, and this requires that you precede its name with the name of the object (`Application`). Note that the following code uses the line continuation character (an underscore) to break up the long statement that you may end up with when supplying the arguments to this method. You will find the list of arguments and their descriptions in Chapter 4. One of the arguments we absolutely must add to the `InputBox` method to get the expected results with the Cancel button is called "type" and it specifies the return data type. When the user clicks Cancel the `Application.InputBox` method returns *False*. Therefore, we need to introduce some conditional logic to test for the return type. We also need to prevent the user from feeding us blank spaces for the sheet name. By now you should be familiar with writing VBA conditional statements. Conditional logic will allow you to make many enhancements to your recorded macro code. Let's look at the revised Insert_NewSheet procedure.

```
Option Explicit

Sub Insert_NewSheet()
'
' Insert_NewSheet Macro revised
' Insert and rename a worksheet
'

    Dim userInput As Variant

    userInput = Application.InputBox _
      ("Enter the name for your worksheet:", _
         "Rename This Sheet", , , , , , 2)
    If userInput = False Then
        MsgBox ("You pressed the Cancel button." & _
            "The procedure will terminate.")
        sFlag = True
        Exit Sub
    ElseIf userInput = "" Or Trim(userInput) = "" Then
```

```
        MsgBox "Please enter the sheet name or press Cancel to
               exit."
        Insert_NewSheet

    Else
        Sheets.Add After:=ActiveSheet
        ActiveSheet.Name = userInput
    End If
End Sub
```

Note that we will now store the user supplied sheet name in the userInput variable. This variable is declared as Variant data type because the Input-Box method can return different types of data and we want Excel to handle it for us. We begin by asking the user for the input. First, we must define the message that the user will see. Next, we specify the text that appears in the title bar of the dialog box. We don't care about the five arguments that follow, so you will see commas as their placeholders, or you can forgo commas when you specify the names for your arguments as shown in Chapter 4 procedures.

Recall that you can use named arguments to make your methods easier to understand. What we care about is the last argument. The value of 2 specifies that we expect to get a string (text). Once the result of the user interaction with the InputBox is in the userInput variable, it's time for the if statements. If the contents of the variable are False, then we want to display a message to the user and terminate the procedure. You already know that you can exit early from a VBA procedure by using the Exit Sub statement. Before terminating the procedure, however, you may want to store some vital piece of information in additional variables. In the case of the Insert_NewSheet procedure, we need to remember that we exited the procedure, so we don't run other procedures that may depend on this one. Recall that our Insert_NewSheet procedure is a part of a larger master procedure which will also need to be terminated. The sFlag variable will hold a Boolean value of True if the user clicked Cancel and False otherwise. You are free to choose names for your variables. Notice that the sFlag variable is not declared anywhere in the Insert_NewSheet procedure. Since we must use it also in the CreateEmployeeWorksheet master procedure, we need a project-level scope declaration.

Recall from Chapter 3 that public variables can be used in any module. Here is the perfect opportunity to utilize them. Figure 9.18 shows the revised CreateEmployeeWorksheet procedure from Chapter 1. Notice the declaration of the sFlag variable at the top of the module. The first line of code in the procedure makes sure that sFlag is set to False when we start. When the Insert_NewSheet procedure has finished running, the sFlag will be True if the user clicked Cancel. Again, we can use the Exit Sub statement to stop further code execution. And if `sFlag` is False we will continue with the remaining statements.

```
(General)                              CreateEmployeeWorksheet

Option Explicit
Public sFlag As Boolean

Sub CreateEmployeeWorksheet()
    Insert_NewSheet
    If sFlag = True Then Exit Sub
    Insert_Headings
    Insert_EmployeeData
    Get_FirstName
    Get_LastName
    CalculateWages
    FormatTable
End Sub
```

FIGURE 9.18 The revised CreateEmployeeWorksheet procedure uses a public variable of Boolean data type.

Note that the Insert_NewSheet procedure also checks in the `Elseif` clause whether the user clicked OK without supplying any data or entered a space or several spaces. The VBA Trim function removes the leading and trailing spaces from a supplied text string. If the value of the `userInput` variable is an empty string (`""`), then we display a message to the user and call the procedure again. This way the user has a chance to either enter the required data or click Cancel. Finally, if everything looks good, then we execute the statements in the `Else` clause. A new worksheet is inserted after the current sheet and is renamed with the text stored in the `userInput` variable.

⊙ Hands-On 9.8   Working with all the Debugging Tools

1. The revised Chap01_ExcelPrimer.xlsm file can be found in the companion files (Chap01_ExcelPrimer_Revised_in_Chapter9.xlsm). Be sure to run the CreateEmployeeWorksheet master procedure at least three times to check all the conditions used in the Insert_NewSheet procedure.

SUMMARY

In this chapter, you learned how to trap errors and test your VBA procedures to make sure they behave as planned. You debugged your code by stepping through it using breakpoints and watches. You learned how to work with the Immediate window in break mode, and you found out how the Locals window can help you monitor the values of variables and how the Call Stack dialog box can be helpful in keeping track of where you are in a complex program.

By using the built-in debugging tools, you can quickly pinpoint the problem spots in your procedures. Try to spend more time getting acquainted with the Debug menu options and debugging tools discussed in this chapter. Mastering the art of debugging can save you hours of trial and error.

Congratulations on reaching the end of this quick Excel VBA programming primer book. If you wish to continue your journey into using Excel VBA, you will find the continuation of topics presented here in my more advanced book titled *"Excel 2021 / Microsoft 365 Programming By Example."*

INDEX